The Invisible Front

The Invisible Front

Love and Loss in an Era of Endless War

Yochi Dreazen

CROWN PUBLISHERS

NEW YORK

Copyright © 2014 by Yochi J. Dreazen

Published in the United States by Crown Publishers, an imprint of the Crown Publishing
Group, a division of Random House LLC, a Penguin Random House Company, New York.
www.crownpublishing.com
CROWN and the Crown colophon are registered trademarks of Random House LLC.

Library of Congress Cataloging-in-Publication Data
Dreazen, Yochi.
The invisible front : love and loss in an era of endless war / Yochi Dreazen.—First edition.
pages cm
1. Graham, Mark (Mark A.). 2. Graham, Mark (Mark A.)—Family.
3. Generals—United States—Biography. 4. United States. Army—Biography.
5. Soldiers—Mental health—United States. 6. Post-traumatic stress disorder—United States.
7. Suicide—United States. 8. Sons—United States—Death. 9. War—Psychological aspects.
10. Sociology, Military—United States. I. Title.
E897.4.G72D73 2014fr
355.0092—dc23
[B]
2014007360

ISBN 978-0-385-34783-9
eBook ISBN 978-0-385-34784-6

Printed in the United States of America

Jacket design by Eric White
Jacket photograph: George Baier IV

10 9 8 7 6 5 4 3 2 1

First Edition

For Annie, always

They say, Our deaths are not ours; they are yours;
they will mean what you make them.

—Archibald MacLeish, "The Young Dead Soldiers"

For such closeness, there should be a word beyond love.

—Shirley Hazzard, *The Great Fire*

CONTENTS

CONTENTS

PROLOGUE
THE LOST BOYS

Seoul, South Korea, June 2003

The call came just after midnight, waking Colonel Mark Graham and his wife, Carol, instantly. Mark worked for the four-star American general charged with protecting South Korea from a sudden attack by its mercurial neighbor to the north, and his job required that he be notified of any emergency, regardless of the hour. He reached for the phone expecting to hear one of his subordinates. Instead, Mark heard the muffled voice of his older son, Jeff, an army lieutenant stationed in Kentucky who was getting ready to deploy to the battlefields of Iraq.

"No, Jeff, no," Mark said, shaking. "Tell me it's something else."

Carol, who had put her own life on hold to follow Mark to postings around the world, sat up in bed, her mind spinning. She knew that her three children partied hard and had a weakness for alcohol. Had one of them gotten into an accident or been arrested for drunk driving? Melanie, the youngest member of the family, had once downed so much alcohol during a frat party her freshman year that she passed out and had to be carried back to the off-campus apartment she shared with her two brothers. Had she done so again? Carol realized it was something much worse when Mark put his arms around her and dropped his voice to such a quiet whisper that she initially had a hard time hearing him.

"Kevin hung himself," Mark told her. "He's gone."

Carol tried to stand and then crumpled to the floor. She loved all of her kids, but Kevin, the middle child, had always been particularly special to her. Tall and burly, with a shy smile and a dry sense of humor, he was the perfect son—brilliant, kind, and always willing to put others before himself. When the children were young, Jeff sometimes locked Melanie into a closet as a joke. Kevin would wait for his older brother to leave and then open the door and let her out. As a senior in high school Kevin notched a 1310 on his SAT and graduated with a 4.07 GPA. He won a full academic scholarship to the University of Kentucky and was a top cadet in the same Reserve Officers' Training Corps program that Jeff had completed just one year earlier. Kevin's ROTC instructors regularly told him that his future in the military was boundless, that his career might one day outshine his father's.

But Kevin had another side, one that his parents didn't discover until after his death. He had been diagnosed with depression during his junior year at Kentucky, and prescribed Prozac. Kevin hadn't told many people that he had begun taking an antidepressant. Depression was seen as a sign of weakness in the military world that Kevin was preparing to enter, and psychiatric medications such as Prozac were thought to make soldiers unreliable and unstable. Kevin wasn't in the army yet, and his military career wouldn't begin until he finished ROTC the following year. But he began to worry that he wasn't going to make it. He was set to spend his entire summer in army-run training courses, and he felt increasingly certain that his ROTC instructors would discover that he was taking the medication and boot him out of the entire program. The risks of staying on Prozac, he concluded, far outweighed the benefits, so Kevin abruptly stopped taking the medication. Alone with his disease, Kevin Graham began spiraling downward. His grades plummeted, and he cut ties with most of his friends. On June 21, Jeff stood in the parking lot of a nearby golf course and scanned the road for his brother's aging green Honda. They'd made plans to play a round of golf that Saturday morning, but Kevin hadn't shown up. Jeff called his brother's cell phone again and again, but the calls went straight to voice mail. Suddenly alarmed, Jeff called Melanie and asked her to check in on Kevin. Phone in hand, she opened the door to Kevin's bedroom and suddenly went completely silent. Her brother was hanging from the ceiling fan, his feet almost touching the floor.

Mark and Carol made it onto the first plane back to the United States and landed in Louisville on June 22, less than a day after Kevin's death. Numb with shock and grief, they struggled to keep their composure as Kevin was buried on a grassy bluff overlooking the slow-moving Kentucky River.

Less than a year after Kevin's suicide, Second Lieutenant Jeffrey Graham was on a foot patrol near the insurgent stronghold of Khaldiyah when he spotted a buried IED. It exploded just as he turned to warn his men to stay back, killing him and one of his soldiers but saving the lives of the rest of the platoon. Jeff was buried next to his brother, which struck Mark and Carol as appropriate. Their sons had been inseparable in life. They would be inseparable in death as well.

In the years ahead, Mark and Carol would struggle to come to terms with their twin losses. They would draw purpose from their sons' deaths by working to change the military that defined both their lives and those of Jeff and Kevin. They would fight to erase the stigma surrounding mental health in the army and battle its growing suicide problem. Kevin hadn't served a day in the military when he killed himself, but Mark and Carol would come to understand that the factors that kept him from seeking help—stigma and the legitimate fear that he'd be drummed out of the military if his commanders discovered that he was on prescription medication—were the exact same ones that would lead hundreds of soldiers to take their own lives in the years ahead. They would become experts in post-traumatic stress disorder, the signature wound of the wars in Iraq and Afghanistan and one of the biggest causes of the suicide epidemic just beginning to spread through the military. They would learn that the Pentagon hadn't had remotely enough psychologists and psychiatrists to handle the flood of troops returning home from the wars with PTSD or depression, forcing some soldiers to wait so long for an appointment that they killed themselves before ever seeing a counselor.

Mark and Carol would also watch, horrified, as the numbers of soldiers taking their own lives grew larger and larger. The military's suicide rate jumped more than 80 percent between 2002 and 2009, the first year that the percentage of troops who took their own lives was higher than the percentage of civilians who did so. In 2012 more soldiers died by their own hand than in combat. In 2013 the total number of military suicides since the start of the wars in Iraq and Afghanistan passed the 1,000 mark. In 2014 the Pentagon disclosed that the suicide rate for male veterans age thirty and younger had jumped 44 percent between 2009 and 2011, a startling figure that suggested that the number of younger soldiers choosing to take their own lives would continue to increase well into the future.

Mark and Carol Graham have devoted their lives to preventing that problem from getting worse. Mark rose through the ranks of the army and was eventually promoted to general, a post that gave him the power to develop innovative suicide prevention tactics that dramatically reduced the suicide rate at the base he commanded and would later be replicated throughout the military. Carol told the story of her lost sons to audiences of strangers all over the country, publicly reliving the most painful moments of her life in the hope of persuading troubled young people to seek help before making the darkest of choices. Suicide has become the military's newest war, and Mark and Carol are squarely on the front lines. Ten years after their sons' deaths, they're still fighting.

CHAPTER 1

Murray, Kentucky, July 1976

Mark Graham had a plan. It was the summer of 1976, and he was finally ready to propose to Carol Shroat, his girlfriend of almost twelve months. Like the military officer he was training to become, Mark had spent months secretly working over the details of how he would ask Carol to marry him. Earlier that summer he snuck away from Murray State, the small state university he and Carol attended, and purchased an engagement ring from a pawnshop in St. Louis. He spent pretty much every dollar he had, but Mark smiled every time he looked into the small white box holding the ring and saw its diamond sparkle brightly in the light.

The second part of Mark's plan involved taking Carol to nearby Kentucky Lake, rowing her out to the middle of the water, and then gazing deeply into her eyes as he told her how much he loved her and how excited he was for the two of them to build a life together. He was certain that it would be both romantic and memorable. It was, though not for the reasons he'd thought. Mark had hidden the ring inside a rolled-up magazine so Carol wouldn't see it during their walk to the lake. He stumbled as they left his apartment, and the ring slipped out and bounced down the stairs.

"Don't move," Mark said quickly. "That's your engagement ring."

"My what?" Carol replied.

Mark picked up the ring and got down on one knee. Carol, laughing, said yes.

Mark and Carol had taken very different paths to Murray State. Carol saw it as the family school; her parents were alumni, as were two of her three sisters. Carl, her father, had met her mother, Jackie, when he gave her a ride home from class in his blue Studebaker during a heavy rainstorm. Jackie soon began noticing that Carl would park near her house virtually every morning to offer her a ride back to campus. A few months later Carl asked her out to a local drive-in movie theater to see a western starring Randolph Scott. They got engaged in the summer of 1952 and married the following year.

Carl attended medical school and then moved to Frankfort to start his own practice. He became one of the city's best-known doctors, famous for serving as the personal physician of Kentucky governor Wendell Ford—he saved the politician's life by diagnosing a brain aneurysm before it could do much harm—while still finding time to make house calls to ordinary citizens throughout Frankfort. The Shroats enjoyed a comfortable, upper-middle-class life. They drove late-model luxury cars like Chrysler Fifth Avenues and lived in a custom-built three-story house in an upscale part of town. A white brick post at the edge of the driveway was engraved with the words C. E. SHROAT M.D. When they graduated from high school, Carl paid for each of his daughters to take a monthlong trip through Europe. Carol never worried about how she'd afford Murray State. Thanks to her father, she didn't need to.

———

Mark wasn't so fortunate. He was born in St. Louis, the only child of Russel and Pat Graham. Russel was a self-educated truck driver who switched to the real estate business and quickly found success selling condominiums throughout St. Louis. Russel used his year-end bonuses to send Mark to summer baseball camps and told Pat to quit her job at the grocery warehouse where she worked. She put in her two weeks' notice and started to prepare for a new life as a stay-at-home wife and mother. Russel began telling friends that he would take Mark into the family business and one day open a real estate company called Graham and Son.

A few days later Pat noticed that her husband's nose had started bleeding and wouldn't stop. Alarmed, she had him rushed to the hospital. The doctors assured her that he'd be out in a few days, but Russel's condition worsened and he began spitting up large amounts of blood. One afternoon a doctor walked into the room and brusquely said, "This man is dying." Russel died from a heart attack a few hours later, barely three days after he'd checked in. He was thirty-three; Mark was eleven and still very much a boy. When a neighbor knocked on his door to say that Russel wouldn't go to heaven because he hadn't been religious, Mark promptly flattened him with a punch to the face.

With her husband gone, Pat took a new job at a factory that supplied parts to Westinghouse and spent long hours painstakingly winding copper wire onto spools for its washing machines and dryers. At night Mark watched his mother put Vaseline on her chafed and cut-up fingers and then gingerly slip them into a pair of white cotton gloves. The little family held on, but just barely. Pat would sometimes drive to work with only a quarter in her purse in case she had to use the telephone in an emergency. She spent evenings counting nickels, quarters, and dimes at the kitchen table, sorting the coins into neat piles. Mark, watching her work, often wondered why the stacks were so small.

After his father's death, Mark stopped going to summer baseball camp and started taking odd jobs to earn spending money. He bused tables at a country club restaurant, mowed lawns, raked leaves, sold greeting cards, and served as a Little League baseball umpire. He didn't take a full-time job until he joined his mother at the grocery warehouse the summer after his senior year in high school. Pat had married a sweet-natured bricklayer named Bill Conrad and returned to her old position with the wholesaler, and Mark worked eight-hour shifts filling trucks bound for individual grocers with boxes of milk, meat, and produce. He joined the Teamsters at age eighteen, and Pat jokes that he may have been the youngest union member in the entire state of Missouri. It was a physically taxing job, and Mark would occasionally nap on a grassy field outside the warehouse. One afternoon Mark and a friend were sleeping when a coworker stumbled across their prone bodies and worried that both young men were dead. He kicked their feet to be sure. When Mark opened his eyes, the man screamed and ran into the warehouse.

Shortly before his death Russel took out a $10,000 life insurance policy that listed Pat as the sole beneficiary. When Mark was getting ready to graduate high school, Pat told him that she'd be able to use the money to help pay for college. Those funds, plus the money he'd earned over the summers, meant that Mark was able to afford the tuition at Murray State, which he'd visited as a senior and fallen in love with because of its bucolic campus and small-town feel. His high school guidance counselor told him that the military's Reserve Officers' Training Corps would pay part of his tuition if he agreed to spend a few years in the army after he graduated. Mark enrolled in the school's ROTC program, figuring it would help him quickly decide if the military was right for him.

Mark's army career almost ended before it started. Murray State's ROTC cadets spent most of their time marching through empty classrooms and practicing military formations. Mark found those exercises so boring that he quickly dropped out of ROTC altogether. Mark had barely resumed his classes the following semester when one of the professors running the program called and asked that he give it another chance.

"We've got some different things we're doing with the program here, and I think you'll like it," the professor told him. "Why don't you just try one class?"

The instructor was right—Murray State's program had changed significantly. The cadets practiced rappelling down mountains and conducting mock patrols of potentially hostile areas rather than endlessly drilling proper military formations. They studied marksmanship and practiced firing M16s and .22 rifles, which was an entirely new experience for a nonhunter such as Mark. They ditched the classroom and spent long, happy days in a nearby national park learning how to read maps and navigate using nothing but the sun and stars. Mark thrived; he was finally spending time in the outdoors with other driven young men who were willing to serve in the military during a time of war. When a military recruiter offered him a formal ROTC scholarship that would pay for his senior year at Murray State in exchange for four years of army service, Mark said yes. It was a chance to see the world and have the kinds of adventures that he'd dreamed about growing up. He planned to do his stint in the army and then go to law school. It was the start of what would eventually be a thirty-four-year army career.

Carol was just as driven, but in a very different direction. She studied social work and psychology with an eye toward helping others deal with the kinds of depression and anxiety that had hung over her own life like dark clouds. "My favorite class was abnormal psychology, because it was the one thing that made me feel normal," she said. During the summers Carol stayed at Murray State to take extra classes and work as a campus phone operator, answering calls with a chirpy "Good morning, Murray State." The summer classes allowed her to finish her undergraduate degree in three years, but she decided to spend an additional year at Murray State so she could get a master's degree in counseling while waiting for Mark to graduate. Her father, old-fashioned and protective, wouldn't allow her to get her own off-campus apartment. Carol dutifully stayed in the dorms.

She didn't wear jeans. Mark tried, but he just couldn't get past that one detail. *She didn't wear jeans.* It was the early 1970s, but Carol looked like she belonged in an earlier, more innocent time. Her classmates wore bell-bottoms, let their hair grow long and unkempt, and made a point of not wearing lipstick or eyeliner. Carol wore skirts or dress pants around campus, carefully styled and blow-dried her hair, and wore makeup to class. Her classmates drank, smoked pot, and had sex. Carol played the tenor saxophone in Murray State's marching band and largely focused on her rehearsals and schoolwork. "I was a bit of a nerd," she said. But Carol wasn't a saint; in high school, she and her younger sister Debbie had snuck out of their house and driven to parties where they could drink with their friends years before any of them were of age. Still, she stood out on the Murray State campus for her dignified appearance and demure behavior. Before meeting Mark, Carol had been dating a devout young man who was now in Scotland studying for a degree in theology and preparing for a life as a Methodist minister.

Mark was leading a very different kind of life. He and his best friend, Jeff Hohman, pledged Kappa Alpha, one of the wildest fraternities on Murray State's campus. KA brothers tied pledges to trees and pelted them with spoiled food. They'd replace each other's shampoo with baby oil. During Mark and Jeff's freshman year, the KA brothers took a group road trip to a nearby strip club called the Black Poodle to party with dancers with names like Heaven Lee and EZ Rider. It wouldn't be their only visit.

The KA house had grimy bathrooms that women were reluctant to use and decrepit furniture speckled with mysterious stains. Jeff lived in a basement bedroom that had no real ceiling; any movement upstairs, especially dancing, would send dust and dirt cascading down onto his mattress. Mark's room was covered with so many loose mounds of socks, underwear, jeans, and T-shirts that Pat remembers being shocked and somewhat horrified when she first visited the house. Mark and Jeff both had beards and flowing, shoulder-length hair. "We looked like Jesus and the apostles," Jeff said.

Appearances aside, Mark was flourishing. He was elected president of his pledge class and was quickly tapped to oversee the fraternity's finances. KA was broke, and Mark devised a plan to sell small books of coupons for local restaurants and stores. He and his frat brothers stayed up late at night stapling the crude packets together, and the project was an immediate success. Mark also worked to improve KA's crumbling headquarters. His stepfather, Bill Conrad, had taught him to mix mortar and lay bricks, and Mark used those skills to build a new cement deck, bar, and grill at the back of the house. He was elected president of the entire fraternity a short time later.

He settled on political science as a major and watched his grades steadily improve. Academics seemed to come fairly easily to him, and so did girls. Mark was tall and thin, with piercing eyes and a muscular physique honed by the ROTC program's grueling early-morning workouts, and he quickly earned a reputation as a campus Lothario. Jeff knew Carol from Frankfort and kept thinking that she and Mark would be a good match. He invited her to a KA party, and she was smitten with Mark the first time she laid eyes on him. "I just introduced them, and Carol kind of took it from there," Jeff said. "Mark never knew what hit him."

Mark initially had his doubts about Carol, though they had nothing to do with her looks. She was a thin brunette with a radiant smile. She had been a baton twirler in her high school marching band and could easily have passed for a Murray State cheerleader. But Mark just couldn't shake the feeling that she was too straitlaced for his taste. "She was a bookworm, studying all the time, and I didn't even know where the library was," Mark said. "She smiled so much that I thought it had to be fake. I just felt like no one could possibly be that happy."

A few months later Carol was at the KA house for a party, looking and feeling uncomfortable. There was a jukebox in the back room, and Mark asked her to dance. He didn't think things would go much further, but when he leaned in to kiss her, she kissed him right back. It wasn't the chaste, quick peck he'd expected. It was a full-on *kiss*. "I was like, 'Wow, she kisses really good,'" Mark said. "I knew right away that there was something there. I just knew."

Their first real date was far from romantic. Mark took Carol to see *Carrie*, a horror movie, which she sat through mostly with her eyes clenched shut. As their relationship progressed, another issue surfaced: Carol's parents were deeply uncomfortable about their eldest daughter dating a bearded young man who didn't look like any of her male friends and classmates from Frankfort. Carl Shroat wore a dark suit to work every day and kept his hair cut short. Mark favored jeans and T-shirts and wore his hair long. "Daddy just didn't know what to make of Mark the first time they met," Carol said. "It was like opposites colliding." Carl and Jackie eventually came to cherish Mark and treat him like the son they never had, but it took time.

The biggest challenge facing the young couple was that Carol, despite her deep attraction to Mark, wasn't sure she wanted to spend the rest of her life with him. When they first met, Carol was still loosely involved with Greg Waldrop, the minister-in-training. Greg knew about Mark, but Mark didn't know about him. Carol felt torn between the two men and the very different lives they were offering her, and her indecision grew even stronger when Greg returned home to Kentucky.

"I was nuts about Mark, but in my head I really thought that God wanted me to marry Greg," Carol said. "He was a minister, and I had it in my head that that was what I was supposed to do."

One afternoon Greg drove her to Kentucky Lake. Carol poured her heart out to him about Mark and her difficulty choosing between the two men. Greg had a simple solution.

"I'm home for the summer," he told her. "You can date Mark and you can date me, and you can kind of see where God leads you."

It seemed like a perfect solution to Carol, but Mark saw it very differently. He felt ambushed by the news about Carol's relationship with Greg and had no intention of effectively sharing his girlfriend with another man. Mark had a simple solution of his own to Carol's dilemma: He broke up with her.

Carol was devastated, which she saw as a clear sign of which man she was meant to be with. "I thought, 'Gee, if this hurts so much, it means Mark is the one I can't live without,'" she said. "I pretty much had to grovel to convince him to take me back."

Carol and Mark were soon inseparable, each subtly changing to accommodate the other's lifestyle. Carol began wearing jeans; Mark cut back on his drinking and moved out of the KA house and into an off-campus apartment with Jeff, who had started dating Carol's sister Debbie, another Murray State student. Most evenings, the young couples would stay in, cook dinner together, and play bridge. On Sundays, the four of them went to church. They created a small world of their own and lived comfortably inside of it.

From the outside, Mark and Carol were a golden couple, the kind of good-looking, accomplished young adults that other college students envied. Unlike those of many of their friends, their futures seemed clear: Carol was finishing a master's degree in counseling, with a job lined up at a nearby mental health institution, and Mark was preparing to be commissioned into the army as a second lieutenant.

But although neither knew it at the time, both were bringing baggage into the relationship: extensive, if unspoken, family histories of depression and suicide. Carol's aunt was diagnosed with bipolar disorder as a teenager and had to undergo regular electroshock treatments; her uncle had a depressive episode so severe that he committed himself to a mental hospital in Louisville and has lived as a recluse ever since. Carl Shroat's grandfather killed himself, and the problems continued down through the generations. Carol's younger sister Sandra has been bipolar her entire adult life and would later develop a detailed—though unfulfilled—plan for taking her own life. Carl rarely spoke to his children about their dark inheritance, but he didn't entirely avoid it. In 1992, the year before he died, Carl stood in Sandra's living room, staring blankly at her stone fireplace and wooden mantel. "I'm so sorry," he told her. "You're the one who got it in the family." Sandra took her father's comments to mean that she was the latest in a long line of Shroats battling severe mental illness.

Carol wasn't immune. She went to a majorette tryout to show off her baton-twirling skills during the summer between her sophomore and junior years in high school and was devastated when the judge told her that she had the skills to make the team but was five or ten pounds too heavy. The rejection hit Carol so hard that she thought about killing herself by jumping off a cliff overlooking the Kentucky River or driving her car off a bridge. "I would look in the mirror and see a fat person, and I couldn't deal with it," Carol said. "I just went to a very dark place, very quickly." She decided to starve herself. Carol often ate just a boiled egg for breakfast and some plain lettuce for lunch. Her parents, alarmed, made her eat pizza or steak so that she would gain weight. She would dutifully clear her plate, then sneak away and force herself to vomit. Carol's weight plummeted from 118 pounds to 95, and she sometimes blacked out from malnutrition. One night she decided that the only way of staying thin was to destroy the parts of her body that allowed her to eat. She crept downstairs to a utility room near the kitchen, carefully poured out a cup of Clorox bleach, and swallowed down as much she could. Her stomach and throat began to burn so badly that she ran to the kitchen and began frantically gulping down milk to ease the pain. Carl rushed her to the hospital and later told his daughter that she had almost damaged her throat badly enough that she'd have had to spend the rest of her life eating through a feeding tube. Carl bought her cassettes on eating disorders, but the bulimia and anorexia didn't begin to disappear until her father put her on Valium while she was at Murray State.

Mark's family had its own secrets. His maternal grandmother suffered a mental breakdown so severe that she had to be hospitalized for a month under heavy sedation. One of Mark's second cousins hanged himself with a bicycle chain. His mother has battled depression her entire life and spent years taking Zoloft, a fact she long kept from her only son. "It would be these deep feelings of melancholy," she said. "I would feel sorry for myself even though I had no real reason to."

Mark himself was prone to deep feelings of pessimism about the future. In the run-up to his wedding, he regularly warned Carol that they'd probably have only a small amount of time together. "Just know that if you marry me, I probably won't live very long because my dad died so young," he told her. Deeply in love, she did her best not to take the comments too seriously.

Mark and Carol got married on August 13, 1977, just eight months after they'd graduated, in Frankfort's First United Methodist Church, a 121-year-old gray stone building in the city's historic district that the Shroats had attended for years. Mark and his groomsmen wore white tuxedoes with brown trim; Carol wore a long-sleeved wedding gown and veil. He was twenty-two and she was just twenty-one. On that sunny afternoon their futures seemed boundless and full of promise.

CHAPTER 2

Baumholder, Germany, 1978

"Just sign here, sir," the young sergeant said as he handed Mark a loaded Colt .45 handgun. "Please don't forget to bring it back when you're done."

Mark hadn't realized that he'd need a gun. It was the summer of 1978, and the newly minted second lieutenant had just arrived in Germany for the first deployment of his military career. Mark had never been out of the continental United States before, so he had felt the nervous giddiness of a tourist when his plane touched down in Frankfurt for the hour-long drive to Baumholder. The base was a mini-America, complete with a pair of tidy baseball diamonds, a football field, and a network of roads with names such as Chicago Street and Theater Road. The maroon-and-gold Buccaneers of Baumholder's on-base high school battled football teams from other U.S. posts. Its commissary sold potato chips, candy bars, magazines, and cereal imported from the States. The officers' club sold Jim Beam, Jack Daniel's, and cold American beer by the bottle or glass. The base was carefully designed to help soldiers forget that they were far from home.

It was the height of the Cold War, but Mark hadn't been given the gun to protect the base against a Soviet assault. He had been given the powerful weapon to defend himself against other U.S. soldiers. The military Mark had just entered had largely been shattered by the Vietnam War. During that conflict, discipline had broken down in many units, with enlisted personnel refusing to undertake dangerous missions and routinely getting into fistfights with higher-ranking sergeants and officers. Racially motivated violence and rampant drug and alcohol use had cast a pall over the entire force. In May of 1971, at the height of the war, a small altercation between black and white troops at California's Travis Air Force Base erupted into a full-blown riot that raged for four days. The violence left more than thirty troops injured, some severely.

One month later, marine colonel Robert Heinl, a twenty-seven-year military veteran, offered a grim assessment of the military personnel who would soon start leaving Vietnam and returning to bases such as Baumholder. "The morale, discipline and battleworthiness of the U.S. Armed Forces are, with a few salient exceptions, lower and worse than at any time in this century and possibly in the history of the United States," Heinl wrote in a blunt June 1971 essay. "By every conceivable indicator, our army that remains in Vietnam is in a state approaching collapse, with individual units avoiding or having refused combat, murdering their officers and non-commissioned officers, drug-ridden, and dispirited where not near mutinous."

Those problems didn't go away when the war ended in 1975. Five years later army chief of staff Edward "Shy" Meyer told Congress that the post-Vietnam army was "hollow" because of the long conflict's heavy human and financial toll. But it wasn't just the force itself that had been hollowed out by years of grueling combat. As with so many earlier conflicts, the men and women who fought in Vietnam had been hollowed out as well. "The army was in a downward spiral," retired colonel Michael Thompson, one of Mark's best friends in Germany, recalled. "We were struggling professionally. We were struggling with men who had no business still being in the army. We were struggling financially. Name the issue, and we were struggling with it."

Thompson's first exposure to the hollow force came when he was walking past a barracks building in early 1974, shortly before Dr. Martin Luther King's birthday, and heard a commotion inside. Yanking open the door, he saw a handful of young black privates trying to push a black sergeant out a second-floor window. A few feet away, other low-ranking black soldiers were cursing and screaming at their sergeants, who were cursing and screaming right back.

The shoving and yelling died down when Thompson entered the room and asked what the fight was about. The enlisted soldiers had told their NCOs that they would refuse to do any work that day, to protest the army's failure to create a holiday formally honoring the slain civil rights leader. The NCOs told them that they sympathized but couldn't let their personal feelings get in the way of their duties as soldiers. The sparring had broken out a few minutes later, with the young soldiers deriding the black NCOs as Uncle Toms and attacking them for being symbols of what they saw as an unfair and even racist military power structure.

Officers at Baumholder weren't always so successful in disciplining their troops.

Early in Mark's tour a young lieutenant who had pulled night-watch duty was making his rounds through a small complex of military office buildings. He spotted a group of soldiers who had climbed up some nearby scaffolding and were sitting there, in violation of base regulations, drinking large bottles of German beer.

"You're not supposed to be up there," the officer told them. "Get back in the building."

"Screw you, Lieutenant," one of the soldiers shouted back.

Before the officer could respond, the soldier picked up one of the empty bottles, reared back, and hurled it at the lieutenant, hitting him square in the head and knocking him out cold. The soldiers calmly finished their beers and then climbed back down. They were never identified or punished.

Shortly after he arrived in Germany, Mark himself was forced to confront a different facet of the army's discipline breakdown: the widespread use of marijuana, hashish, and other drugs, particularly among the thousands of troops who'd gotten hooked in Vietnam. The military's narcotics problem was so severe that Mark would routinely order his troops to leave their barracks so armed military policeman could use a drug-sniffing dog to search the long, narrow room. One evening in 1979 a specially trained German shepherd was sniffing around the lockers and bunk beds when it gave a sudden bark and hurled itself at a young soldier. The dog tore at the soldier's front pocket and started thrashing its snout from side to side, shredding his uniform. It finally ripped the pocket clean off, sending silver packets of hashish cascading down to the floor like snowflakes. The soldier was arrested and kicked out of the army, but Mark's soldiers—like others throughout the military—continued to find other ways of hiding drugs.

Few officers realized it at the time, but many of those soldiers weren't simply trying to get high. Hundreds of thousands of American troops fought in Vietnam and returned home burdened by horrific memories of friends torn apart by buried bombs or shot down by unseen enemies. Others were haunted by images of Vietnamese villagers burning from American napalm or sobbing as they huddled over the bodies of their dead parents, spouses, or children. There is no question that some of the soldiers Mark Graham found drinking and abusing drugs in their barracks were undisciplined kids looking for a good time. Many others, however, were trying to evade the demons that had haunted them since the guns fell silent across the jungles, villages, and cities of Vietnam. They were battling what would later come to be known as posttraumatic stress disorder, an invisible wound many would struggle with for the rest of their lives.

Soldiers have buckled under the strain of witnessing and committing horrific acts of violence for as long as humans have taken up weapons against one another. In the *Iliad,* Achilles experiences such overpowering sadness and rage after his closest friend dies outside the walls of Troy that he contemplates suicide. Later Achilles publicly mutilates his friend's killer in revenge. In the *Odyssey,* Homer plaintively asks, "Must you carry the bloody horror of combat in your heart forever?" For centuries, the answer has been yes. Soldiers have returned from combat beset by lifelong bouts of depression, anxiety, and sleeplessness. They have felt disfigured and debased by war, even if they suffered no physical injuries. "I don't believe I am the same being I was two weeks ago," a young Civil War soldier named Walter Lee wrote to his mother in 1862. "I don't think as I used to and things don't seem as they did."

Civil War physicians tried to prepare soldiers for the horrors they'd see, hoping that written warnings would prevent troops from being fundamentally changed by the long and bloody conflict. Before heading into combat, newly minted Confederate troops received letters emphasizing that "familiarity with scenes of violence and death [means that] soldiers often became apparently indifferent to suffering and anguish, and appear to be destitute of the ordinary sensibilities of our humanity."

Union troops received similar warnings, but the efforts didn't work. The Civil War claimed the lives of more than six hundred thousand Union and Confederate troops, and hundreds of thousands of others returned home with deep psychological wounds that never fully healed. In the years after the long war, half the patients in the nation's mental institutions were veterans. Countless returning troops suffered from depression, anxiety, and mood swings that left them unable to eat, sleep, or hold regular jobs. Veterans beset by nightmares and unable to readjust to civilian life received little public sympathy, with the doctors of the time icily diagnosing them with hysteria, melancholy, and even insanity.

The names given to such invisible wounds have changed over time, but their high human toll has remained grimly constant. Soldiers shattered by the carnage of World War I were told they had "shell shock." By 1919, 38 percent of the veterans in U.S. military hospitals were "mental and nervous cases"; by the mid-1930s, that number had spiked to more than 56 percent. In World War II, military doctors said soldiers who were unable to return to the fight because of anxiety, depression, and listlessness were suffering from "combat fatigue." The mental and emotional strains were so intense that military physicians later estimated that one out of every two troops on the front lines suffered from some form of psychological malady.

Charles Kuhl was one of them. In 1943, General George Patton was visiting a military hospital in Italy when he stopped by Kuhl's bed and noticed that the young man had no visible physical injuries. When the general asked him where he had been wounded, Kuhl—who'd just returned from months of frontline combat against the Germans—put his head in his hands and said, "I just can't take it, sir." Patton, furious, called Kuhl a coward, grabbed him by the scruff of his neck, and shouted to a nearby doctor, "Don't admit this sonofabitch." He turned to Kuhl, eighteen, and yelled directly into the soldier's face. "You hear me, you gutless bastard? You're going back to the front at once." Patton, military historian Mark Perry wrote, "literally kicked him in the pants and dragged him out of the tent."

Kuhl was far from the only American soldier to break down amid the carnage of Europe and the Pacific. Eugene Bondurant Sledge was the son of a prominent doctor in Mobile, Alabama, but dropped out of college to ensure that he'd see combat. He later fought in both Peleliu and Okinawa, and his memoir, *With the Old Breed*—which draws from notes Sledge scribbled in the margins of his Bible during the fighting—offers an unsettlingly vivid account of the psychological wounds of war.

During his time on Okinawa, Sledge saw an experienced marine begin babbling incoherently before picking up his rifle and rushing toward an entrenched Japanese position. It would have been a suicide mission, but a nearby sergeant managed to grab hold of the man and pull him back into a trench before he could get himself killed. "He's a damn good marine," the sergeant said. "But he's just had all he can take. That's it. He's just had all he can take."

Roughly 438,000 U.S. troops were discharged from the military for so-called psychiatric reasons during World War II, but military physicians of the time were no better at understanding the veterans' anger, depression, and guilt than their predecessors had been. It had been clear for centuries that soldiers returned from combat far different from when they'd deployed. It wasn't until Vietnam that doctors finally began to understand why.

In April 1971, Democratic senator Mike Mansfield of Montana took to the floor of the U.S. Senate and told an unusually vivid and disturbing story. One month earlier a young lieutenant named Thomas Dellwo had been sleeping in his tent in Vietnam when a grenade rolled in through an open flap and detonated, killing him instantly. The culprit, Mansfield told the lawmakers, wasn't a North Vietnamese soldier or a guerilla fighter from the Vietcong. It was another American soldier. "In every respect, this young man had every right and every reason to live," Mansfield said. "He was 'fragged' to death as he lay sleeping in his billet. He was murdered by a serviceman, a fellow American GI."

The speech was the first time most Americans were exposed to an unusually dark and unknown aspect of the Vietnam War: the large and growing number of troops, particularly officers, who were being murdered by those serving under them. There were 96 such fragging incidents in 1969. Two years later the number spiked to 333. Some units reportedly offered bounties for the murders of particularly unpopular officers and NCOs. Military historian Richard Holmes estimates that

20 percent of the American officers lost in Vietnam died at the hands of other troops. Senior enlisted personnel were no safer. In 1969 a young specialist named Enoch "Doc" Hampton walked into an office on his small base near the Cambodian border, pointed his M16 at a particularly hated NCO named Clarence Lowder, and pulled the trigger. Hampton then shot himself.

Such troop-on-troop violence was a symptom of a larger problem. Many of those who served in Vietnam did and saw things that would have been unimaginable to them just months earlier. They responded with feelings of uncontrollable fury. On the battlefield, some U.S. soldiers tried to kill as many Vietnamese fighters as they could, as violently as possible. Others targeted Vietnamese civilians, burning villages and killing women, children, and even babies. American soldiers killed their fellow troops and violently hazed younger compatriots. War had always taken a toll on those sent to fight in distant lands, but Vietnam was different. Troops fought guerillas who wore no uniforms, hid among civilians, and emerged from the shadows to kill and maim American soldiers before disappearing again. U.S. forces responded with acts of savagery many would spend the rest of their lives struggling to forget. Veterans came home feeling like they'd left essential parts of their humanity on the battlefields of Vietnam. The war had fundamentally changed them, and there was no going back.

Karl Marlantes grew up in the small town of Seaside, Oregon, and spent his summers working alongside his grandfather Axel on a fishing boat in the nearby Columbia River. A classic overachiever, he won a National Merit Scholarship and graduated from Yale before attending Oxford on a Rhodes Scholarship. He came from a left-leaning family and strongly opposed the Vietnam War. But walking Oxford's narrow streets, Marlantes was consumed with the thought, as he writes in a memoir, that he was "hiding behind privilege." His high school friends were already fighting and dying in Vietnam; Marlantes decided it would be cowardly for him to sit out the war. He traveled to Africa and showed up at an American base near Casablanca, looking like a "desert-darkened hippie," to volunteer for the war.

A short time later Marlantes was in Vietnam as a second lieutenant, leading marines into battle and both witnessing and committing acts of brutal violence. He returned home with a Navy Cross, a pair of Purple Hearts, and a long list of other military commendations. But Marlantes quickly realized that part of him would always remain in Vietnam, and that it would be impossible for him to fully transition from war to peace. "This 'adjustment' is akin to asking Saint John of the Cross to be happy flipping burgers at McDonald's after he's left the monastery," he writes.

When he returned home to Oregon, Marlantes was greeted at the airport by his parents and a former high school girlfriend looking to re-kindle their relationship. He couldn't bring himself to do it. Marlantes had left Vietnam as a shell of his former self, both physically and emo-tionally. It would take years for him to feel capable of giving or receiving love. "The fact was I felt unclean, insecure, strange, and awkward," he writes. "I didn't feel right—with anyone."

One veteran of three combat tours told psychiatrist Jonathan Shay that he returned from Vietnam looking almost exactly the same as when he had left. But those who had known him the best before he shipped off to war didn't recognize the angry, moody, and occasionally violent man who came home. "I'd be sitting there as calm as could be, and this mon-ster would come out of me with a fury that most people didn't want to be around," he told Shay. "It wasn't just over there. I brought it back here with me."

Few veterans were even willing to talk to doctors like Shay. Return-ing troops who sought psychiatric or psychological treatment were rou-tinely denied promotions or pushed out of the military. War-damaged soldiers left in droves, flooding into a civilian world that wasn't prepared to receive them. It was the era of *The Deer Hunter,* with movies and television shows portraying returning soldiers as unstable, violence-prone men capable of exploding at any moment. Veterans were left largely alone to battle their depression and anxiety, often with tragic results. *The Things They Carried*, Tim O'Brien's classic book of short stories about a platoon of U.S. soldiers in Vietnam, closes with a tribute to a close friend named Norman Bowker, who hung himself in a YMCA locker room in Iowa after playing a pickup basketball game. The war in Vietnam had ended eight years earlier, but Bowker was still fighting his own personal battle. Like an alarmingly high number of other veterans, he lost.

In 1980 the American Psychiatric Association finally gave a name to the invisible enemy that had killed Bowker and countless other veterans: post-traumatic stress disorder, or PTSD. The association's official diagnostic manual used the dry language of the clinician to describe a malady that often provokes sheer terror and debilitating feelings of powerlessness in those suffering from it. A diagnosis of PTSD, the psychiatrists write, could come only if a patient had "experienced an event that is outside the range of usual human experience and that would be markedly distressing to almost anyone," such as a serious threat to the patient's own life or the sight of other people who had been killed or grievously wounded. Patients with the disorder would suffer from vivid nightmares, hallucinations, and flashbacks. They'd have trouble concentrating or falling asleep, startle easily, and be prone to flashes of anger. They'd have physical reactions to loud noises or anything else that reminded them of the initial trauma.

Hundreds of thousands of Vietnam veterans would later be diagnosed with those exact symptoms. They had come back to the United States burdened by invisible wounds that their friends and families couldn't understand. Many veterans would tell their own loved ones that they hadn't expected to return from Vietnam alive and sometimes wished they hadn't. They would feel jittery in crowds, fight with their wives and children, and have difficulty eating, working, or sleeping.

Many would simply give up, overdosing on drugs, smashing their cars into trees, or using the guns and knives they had used to take enemy lives in Vietnam to take their own lives as well. Bowker, the veteran who killed himself eight years after Vietnam ended, may well have been one of them.

In 1983, Congress ordered the Department of Veterans Affairs to provide hard data on what was happening to soldiers after they returned home. The results, released in 1988, were shocking. The VA concluded that 15 percent of the men who'd fought in Vietnam had experienced PTSD in the previous six months and estimated that 31 percent would suffer it at some point in their lives. With roughly 2.5 million men serving in Vietnam over the course of the long war, those numbers meant that roughly 750,000 veterans were at risk of developing some form of PTSD.

Later studies have argued that PTSD rates were slightly lower, but there is no question that PTSD is the single darkest legacy of the Vietnam War. In 2011, nearly four decades after the last U.S. troops were airlifted out of Saigon, 299,076 Vietnam veterans were still receiving VA benefits for PTSD, far more than for any physical wound. Just as strikingly, the VA was continuing to provide PTSD-related financial assistance to 19,064 veterans of World War II and 12,745 veterans from the Korean War. Physical injuries heal; the mental and emotional ones often grow worse over time.

CHAPTER 3

Iraq, February 1991

The Chinook helicopter kicked up mottled clouds of sand and dirt as it flew over southern Iraq, moving low and fast to avoid being spotted by the Iraqi forces fighting the American ground troops who had poured into their country just days earlier. Major Mark Graham peered through the helicopter's small glass portholes for a glimpse of the tanks rumbling across the desert below, but it was too dark for him to see much of anything. He leaned back in his seat and listened to the rhythmic thumping of the helicopter's giant rotors, mentally preparing for his first mission of the Gulf War.

It was supposed to be a fairly routine assignment: fly to a small U.S. outpost in southern Iraq, drop off a handful of new troops and supplies, then fly back. Mark was excited all the same. He'd spent months cooling his heels in Saudi Arabia while the administration of President George H. W. Bush gave Iraqi dictator Saddam Hussein a final chance to remove his forces from Kuwait. War broke out when U.S. jets began pounding targets throughout Iraq in mid-January, but Mark was far from the front lines. He spent the first hours of the conflict huddled inside a sandbagged bunker in the Saudi Arabian desert, sweating under the bulky gas mask he was ordered to wear in case of an Iraqi chemical weapons attack. The ground invasion of Iraq and Kuwait began just after midnight on February 24. Mark flew into Iraq the next day.

It was dark and cold when Mark's Chinook touched down at the base. He got off to stretch his legs and walk around the small outpost, making mental recordings of the sights, smells, and sounds of the war zone. Mark was on his way back to the helicopter about an hour later when a grim-faced member of the flight crew stopped him and gestured toward the waiting Chinook.

"Sir, we have a couple of men who were killed in action," the soldier told him. "We need to get their remains to the mortuary. Can you take them back?"

Mark nodded immediately, but the full meaning of the soldier's words didn't hit him until he climbed up the Chinook's loading ramp and saw a pair of black body bags arrayed carefully at the front of the helicopter, just behind the cockpit. The rest of the cavernous helicopter was empty, leaving Mark alone with the two corpses. He didn't know their names, but he couldn't stop thinking about the men who'd died and the families back home who would soon be receiving the news. Mark had been in the military for more than thirteen years, but it was the first time he'd been in a war zone and the first time he'd been exposed to its human costs. The flight back to Saudi Arabia lasted only about forty-five minutes, but Mark remembers it as one of the longest journeys of his life. "That was when it really kind of sets in and hits you that 'Hey, this is real, no kidding, life-and-death stuff,'" he said. "Training accidents happen and car accidents happen, but these guys were killed fighting, and I'd never been exposed to that before."

Thousands of miles away in Augsburg, Germany, Carol was facing a challenge of her own. She was an army mom as well as an army wife, which meant she had to set her own fears about Mark's safety aside so that she could put on a brave face for her three young children, each of whom had reacted differently when the family got word that Mark would be deployed to the Middle East. Melanie, six, had hatched an elaborate plan to hide Mark under her bed so he wouldn't have to leave. She promised to sneak him food and water each day so he wouldn't be hungry or thirsty. Jeff, ten, and Kevin, eight, assured Mark that they'd be the men of the house and look after Carol and Melanie while he was away. They did their best to look strong, but Carol would sometimes hear them crying when they thought she wasn't around.

Shortly after Mark left for the Persian Gulf, Carol walked into the bedroom Jeff and Kevin shared so they could say the family's nightly prayers for the safety of Mark and all of his fellow soldiers. Bette Midler's "Wind Beneath My Wings" had become an enormously popular song during the run-up to the war, and the boys listened to it incessantly. As she was turning off the lights, Carol heard Kevin thank Jeff for always picking him first during pickup games of baseball and football even though other kids were far more athletic. "You are the wind beneath my wings," Kevin said.

Carol's stomach fell. Kevin was a serious and deeply sensitive boy who had no idea how corny that line would sound to his older, more irreverent brother. She expected Jeff to say something cutting and sarcastic in response. He surprised her.

"Kevin, you always tell me how smart I am even though you're so much smarter," Jeff said from the bottom bunk. "You are the wind beneath *my* wings."

Carol was deeply touched. At the time she attributed it to the heightened emotions the entire family was feeling with Mark away. But she soon realized it was something else entirely: a sign of the extraordinarily close bond that was developing between her two very different boys.

Try as they might, Carol and Mark couldn't figure out a way of coaxing their first son into the world. It was September 1979, and Carol was three weeks overdue with what would be the first of her three children. Carol's mother, Jackie, had flown in from Kentucky to be there for the birth, but as the days passed it was less and less clear when that would actually be. Jackie suggested that walking might send Carol into labor, so the two women spent hours exploring the winding cobble streets and centuries-old churches of Baumholder, an ancient market town nestled in the rolling green hills of western Germany. When that didn't work, Carol began carrying buckets of water up the narrow stairs of her four-story apartment building. "Looking back, that probably wasn't the smartest thing in the world," Carol said. "But it worked." Carol gave birth on September 22, at a military hospital at Landstuhl. She and Mark named their son Jeff in honor of Jeff Hohman, Mark's fraternity brother, best friend, and brother-in-law.

Even as a child, Jeff Graham was analytical, self-assured, and mischievous, traits that would grow stronger with time. When he was a toddler, Carol decided to teach him the importance of waking up early enough to make his own bed, something he had absolutely no desire to do. Instead, Jeff would finish his nightly bath, put on the clothes he planned to wear the following day, and then go to sleep in his *Star Wars* sleeping bag, leaving his sheets and pillows untouched. The next morning he'd jump out of bed already dressed, zip up his sleeping bag, and be ready for school. The system allowed him to get an extra hour of sleep.

Jeff could also be stubborn. At breakfast he insisted on eating only Cheerios, and only if he could pour the milk himself to make sure it wasn't as soggy as when his mom did it. When Carol would complain that he never listened to her, Jeff would just grin. "Mom, I always listen," he told her. "But then I make up my own mind."

Kevin Graham was born in November 1981, at Oklahoma's Fort Sill, Mark's first assignment after his time in Germany. Carol wanted to surprise her sisters and hadn't told them she was pregnant, so they thought she had simply gotten fat in Germany. Kevin, like Jeff, was late, so Carol drank a little castor oil in the hopes of speeding things along. Kevin was born after just three hours of labor, and Mark and Carol would later joke that he had been a perfect child right from the very start. Unlike his brother, Kevin would go to sleep in pajamas, wake up early, and politely eat whatever Carol had made for breakfast that day. Whenever there was talk of going out for ice cream, Jeff would say, "Me first, me first." Kevin would immediately defer to his brother. "Me last, me last," he'd say, smiling.

Mark and Carol's second son was a gentle child, eager to please both his parents and his grandparents. When Kevin was three, he held on to a small, handmade afghan blanket and sucked his thumb as he was falling asleep each night. During a family visit to Kentucky, his grandfather Carl told him that "big boys don't suck their thumbs" and promised to give him a "big boy trophy" if he dropped the habit. Kevin told Carol that he wanted his grandfather to be proud of him but needed one more night to hold on to the blanket and fall asleep with his thumb nestled reassuringly in his mouth. The next morning Carol was making pancakes when Kevin marched into the kitchen, climbed up on a chair, and ceremonially handed her the neatly folded blanket. He never held on to the afghan or sucked his thumb again. True to his word, Carl shipped Kevin a trophy that the young boy immediately, and proudly, put on his dresser.

Jeff, for his part, thought the whole thing was ridiculous. He slept with a stuffed raccoon and sucked his thumb until he was six years old. When Jeff made up his mind about something, Carol said, he really didn't care what others thought.

Jeff Graham was just two years older than Kevin, but he was fiercely protective of his younger brother and baby sister Melanie, who was born at Fort Sill in 1984. Like most military families, the Grahams were essentially nomads. They left Oklahoma and moved to Stafford, Virginia, so Mark could take a three-year assignment at the army Personnel Command (PERSCOM) in Alexandria, some forty miles south. Mark was promoted to major and then lieutenant colonel several years before most of his peers and did a final stateside tour at the army's Command and General Staff College at Fort Leavenworth, Kansas, a finishing school of sorts for officers preparing for long careers in the military. The Grahams returned to Germany in the summer of 1990.

The constant moves were hard on Jeff, Kevin, and Melanie, who were abruptly yanked out of schools where they had friends and favorite teachers and moved to new schools where they had to build relationships from scratch. That forced the three Graham children to become unusually close to one another. Jeff was painfully shy as a young child and had a severe speech impediment that left him unable to pronounce his *r*'s and *l*'s. He was so self-conscious about it that he would routinely crawl into a cabinet and spend hours talking to an imaginary friend named Steven. Jeff would whisper into Kevin's ear whenever he had something important to say because he knew that his younger brother would articulate every word perfectly. Kevin, for his part, was certain that Jeff could get rid of his speech impediment if he worked hard enough at it. He would repeat words like *la-la-lamp* or *ra-ra-railroad* until his older brother learned to pronounce them correctly. Jeff eventually learned to pronounce both letters perfectly and became the most talkative and extroverted of the three Graham children.

He was also the most protective. When Kevin was in first grade, his most prized possession was a stuffed animal called Tenderheart Bear, which had a large red heart emblazoned on its chest. Kevin would talk to the bear like it was alive, sharing stories from his day at school and jokes about his family and friends. One afternoon Kevin's teacher told him to bring his favorite toy to class for show-and-tell. Kevin was scared to bring Tenderheart Bear to school because he worried that something would happen to it, but Mark and Carol assured him that no one would harm the toy. They were wrong. On the bus ride back home, a group of older kids snatched the teddy bear out of Kevin's hands and tossed it around like a football. Jeff was younger and smaller than the other kids, but he tried pushing and punching them so they'd give the bear back to his brother. When that didn't work, the bus driver searched every kid's backpack but couldn't find Tenderheart. Kevin returned home sobbing.

A few weeks later a group of middle school kids knocked on the Grahams' door with the remains of the bear, which they'd found in a pile of burnt leaves. The bear was covered in dirt and grime, and much of its fur had been singed off. Mark and Carol didn't want Kevin to see what was left of his beloved toy, but he came to the door before they could hide it away. The Grahams ended up giving the teddy bear a funeral of sorts, placing it in a small, felt-lined box, singing hymns, and then burying it under a backyard tree house that Mark had built for his boys. Kevin cried throughout; Jeff looked like he wanted to find the kids who'd stolen his little brother's cherished toy and beat them into the ground.

Jeff and Kevin had a more complex relationship with Melanie. When she was a toddler, Jeff would put her in a laundry basket at the top of the staircase and tell her that if she moved, she'd plunge down the stairs. He'd hide a cup of cold water on the top of her bedroom door so it would splash on her as soon as she walked into the room. He'd lock her in the darkened laundry room and then head out to play with his friends. Kevin was her savior. He'd gently lift his little sister out of the laundry basket or sneak to the laundry room to open the door and let her out. "Jeff was basically acting like a mean older brother," Melanie remembered. "Kevin would be the one trying to figure out a way of protecting me or keeping me from getting hurt."

When it came to other people, however, the two brothers closed ranks around their little sister. The family left Germany and moved back to Fort Sill in 1993, and the Grahams lived in a house overlooking a large lawn that neighborhood kids used for impromptu games of football. One afternoon a family friend named Peter Vangjel tackled Melanie to the ground, knocking the wind out of her. Kevin and Jeff came running from across the field and shoved him down onto the dirt. "Don't touch her!" Jeff yelled, red-faced with anger. "You're never allowed to touch her."

Melanie was shocked, in part because Peter and her brothers were so close and in part because Jeff routinely knocked her down much more forcefully. "You do that all the time," she told him. "Yeah, but you're my sister," he replied. "No one else gets to pick on you besides me." He helped her up off the ground and went right back to the game.

How many kids back home, Melanie thought, *will ever get a chance to do anything like this?* She was standing on the edge of Munich's former Olympic pool, gazing down into the placid aqua waters that Mark Spitz had made famous decades earlier. Melanie, six, was a gifted, graceful swimmer who dominated the other girls in her age group from the Augsburg Otters, a swim team for local military children. Jeff, ten, and Kevin, eight, were already on the team, though Jeff's skills and drive largely overshadowed those of his younger brother. The day before, the Otters had traveled to Munich for a swim meet on a chartered bus, Mark and Carol sitting a few rows away from their boys. Jeff had a fever of 102 degrees but insisted on swimming in both the individual and relay races; the meet would determine whether the Otters beat out teams from all of the other U.S. military bases in Europe, and Jeff was determined not to let his friends down. Melanie was just as motivated to win her part of the meet. She looked over at the older swimmers arrayed beside her, waited for the starting bell, and then dived headfirst into the pool.

Shuttling their kids to swim meets all over Germany was exhausting for Carol and Mark, but they didn't mind. When they got orders to deploy to Germany for the second time, the Grahams decided that they'd try to expose their children to as much of the country as they could. They visited castles, and Melanie and her brothers would sneak away from their parents to explore the buildings' dank underground jails and torture chambers. They trekked to the Felsenkirche, a five-hundred-year-old church carved into a sheer rock wall above the town of Idar-Oberstein. They drove to Trier, Germany's oldest city, and toured the ornate Catholic cathedral that houses a tunic believed to have been worn by Jesus Christ shortly before his crucifixion. They took a cable car to the top of the Zugspitze, Germany's tallest mountain, and gazed out over the towering, snow-covered Alps. They even brought the kids to Munich's legendary Oktoberfest, where Jeff, Melanie, and Kevin spent the day riding the Ferris wheel, merry-go-round, and wooden roller coaster and gorging on giant, heavily salted pretzels. "Their eyes would just be popping when the ladies walked by with those huge plates of pretzels and those giant steins of beer," Mark said.

The kids played American sports such as football, baseball, and basketball, but they also quickly took to Germany's traditional *volksmarsches,* long, leisurely hikes organized by private clubs throughout the country. The *volksmarsch* world was a lot like the Boy Scouts; the more hikes you completed, the more medals, pins, and badges you collected. Jeff, Kevin, and Melanie would all wear the traditional green wool hats, complete with a single feather in the brim, which were part of the unofficial uniforms of the rural Germans who led the marches. Each time they finished a hike, the Graham children added a new patch of cloth to their hats. Kevin took the hikes especially seriously. After finishing one particularly grueling march, he asked his parents if he could have one of the wooden canes that older Germans used to maneuver themselves up steep hills or across muddy terrain. Mark and Carol thought their little boy would look a bit strange walking with a cane, but Kevin had never asked them to buy him anything before. Kevin took the cane with him on every hike and occasionally brought it to school. It was leaning against their fireplace decades later.

Mark and Carol hoped that all of their children would pick up Ger-man, but that didn't happen. Jeff and Melanie learned how to order schnit-zel and ask where the bathrooms were, but that was about it. Kevin was different. He quickly developed the language skills to read and write in German and hold entire conversations with native speakers. He was the only one of the Graham children to ace his German classes at Augsburg's elementary school. A different side of Kevin was also emerging, though the family wouldn't grasp that it was a sign of his growing depression until much later. He would fall into dark moods that lasted for days when he learned about such tragedies as slavery or the diseases that wiped out hundreds of thousands of Indians after the Spanish discovered America. The Holocaust hit him even harder, and Kevin stopped eating or sleep-ing for nearly a week when he realized that the mass genocide had been planned just a short distance from the family home in Germany. Kevin would ask his parents how people could be so cruel and how God could stand aside and allow evil into the world. Their answers never satisfied him, and he'd disappear for hours at a time into the room he shared with his brother. Melanie and Jeff would knock on the door and ask him to come outside to play baseball or basketball, but Kevin wouldn't respond. "It was like he had just gone to a different place," Carol said. "He'd hear about these things and have trouble understanding how they happened. He'd obsess about it for days." At the time, Mark and Carol attributed their son's hypersensitivity and mood swings to puberty. It was a serious miscalculation.

Most of the time, though, Kevin was the same cheerful, happy-go-lucky kid that he'd been since he was old enough to walk and talk. He was the smartest of the three Graham children, and he would occasion-ally use his intelligence to gently mock his older brother. Shortly after he turned ten, Jeff called his brother into the bathroom and shut the door. Carol stood in the hallway and heard the two boys whisper to each other and then burst out laughing. When they came out, Jeff said he'd found his first "man hairs" that morning and wanted to show his brother that he was hitting puberty. Kevin then made a point of completely examining Jeff's lower body before solemnly pointing out that the "man hair" was actually just lint from the brand-new pajamas Jeff had worn to sleep. The brothers laughed about it for weeks. Years later they were playing Pictionary one afternoon when Jeff kept stumbling over the pronunciation of the same word. "Mare and guey?" he asked. "What the hell is that?" Without missing a beat, Kevin glanced at his brother and said, "It's *meringue,* you idiot," cracking up the entire room.

Jeff wouldn't come down from the roof. It was the fall of 1984, and Carol had just taken a new job as a substitute teacher at an elementary school at Fort Sill. Melanie was an infant, Kevin was two, and Jeff was about to turn five. None of the kids had ever spent a day without their mom before, and they did their best to make sure it didn't happen again. Carol came home at the end of her first day to find Melanie bawling uncontrollably and Jeff sitting on the roof of their babysitter's house and promising not to come down until Carol quit her job. She didn't go back to work for almost seven years.

The sacrifice was a typical one for Carol, who quickly learned that life as an army wife and mom meant that her husband's career would always come first and that it would be difficult—if not impossible—for her to hold down a steady job. She'd had to leave behind a promising mental health career in Kentucky when Mark received his initial deployment orders for Germany. She took a job at Baumholder teaching English classes to the Korean, Vietnamese, Hispanic, and German wives of some of the soldiers there, and frequently had to fend off lighthearted complaints that she was teaching them to speak with a southern accent. When Jeff was born she switched to part-time work at the base. His meltdown four years later meant the end of her teaching job at Fort Sill.

Carol also had to adjust to the stress of knowing that Mark could abruptly be sent to a dangerous place at any time. In 1990 the family had been back in Germany for only a few months when Mark got his deployment orders for Saudi Arabia. The family celebrated an early, sad Christmas on December 15, just before Mark left. A few weeks later Carol came home and found that Jeff had moved all of the furniture in the living room back against the wall, popped a videotape of Richard Simmons's *Sweatin' to the Oldies* into the VCR, and invited his siblings and a small group of neighborhood kids over for an impromptu aerobics class. Everyone in the house had a parent deployed to the war zone, and Carol immediately understood that her oldest son was trying to distract the kids for a few hours and give them some time to just laugh and goof around.

Mark returned home the following spring but soon got word of another potential deployment, this time to Bosnia. "We all thought it would happen any day," Carol said. "It seemed like his duffel bag was packed for months."

Despite the stress of Mark's preparations for the prospect of heading back to a war zone, Carol finally managed to find a way to go back to work. When Melanie started first grade in Augsburg, Carol decided to give substitute teaching another try. Her first day wasn't promising. She was assigned to fill in for a second-grade teacher but tried hugging the kids and letting them tell goofy stories instead of quickly making clear that she was in charge. She lost control of the classroom almost immediately, and the principal ultimately had to rush into the room, flip the lights on and off to get the kids' attention, and then scream at them to stay in their seats and be quiet. "It was like a scene from *Kindergarten Cop*," she said.

Her next assignment went more smoothly. The principal moved her over to the base's high school, and Carol formed close ties with the captain of the football team and some of the school's cheerleaders, rightly assuming that other students would follow their lead. The strategy paid off, and Carol was able to maintain discipline in her classrooms and make sure that her students turned in their assignments on time and did well on their exams. She taught at the school until Mark moved the family to Baumholder in the summer of 1991, their third move in as many years. Despite all of his preparations, he never did deploy to Bosnia.

The constant relocations were a welcome distraction for Carol, who was suffering through one of the most difficult periods of her life. Her father had been diagnosed with an inoperable brain tumor in early 1991, and his condition had been steadily worsening. Carl wanted to see the remains of the Berlin Wall before he died, so he and Jackie flew to Germany in March of 1992 to visit the wreckage and say good-bye to Mark, Carol, and the kids. The family took a bus trip to Berlin, but Carl was too weak to get off and walk the short distance to the wall. The kids went instead, chipping off a small piece of a graffiti-covered brick and giving it to their grandfather as a makeshift souvenir. Mark and the kids never saw Carl again after he flew back to Kentucky, but Carol managed to make it home a week before he died. She was sitting at her father's bedside when Carl Shroat drew his last breath on May 28, 1993.

Mark, meanwhile, was earning a reputation as one of the army's most promising young officers. He was handpicked for jobs normally reserved for higher-ranking soldiers and given a Bronze Star, one of the military's highest commendations, for handling the logistics of bringing tens of thousands of troops into and out of the war zone. Back in Germany, the officers in Mark's chain of command made clear that they believed he was bound for bigger things. Lieutenant Colonel Stephen Whittenberg, Mark's direct boss, wrote in a formal performance review that Mark was "definitely one of the army's top 5 percent." Colonel Thurman Smith said that Mark had "unlimited potential." Brigadier General Creighton Abrams wrote that Mark was the "best G1 and maybe the best staff officer I have ever known." The general praised Mark's foresight, problem-solving abilities, and sheer intelligence. And then Abrams paid Mark the biggest compliment a general can give a younger officer. Mark Graham, he wrote presciently, had "General Officer potential."

The late 1990s were heady times for the Grahams. Their children were young and popular. Mark's career was on the ascent, and they were about to move back to the States for what promised to be a long enough stint that Jeff would be able to begin and finish high school in the same place. It sometimes felt too good to be true, but Carol wasn't complaining. She had, in her words, the "Walt Disney family" that she'd always wanted.

CHAPTER 4

Stafford, Virginia, October 1997

Jeff Graham didn't try to be subtle. It was his senior year in high school, and he had turned the cavernous basement of his parents' new house in northern Virginia into a rec room of sorts for a growing number of friends and classmates. The teens would hold marathon Ping-Pong tournaments on the Grahams' downstairs table, watch and rewatch movies such as *The Wizard of Oz,* and down the occasional beer. The basement became even more popular as word spread that there were usually girls there, and at a certain point Jeff had enough. He began to keep an informal list of who was welcome in the basement and who wasn't. He had a simple but devastatingly effective way of turning away people he didn't know very well or simply didn't like. He'd invite them downstairs and ask them to sit down on one of the couches. Ten minutes later he would sidle over and gently ask, "So, where are you heading?" The unwanted visitors would quickly get the hint.

The Grahams had moved back to Stafford in 1996, just after Jeff finished his sophomore year of high school in Oklahoma, so Mark could start another job in the army's Personnel Command Headquarters. They bought a two-story house, sight unseen, in a gated community called

Aquia Harbour. It was a big change for Mark and Carol, who'd spent their entire married life living in either military housing or rented apartments. It was an even bigger change for Kevin and Jeff, who used the spacious new house in vastly different ways. Kevin had been prone to sharp mood swings since he was a child, but they became far more pronounced as he got older. There were long stretches when he would suddenly look visibly sad and then abruptly stop talking to his parents or siblings. Aquia Harbour—where he had his own room for the very first time—gave Kevin a place to retreat to when he didn't want to be around his family. He would go into the room, shut the door, and refuse to come out for hours. Mark and Carol chalked it up to normal teenage angst and didn't get him into counseling. Jeff, by contrast, turned the basement into a central gathering place for his friends and classmates. They would come over after school to spend afternoons bouncing on the Grahams' outdoor trampoline and evenings hanging out in the basement. Jeff's friends felt comfortable talking about virtually anything with Carol, including girls, but they were careful to keep the Grahams in the dark about the drinking sometimes taking place downstairs. "It was understood that having a bit of beer was okay if everyone followed one rule: If someone had a drink, even just one, they couldn't get on the road until the morning," said Grant Breithaupt, one of Jeff's closest friends. "Mr. and Mrs. Graham treated us like adults and trusted that we weren't going to do something stupid. No one wanted to abuse that trust."

Six or seven of Jeff's male friends would often wind up sleeping over. When they woke up the next day, Carol would be in the kitchen, humming to herself as she made mounds of pancakes.

If my mom could do this, Jeff thought as he looked down at the wriggling, slimy fish, *so can I.* It was the summer of 1998, just weeks before graduation, and Jeff was on a mission. Carol had mentioned offhandedly that she had swallowed a goldfish on a dare in middle school. That was enough for Jeff, who decided he'd have to follow suit before he left for college. One afternoon he sent a friend to a nearby pet store, but he came back with fully grown goldfish that were far too big to swallow. Carol drove over to the nearby Potomac Mills mall and bought clear Ziploc bags full of tiny baby goldfish. Jeff and nearly two dozen of his classmates and teachers gathered in a crowded classroom at Brooke Point High School and passed around the bags. Jeff went first, reaching into the murky water, pulling out one of the tiny fishes, and swallowing it whole. Some of his friends looked nauseous, but they all eventually followed suit. The school's branch of People for the Ethical Treatment of Animals, Carol later recalled, filed a formal letter of protest with the Brooke Point administration.

Jeff was used to having classmates follow his lead. A gifted football player, swimmer, and golfer with a quick smile and an offbeat sense of humor, he was the most outgoing of the three Graham children and the one who had the easiest time making friends. He looked like Mark, and sounded so much like him that Carol's mother, Jackie, and most of her other relatives couldn't tell them apart on the phone. But he didn't have Mark's quiet, introverted nature. Put him in a room and he would immediately turn into a male version of Carol: charismatic, engaging, and quick to turn strangers into friends.

Jeff did well in high school, but academics weren't remotely as important to him as they would later be to Kevin. He found out early on that he needed a 3.5 grade point average to qualify for the National Honor Society, and that's exactly what he earned. He didn't take any AP or honors courses, and he made a point of finishing his homework at school so he wouldn't need to bring textbooks home or miss out on time with his friends. Carol would occasionally press her son to make academics more of a priority, but Jeff was set in his ways. "I'll do college when I get to college," he told her.

His teachers loved him all the same. Jeff had grown up in the military world, so he was unfailingly polite to all of his instructors and called the male ones "sir" and the female ones "ma'am." Ted Thoerig, who had been one of his closest friends since kindergarten, said that Jeff began to play up his southern drawl and make more of a point of opening doors for his teachers once he realized how much they seemed to like it. "Jeff was the kind of guy who could lay it on thick, and he went a bit overboard when he saw how the teachers responded," he said. "It became a bit of a game to him, like 'just how much of a southerner can I pretend to be?'"

Jeff had another reason for being so polite to his teachers: self-preservation. Carol worked as a full-time substitute teacher at Brooke Point, so she was in the school building virtually all day, every day. That allowed her to keep close tabs on her oldest son and bluntly ask her fellow teachers how Jeff was doing, and behaving, in their classes.

"Mrs. Graham would have found out immediately if he was misbehaving, and she would have just killed him for it," Ted said, laughing. "She was this sweet, kind woman, but you didn't want to push her."

Like many of his classmates, Jeff's real priorities were sports and girls. He learned how to ski during a trip to the Alps while the Grahams lived in Germany, and he took up football once the family moved to Fort Sill. Jeff was an undersized starter on the football team during his freshman year, doing double duty as a defensive back and a guard on the team's offensive line, but his sophomore-year coach told Jeff that he'd have to get heavier and stronger to keep his starting jobs. Mark installed a pull-up bar in Jeff's bedroom and a weight machine downstairs, and Jeff diligently wolfed down protein bars, supplements, and vitamins. None of it made him taller or more muscular. Relegated to a backup position as a sophomore, Jeff dropped off the team after the season ended.

He instead focused his time and energy on swimming and golf, a pair of sports where size didn't matter. Jeff's high school swim team in Lawton, Oklahoma, just outside of Fort Sill, made it to the state finals his sophomore year; he made it to the state finals again as a senior in Stafford. He had just as much success in golf, leading Brooke Point's golf team to Virginia's regional play-offs as a junior. The Brooke Point yearbook ran a picture of Jeff calmly sinking a thirty-five-foot putt. It also ran a picture of Jeff and his teammates carrying their golf clubs around on their foreheads, a testament to his genial goofiness.

He didn't look or act or like an athlete. Jeff stood just a shade over five foot six and had been wearing glasses since elementary school. He drank, smoked, and had a small but noticeable paunch that he proudly referred to as his jelly roll. His height and weight didn't get in the way in the pool or on the golf course. They also didn't get in the way with women, inside and outside of school.

At Brooke Point Jeff dated both the prom queen, Erin Cahill, who later worked as a model and an actress on shows such as *General Hospital* and *Saving Grace*, and an array of other girls. Adrienne Bory, another classmate, believes that Kevin came to have a crush on her at least in part because she was one of the few in their social circle who hadn't dated Jeff. "He saw me as the untainted one who hadn't had Jeff's paws on me," she said. "I was the only one of my girlfriends who went unsmooched by Mr. Jeff Graham."

Jeff and Kevin remained exceptionally close throughout high school, with the older Graham making a point of always inviting his younger brother to hang out and drink with his friends. Jeff also did his best to help his brother find a girlfriend. Early in their senior year Jeff and his friends began telling classmates that Kevin was great in bed and physically well endowed. The idea was to build up Kevin's reputation around school so that girls would approach him without waiting for the notoriously shy young man to ask them out first. "Jeff thought that if he said it enough times, there would get to be a point where girls started hearing the same thing from different people and deciding that it had to be true," Bory said. "It didn't work, but it was kind of sweet in its own weird way."

Ironically, a fight over a girl later caused a major rupture between the two brothers. During his sophomore year, Kevin asked Carrie Saunders to be his date to homecoming, and she said yes. "I thought he knew we'd just be going as friends and was cool with that," she said.

Shortly before the dance, Kevin found out that Carrie had been having a fling with Jeff, whom she'd met in a high school drama class. He was decidedly not cool with it.

"Why her, Jeff?" he yelled at his older brother. "You could have had anyone, so why her?"

Friends would remember it years later as one of the only times they ever saw the brothers fight.

By the start of his senior year Jeff felt like he had his future planned out. He had grown up hearing about Kentucky from his parents and was close to all of his relatives there, particularly his grandmother Jackie. Visits to Frankfort for Christmas and Thanksgiving left Jeff with an addiction to University of Kentucky basketball, a statewide obsession. He also knew that the school had a large and respected ROTC program. Murray State, which he'd strongly considered, did not, so the choice was an easy one. Jeff applied to Kentucky in the fall of 1997 and was quickly accepted. He was also given a four-year ROTC scholarship, making school free in exchange for a commitment to several years of military service. Jeff was fine with the trade; there had been only one school he ever wanted to attend and only one thing he wanted to do after graduation.

He had always dreamed of being a soldier. As kids, he and Kevin played around in miniature army uniforms and went to bed in matching army T-shirts and camouflage underwear. When he was in first grade, Jeff spent Christmas Day building a giant fort in the living room out of the gift boxes he'd found under the family tree. During the winters he and his brother built outdoor snow castles that were large enough to include tunnels, hiding places, and caches of snowballs. In the summers the boys climbed into a tree house Mark had built for them and scanned their backyard for imaginary invaders. They even invented an army-themed game called Man Hunt, which involved heading out into the woods behind their house in dark clothes and face paint and trying to avoid being captured by their friends for as long as possible.

Both Graham boys had the army in their blood. They had grown up in army housing, attending army schools, and playing with the children of other soldiers. They were unabashedly patriotic and saw their father as a genuine hero. They stuck yellow ribbons to their front door when he deployed and waved miniature American flags when he returned home. Jeff and Kevin stood alongside their father whenever he was promoted and clipped the metal insignia of his new rank to his uniform. He would smile for the camera, but the boys always looked even happier.

Jeff had another reason for wanting an army career: He felt far more comfortable in the military world than in the civilian one. Shortly after moving to Aquia Harbour, Jeff came home from a day of golf with his brother and angrily told Mark and Carol that he'd been treated like a child on the course, with older golfers condescendingly offering pointers or suggesting that he shouldn't be out there without an adult. Jeff had been golfing since childhood and was used to playing on military courses where age didn't matter and older golfers recognized his talent; the experience at Aquia Harbour left a bad taste in his mouth. He was also surprised that so few of the Grahams' new neighbors had come over to introduce themselves or bring some food as a welcome gift. When the Grahams moved onto army bases such as Fort Sill, by contrast, other military families came by with so many casseroles and pies that Mark and Carol literally had no place to put it all. Jeff was blunt about which kind of neighbors he preferred. "I don't like civilians," he told Carol. "I belong in the army."

Jeff knew that making it through the University of Kentucky's ROTC program would set the stage for him to follow in his father's footsteps and start his own career as an army officer. It wouldn't be easy: ROTC cadets went running three days a week at 6:30 A.M. and spent roughly six hours per week in the classroom, a heavy load to bear alongside the courses he would be taking for his engineering degree. He couldn't wait to start, but Jeff had one summer left in Stafford before he and his friends went their separate ways. He was determined to make the most of it.

The three friends would come to call it their summer of freedom. The Grahams had moved to California right after Jeff's graduation so Mark could start a new job at a base near Los Angeles. Jeff decided to stay behind; he didn't see the point of making two major moves within a few months. His classmate Ted was also looking for a new place to live. He had been fighting with his parents and wanted to move somewhere else until things settled down. Jeff and Ted decided to move in together for the summer. The only question was where.

In the end, it all came down to the futons. The third member of the group, Grant Breithaupt, came from a military family, and his parents had returned from an earlier deployment to Okinawa with a stack of the thin, cotton-stuffed mattresses. Grant and his friends would sleep on the futons when they got back to his house after a night of drinking. The basement of the Breithaupts' house had a large TV, a refrigerator stuffed with soda and beer, and a side door that allowed them to sneak in and out to avoid being spotted by Grant's parents. Jeff and Ted had spent a lot of time in that basement over the years. It was, they decided, a perfect place to spend the summer.

Jeff was already beginning to think like an engineer, so he set out to build himself a makeshift bedroom. He decided it should go in the corner of the basement farthest from the staircase, reasoning that that would be the quietest spot. He flattened a pair of cardboard boxes and taped them to the basement's concrete walls to create a small, four-sided space. He slung a couple of sheets over the cardboard walls, including one that he could pull back to enter the new room, and used another sheet as a roof. He dumped a mound of clothing near the futon, stacked some books and magazines, and plugged in a lamp and an alarm clock. It wasn't a big space, but Jeff wasn't a big guy.

The three friends weren't limited to Grant's basement. Jeff had kept the code to the garage door of his old house, and the new owners hadn't moved in yet. That meant that he, Ted, and Grant could sneak over and use it as a second home of sorts for drinking, eating pizza, and watching movies. Mark and Carol never found out. To Ted, it was a summer of complete and utter freedom. "We were basically living like we were in college already," he said.

It ended far too soon. They all had summer jobs—Jeff was coaching the swim team and working as a lifeguard at a local pool, Grant was painting fences, and Ted was parking cars at a nearby fairground—but none of them took the work particularly seriously. College was looming for the three of them, and they spent most of their time talking about their plans for the future. Ted and Grant weren't sure what they wanted to do after they graduated. Jeff was.

In August 1998, Jeff Graham dismantled the walls of his little basement bedroom and boxed up his clothes and books. He was preparing to fulfill one dream by beginning school at the University of Kentucky and another by entering the ROTC program that would mark the formal start to his military career. His friends would later wonder which he had been more excited about.

CHAPTER 5

Lexington, Kentucky, September 1999

Jeff Graham couldn't believe what he was seeing. He was sitting at a bustling off-campus restaurant with Stacey Martinez, a petite, pretty brunette he'd met at a party a couple of weeks earlier. They'd hung out regularly since then, but this was their first real date. Jeff ordered a salad, Stacey a mammoth cheeseburger and a mound of french fries. The waiter assumed Jeff had ordered the burger and slid it in front of him. He and Stacey swapped plates, and Jeff watched, both amazed and amused, as Stacey wolfed down the entire cheeseburger and every last fry. Jeff had never met a woman who could eat like that. Most young men would have kept that observation to themselves in the hopes of getting a second date. Jeff couldn't let the moment pass without a bit of sarcasm.

"You need anything else to eat?" he asked, straight-faced. "Another burger or some more fries?"

"No, I'm good," Stacey responded, and then smiled. "But I could be up for some dessert."

Jeff and Stacey made for an unlikely couple. He was a ladies' man and party animal like his father had been at Murray State, and Jeff's off-campus apartment was the place friends and neighbors gathered to plow through cases of beer, hold late-night video-game tournaments, and huddle around the TV for Kentucky basketball games. Stacey, like Carol, was a bookish young woman who didn't date much, rarely drank, and spent most of her nights in the university library poring over a stack of textbooks and note cards. Jeff was studying engineering, earning top honors as an ROTC cadet, and looking forward to a long career in the army. He had promised Carol that he would do college once he was in college, and he had kept his word. Stacey was taking grueling courses in biology and organic chemistry and hoping to start a three-year pharmacy program as soon as she graduated from Kentucky. They lived vastly different lives and were even part of different social circles.

Jeff and Stacey had met two weeks earlier at a party she hadn't wanted to attend. One of Stacey's roommates was dating one of Jeff's friends, and was convinced—despite all evidence to the contrary—that Jeff and Stacey would hit it off. It was a Saturday night, and Stacey was back in her apartment getting ready to go to sleep after a day of shopping with her mom. She'd washed off her makeup, changed into sweatpants and a T-shirt, and was about to lie down when the phone rang.

"Get dressed," her roommate said. "There's a party I want to go to, and I want you to come with me."

Stacey demurred. "Not tonight. I look like crap and I'm just not up for it."

"You have to come," her roommate replied. "You don't have a choice. There's a guy I want you to meet."

Stacey and her roommate arrived with the party already in full swing. Jeff was standing outside, and Stacey somehow knew almost immediately that he was the one her roommate had in mind for her. Jeff waved and walked over to introduce himself. Years later she would remember that his entire face seemed to light up when he smiled at her. She had never seen anything quite like it. "I wasn't that impressed with his looks at first—he was shorter than most of the guys I knew and was wearing this ratty T-shirt that looked like it hadn't been washed in weeks," she said. "But he had this incredible charisma and magnetism. He just sort of seemed larger than life."

Stacey was surprised that she and Jeff actually had quite a bit in common. They both came from military families and had spent several years living in Germany. Stacey's parents, like Mark and Carol, had met at Murray State decades earlier. She and Jeff were even living at the same off-campus apartment complex, the Royal Lexington.

The party wound down just after 2 A.M., and Jeff offered to walk Stacey to her front door. She invited him in for a late-night breakfast, and they wound up talking until dawn. They were soon, in Stacey's words, "pretty much connected at the hip." They lived so close to each other that they never really needed to make formal plans. She would simply walk to Jeff's apartment or he'd make his way to hers. They were spending so much time together that neither one stopped to realize that they'd been dating for weeks without ever actually going out on a date.

Jeff was determined to change that. Stacey laughed when he'd made a point of formally asking her out for dinner at a student hangout near the University of Kentucky's campus in downtown Lexington. Stacey's love of fast food soon became a running joke between them. Within a few months they were looking at engagement rings and talking about marriage, kids, and their dreams for the future. Jeff, a sophomore, wanted to follow his father into the army and one day lead troops into combat. Stacey, a junior, was preparing applications for pharmacy school and hoping to do a residency at a local hospital before beginning her own career. They were young, deeply in love, and certain they wanted to spend the rest of their lives together. Stacey felt that Jeff would eventually ask her to marry him, but she didn't know when or how.

One afternoon in early January 2001, Jeff and Kevin went to a nearby mall and made a point of not inviting Stacey to come along. She assumed Jeff was buying an engagement ring and would propose to her on Valentine's Day. She kept asking Jeff where he'd hidden the ring, and he kept pretending that he had no idea what she was talking about. Stacey had to spend Valentine's Day studying, so they made plans to have dinner the following night. On February 15, Stacey stepped out of the shower, slipped on a terry-cloth robe, and was toweling off her hair when she noticed Jeff walk into the bathroom and get down on one knee, ring in hand. "I can safely say that I never thought someone would propose to me right after I got out of the shower," Stacey said, laughing. "It wasn't romantic by any means, but it caught me completely off guard, which is exactly what Jeff wanted."

The engagement took most of Jeff's friends by surprise as well. They knew he'd fallen for Stacey, but they hadn't realized that he was ready to completely turn his back on the other women of the University of Kentucky. What had happened, they wondered, to the Jeff Graham they'd partied with since freshman year?

Jeff's obsession with the Wildcats began before he ever stepped foot on campus. Kentucky was the only school he applied to, and his friends couldn't imagine him anywhere else. The University of Virginia started classes earlier than the University of Kentucky, so Jeff stopped off to spend a day with his friend Ted Thoerig there before continuing on to Lexington. Jeff was wearing a brand-new Kentucky basketball T-shirt and a Kentucky baseball cap with a price tag still attached. Ted was mortified.

"You look like a dork," Ted said. "You absolutely cannot show up on campus dressed like that. It's like going to a concert wearing the shirt of the band. People will think there's something wrong with you."

"Whatever," Jeff replied, stubborn as ever. "This is my team."

Living in Lexington turned Jeff into a full-blown addict of all things Wildcat. During the NCAA tournament, he and his roommates transformed their apartment into a makeshift private sports bar. Jeff drew an enormous copy of that year's March Madness brackets on one of the walls. They dragged a TV from one of their bedrooms and set it up alongside the TV in their living room so everyone would have a good view. They covered every free surface of their apartment with University of Kentucky basketball calendars and posters. And they hauled in extra couches and chairs from neighboring apartments, planting them in front of a long row of stools to create what they called "stadium seating." Some years they replaced the stools with a second row of couches mounted precariously on a foundation of tables, dressers, and desks. "It was basically anything that looked like it could hold a couch," said Ben Baxter, one of Jeff's closest friends.

Jeff also had an ironclad rule that anyone entering the apartment had to be wearing a University of Kentucky T-shirt or baseball cap. He would unapologetically turn people away at the door, including close friends, if they were dressed in anything else. One year, Jeff Ullmer, a fellow cadet from Kentucky's ROTC program, showed up without the requisite gear. Ullmer's girlfriend, Emily, was already in the apartment, but Jeff wouldn't let his friend in. It got to the point that Jeff's roommates began keeping a stack of spare University of Kentucky basketball gear squirreled away in the kitchen. "They'd come to the door, give you one, and tell you to put it on before Jeff saw," said D. J. Mathis, one of Jeff's best friends.

Jeff's devotion to the Wildcats stood out even in basketball-crazed Lexington. He and his roommates nailed a mounted deer head to the wall and named it after the team's best player, Tayshaun Prince. They put a University of Kentucky Santa Claus hat on Tayshaun's head and draped multicolored beads that they'd picked up in New Orleans around its neck. They'd applaud whenever the real-life Tayshaun Prince scored and then point to the namesake hanging on their wall. They eventually bought a replica Prince jersey and hung that around the deer's neck as well.

Jeff didn't just cheer for the team's stars. The Wildcats had a wildly unpopular player named Saul Smith who was widely thought to have only made the team—let alone been given the chance to play—because his father, Tubby, was the Wildcats' head coach. University of Kentucky fans would loudly boo Smith every time he entered the game, and Jeff would just as loudly tell them to shut up. Smith might have been the worst player on the team, but he was still a Wildcat, and Jeff Graham didn't think any University of Kentucky player should be treated that way. "I think Jeff may have been Saul Smith's only genuine fan," Emily recalled.

In his five years in Lexington Jeff Graham attended virtually every University of Kentucky home game, traveled to dozens of road ones, and watched the rest on TV. He went to the team's midnight pep rallies and spent hours watching its practices. He filled his apartment with dozens of Wildcats T-shirts, hats, sweatshirts, coffee cups, and beer mugs. The University of Kentucky's basketball team was one of Jeff's two main passions. The school's ROTC program was the other.

Jeff Graham peered through his binoculars, searching for an enemy tank. He spotted it in the distance and fired an armor-piercing shell that struck the opposing tank right in its turret. Jeff watched the round hit, high-fived the cadet next to him, and walked away for more coffee.

It was a bloodless battle, part of a simulation Jeff and his fellow cadets practiced at Buell Armory, a redbrick building that had housed the University of Kentucky's officer training program since 1901. The exercise would begin when the instructor, Major Dwayne Edwards, arranged four model U.S. Army tanks at one end of the high-ceilinged room cadets used to practice their drill formations and placed twenty model Russian tanks at the other. Each U.S. tank was controlled by an ROTC cadet, who would move the model vehicle around the mock battlefield and use laser pointers to mark where he wanted his rounds to land. A fifth cadet controlled the entire Russian formation. The simulation ended when each cadet in the course had a chance to control both the American and Russian tanks.

Jeff excelled at the fake tank fights, just as he did in virtually every other part of the ROTC program. He was doing well in his engineering classes, but friends could tell that he was far more interested in his military training. The cadets gathered in the early-morning darkness three times a week for push-ups, sit-ups, and a lengthy jog. Jeff was one of the smallest of the cadets, but he pushed himself hard and held his own with larger and more muscular classmates. He dropped his jelly roll and worked himself into the best physical condition of his life. "Jeff would go running in the morning with the ROTC guys and then go for a jog with me at night, and it got to be a bit of a joke because I'd be panting and out of breath and he'd just be cruising along," Stacey said.

Jeff kept a punishing schedule, balancing his long list of ROTC commitments with challenging courses in engineering and advanced mathematics. He spent two hours every Tuesday and Thursday morning at Buell for courses on military history, the proper ways of giving and receiving orders, and the ins and outs of the army's internal judicial system. He took an additional leadership course on Wednesday afternoon, the one day a week that he and the other cadets wore their dark-green combat fatigues or blue dress uniforms around campus. Friday mornings were set aside for the final workouts of the week, Saturdays for trips to a nearby nature preserve to practice rappelling and learn how to navigate through dense forests at night. Jeff, who had grown up playing war games, mastered both skills so completely that his instructors later tapped him to oversee land navigation training for younger cadets. The cadets also made occasional trips to a local armory to practice handling, disassembling, and firing M16 rifles. Jeff, despite poor eyesight, was one of the best shots in his entire ROTC class.

In high school Jeff had taken the lightest course load possible so that he could spend his evenings hanging out with his friends. College was different. Jeff drank and partied with his friends, particularly during basketball season, but he surprised his parents and siblings by voluntarily applying for the Pershing Rifles, a national organization of high-achieving ROTC cadets. The Pershing Rifles date back to 1891, when John Pershing, who would become a legendary general, was working as a professor of military science at the University of Nebraska at Lincoln. Pershing, worried about the low morale of his ROTC unit, took the best of his cadets and trained them for five hours a day on the finer points of marching in military formation. His team, known as Company A, won a high-profile ROTC competition the following year, and chapters of the Pershing Rifles were soon created across the country. It now functions as a finishing school of sorts for military superstars such as retired generals Hugh Shelton and Colin Powell, each of whom served as a chairman of the Joint Chiefs of Staff, the highest-ranking position in the military. Jeff saw the two men as role models and dreamed of one day following in their footsteps. He made it through the Pershing Rifles' semester-long selection process and was accepted into the elite organization. Within a year he was running its University of Kentucky chapter. Mark hadn't applied to the Pershing Rifles when he was doing ROTC, and Jeff's selection marked one of the first times his nascent military career outstripped that of his father.

Jeff took the job seriously. He drilled the members of his Pershing Rifles team relentlessly and spent hours practicing a countermarch, a complicated maneuver where all the cadets spin on their heels at the same time and then walk back the way they have just come. The team rehearsed holding their ceremonial M1 Garand rifles at their sides, muzzles pointed straight up into the air, and then abruptly angling them toward their right or left shoulders. Would-be members of the Pershing Rifles were summoned to the armory at 3 A.M. so Jeff could shout, "Left shoulder, right shoulder, left shoulder, right shoulder," and make sure they were able to immediately shift their rifles from side to side without bungling.

There were some perks. Jeff and the other members of his team got to show off their membership in the elite group by stitching the Pershing Rifles' official crest—a shield showing a torch partially covered by a pair of crossed rifles—onto their dress uniforms and coiling a blue-and-white cloth cord over their right shoulders. The Pershing Rifles also served as a military color guard before each of the school's basketball games, marching to center court with a pair of Jeff's teammates holding the U.S. and University of Kentucky flags aloft while the rest of the squad flanked them with unloaded wooden rifles slung across their chests. Jeff told his friends that standing on the court, just a few feet from his beloved Wildcats, was one of the coolest things he had ever done.

Jeff and Stacey had just woken up on September 11, 2001, less than seven months after their engagement, when one of his roommates pounded on the door and told them to get dressed and come into the living room. They watched, openmouthed, as the major TV networks showed live footage of the hijacked 767s plowing into the two towers of the World Trade Center. Jeff called Mark, who told him that the attacks meant the United States would soon be at war.

"The war could still be going on when I graduate," Jeff told Stacey after he hung up the phone. "I could be part of it."

At the time she didn't give the comment a second thought. Jeff wasn't slated to start his military career for two more years. She assumed the fighting would long be over by then.

"All I have to do is make a phone call," Stacey's father told Jeff. "If this is what you want, I can make it happen."

It was the fall of 2002, and Jeff was facing the toughest choice of his nascent military career: deciding which branch of the army would be his professional home. He had long conversations with Mark about it but wanted a second opinion and knew just the man to go to. Jeff had grown close to Stacey's father, Toby, a retired lieutenant colonel who had spent his entire career as an armor officer charged with overseeing units of tanks and Bradley fighting vehicles. Stacey's parents had divorced years earlier, but she and Jeff maintained strong relationships with both. Jeff would sit in Toby's living room outside Lexington for hours at a time, discussing the finer points of life as an officer in the United States Army. Toby had one lesson he tried to hammer home to Jeff again and again: Don't try to be friends with your soldiers. Soldiers already have friends, Toby said. What they need is a leader.

One night Jeff told Toby that he was going to apply for a position in the 1st Armored Division, a famed unit nicknamed "Old Ironsides" for its exploits during World War II. Toby said he had a close friend in the division who could easily ensure that Jeff made it in, but Jeff rejected the offer out of hand. "I'll either make it on my own or I won't make it at all," he replied.

Jeff finished school in the summer of 2003 and was sent to Fort Knox for the Armor Basic Officer Leaders Course, an eighteen-week prerequisite for soldiers training to oversee units of tanks and other powerful vehicles. Fort Knox had been used to house Italian and German prisoners during World War II. The barracks and dining facilities those prisoners used had long since been torn down, but their soccer fields remained largely intact. When Jeff got to Fort Knox, soldiers were using the grassy fields for pickup football games.

The armor course was notoriously challenging, but Jeff thrived. He was selected to the Commandant's List, an honor reserved for the top young officers, and won praise for his intelligence, leadership skills, and physical fitness. "2LT Graham is an outstanding officer whose performance in this demanding course was clearly superior to his peers," army captain James Bushong wrote in Jeff's official evaluation. "Easily among the best officers in his class, 2LT Graham's achievements clearly indicate superior potential for the most demanding assignments."

Years later Mark and Carol would wonder how much of Jeff's decision to join an armored division came from genuine professional interest and how much came from a desire to stay as close to Stacey as possible, for as long as possible. Fort Knox sits on the outskirts of Louisville, less than two hours from the University of Kentucky campus in Lexington. That meant Jeff could do his training during the day and then spend nights with his fiancée. They both knew he'd soon be leaving Kentucky, and they wanted to make the most of those final months together. Jeff brought her to University of Kentucky basketball games; Stacey dragged him to a series of romantic comedies. Stacey cheered for the Wildcats because of her love for Jeff. Jeff laughed his way through *Love Actually* and *How to Lose a Guy in 10 Days* because of his love for Stacey.

Jeff finished his training at Fort Knox in October of 2003 and was ordered to Fort Riley, a large base in rural Kansas, where the army was mustering forces for the second war of the post–September 11 era. He was assigned to the 1st Battalion, 34th Armor Regiment, 1st Brigade Team, 1st Infantry Division, a unit that was slated for imminent deployment to Iraq. Shortly before he left for Kansas, Jeff stopped by Toby Martinez's house to say good-bye. Toby asked him if he had any second thoughts about heading into combat.

"The only thing worse than being at war is to be a soldier and watch your country go to war and know that you're not going to be part of the fight," Jeff told him. "Soldiers don't want to be sitting at home."

Jeff didn't have to worry. The 1st Infantry Division had received orders to deploy to Iraq in September. By Thanksgiving, his commanders assured him, he'd be at war.

CHAPTER 6

San Pedro, California, March 2000

It was a challenging homework assignment, but Heather Booty felt like she'd finally nailed it. "Imagine you're putting together a sound track for a movie version of *The Crucible*," the teacher in her senior-year AP English course had said. "What song would you choose?" Booty pored over stacks of her favorite CDs and eventually decided on a Dave Matthews Band song called "The Last Stop." It had some of the darkest and angriest lyrics the group had ever written. "You're righteous, so righteous," Dave Matthews growled near the beginning of the song. "Go ahead believe that you are the chosen one." Heather felt it perfectly captured the themes of religious fundamentalism, intolerance, and blind fury that ran through the Arthur Miller masterpiece. Best of all, she felt, it was such a little-known song that none of her classmates were likely to have heard of it.

Heather was sitting in her classroom at San Pedro High School one afternoon and waiting for the chance to introduce the song when she saw a tall and burly classmate named Kevin Graham walk to a stereo in the front of the room, pop in a CD, and hit Play. The room suddenly echoed with the saxophone and violin chords that open "The Last Stop." Kevin was tapping his foot and mouthing the lyrics, which he clearly

61

knew by heart. Heather was stunned. "I couldn't believe that someone else had even heard that song because it was the number one song that you would skip on that CD," she said. "Kevin had listened to it and felt the same thing that I did. I felt like he must be a kindred spirit. It seemed like it couldn't just be coincidental."

She had met Kevin a few times before, but he hadn't made much of an impression. Both of them were academic superstars, straight-A students who aced tests effortlessly and finished challenging homework assignments quickly. But that was where she had always thought the similarities ended. Heather was a deeply religious young woman who ran San Pedro High School's Christian Club. Kevin told his friends that he was an agnostic and wrote a lengthy essay about what he derided as the Puritans' religious hypocrisy. Heather had a large circle of friends. Kevin spent most of his time hanging out with Melanie and a handful of other bookish classmates. Heather was dating another senior and preparing for college. Kevin was single. As far as she knew, he had never had a girlfriend, which surprised her. Kevin, she thought, had a smile that could light up an entire room. Why didn't he use it to get a girl?

A few weeks before graduation, Heather saw Kevin standing by himself during a party, looking down at the ground and making no attempt to talk to any of their classmates. She walked up to him during a break in the music and tapped him on the shoulder.

"Are you okay?" she asked. "You just don't seem to be in a good mood tonight. What's wrong?"

"I met the perfect girl," Kevin said. "I've had a crush on her for months, but I don't think she's even noticed."

"You never know," Heather replied. "Maybe she likes you but just hasn't told you yet. Who is it?"

Kevin looked up at her and smiled. "I'm talking to her," he said. Then he leaned in and kissed her on the lips.

Years later Heather would laugh at the corniness of the entire exchange. "It seems like a scene from a bad romantic comedy," she said. But that wasn't how it felt at the time. In the moment it felt like the start of something new and wonderful. Heather Booty would quickly fall for Kevin Graham, and he would quickly fall for her. She would be the one great love of his life.

Kevin took a deep breath and leaned into the microphone. It was March 1992, and Kevin had advanced to the third round of the spelling bee at his elementary school in Baumholder.

Kevin, ten, had spent months studying a lengthy word list and believed he would remember the spelling of anything he had ever read. Carl and Jackie Shroat had flown in from Kentucky, and the entire family felt certain that he would win the competition. The judges gave him a relatively easy word, one that he had spelled correctly in dozens of practice quizzes. "Agitated," he repeated back. "A-d-j-e-t-a-t-e-d." When the judges shook their heads, Kevin stormed off the stage without saying a word. Back at home, he went straight to his room and began to sob.

"I called myself an idiot and all of its synonyms that I knew," he remembered later. "I finally gave up and just put my head down on my pillow."

Kevin pulled himself together after about an hour. He had an oral reading contest the following month and resolved to win it. He walked to his bookshelf and picked up his favorite book, Dr. Seuss's *Marvin K. Mooney Will You Please Go Now!* He read and reread the book so many times that he had it memorized by the time the competition rolled around. "I didn't even have to look at it during the contest," Kevin recalled. "I held it for effect." He won his school's competition easily and placed second in the regional.

Academics had always come easily for Kevin. The Grahams moved back to the United States when Kevin was in sixth grade, and he quickly began racking up a string of As at Central Middle School, just outside of Fort Sill. One afternoon Kevin brought home a report card with a B in math, which had always been one of his strongest subjects. When Carol asked him if everything was okay, he calmly replied that he was having problems seeing the blackboards in his classrooms. She took him to an optometrist, who diagnosed him with severe nearsightedness and prescribed glasses. Privately, the doctor told Carol that he was amazed Kevin had been able to make it through everyday life for so long without complaining that anything farther than a few feet away looked blurry.

A short time later Mark and Carol watched Kevin pull off his cleats after a golf tournament and were horrified to see that his socks were covered with blood. He told Carol that his golf shoes were too small but that he hadn't wanted to bother her by asking for a new pair. "I just know how busy you've been," he told her, shrugging. Carol rushed Kevin straight to the emergency room when she saw his feet. His big toes were so infected that he had to wear open-toed sandals for weeks until they healed. Again, he didn't complain.

Kevin did everything he could to please his parents, but his kindness masked a drive that often dwarfed that of his siblings. It wasn't just that he seemed to know exactly what he wanted to do with his life; it was also that he seemed to know exactly what he *didn't* want to do. When the family moved back to Fort Sill, Jeff went out for—and quickly made—the Cougars' basketball, baseball, and football teams. He was so committed to football that Carol remembers seeing him diligently working out first thing every morning and again right before he went to sleep. Kevin, on the other hand, rarely used the equipment. Like his brother, he played football, baseball, and basketball when the Grahams lived at Fort Sill. Kevin dropped those sports in favor of golf and swimming when the family moved to Virginia in 1996, and he routinely told his parents that athletics were simply not as important to him as academics.

Left unsaid was that Kevin was much better in the classroom than he was on the football field or baseball diamond. He won Brooke Point's top award for academic excellence his freshman year after earning As in health, world geography, and English; A pluses in German, band, and geometry; and a B plus in biology. He won another award for academic excellence his sophomore year and was named to the National Honor Society.

The family moved to California after Kevin's sophomore year. The relocation was hard on Melanie, who starred on Brooke Point's field hockey team and was so angry that San Pedro High didn't have a team of its own that she took her hockey stick along for the cross-country trip as a form of silent protest. Kevin struggled as well. One of Kevin's new classmates tripped him as he walked out of a classroom early in the school year, sending him tumbling to the floor in a jumble of textbooks and folders. Others pelted him with M&M's and jelly beans while he sat in the cafeteria, eating lunch with only Melanie.

Kevin adjusted to his new surroundings and eventually did just as well in California as he had in Virginia. He starred on the school's golf team, worked as a volunteer math tutor, and spent much of his spare time pulling weeds from an overgrown waterside park. "Kevin is a joy to have in any surrounding. He has proven a genuine asset at our high school. He will be just as fine an asset in yours," Peggy Coker, the school's guidance counselor, wrote in a recommendation letter. Stacey Michaels, one of Kevin's favorite teachers, wrote that Kevin was an "ideal student" who also "demonstrates the kind and caring qualities of an outstanding human being." In school, as at home, Kevin seemed like the perfect young man.

Heather Booty loved virtually all forms of music, but the metallic screeching of the Nine Inch Nails album was beginning to give her a serious headache. It was a searing July day in California, and she and Kevin had gone to a friend's house to escape the heat and listen to some CDs.

"I really don't like this," she said. "Can we put something else on?"

"Sure," Kevin replied. "How about we put on some gospel music and we can all just praise the Lord?"

A devout Christian, Heather would have been deeply offended if the comment had come from anyone else. With Kevin, she knew it was a joke. When her friends started to laugh, she joined in. "Kevin had such a sweet look on his face," she recalled. "He was making fun of me, but it was somehow also kind of endearing."

Kevin and Jeff had grown to have sharply different personalities and demeanors, with the older Graham becoming the life of any party and the younger one largely melting into the background. Jeff was the one who told the jokes, planned the pranks, and organized the nights out. He tore through life like a motorboat. Kevin always seemed perfectly content to follow along in his wake.

They remained extraordinarily close—Jeff had prevented the other members of his football team from dunking Kevin's head in a toilet as a form of hazing—but their friends were still sometimes surprised that the two Grahams actually came from the same bloodline. Jeff was absolutely fearless when it came to girls. Kevin seemed afraid to even approach them.

"He would say things like 'That girl is so pretty that I don't know why she'd want anything to do with me,'" Ted Thoerig recalled. "Kevin was always putting himself down. I never knew how much was shtick, his way of being funny, and how much was serious."

The one thing that could consistently bring Kevin out of his shell was music. At Fort Sill he played the trombone in the school band and joined his friends Matt Vangjel and Tommy Mayock for impromptu Christmas Eve concerts at different houses on the army base. In Stafford, Kevin and Adrienne, one of his high school classmates, would speed through the darkened streets of Aquia Harbour in her mint-green Toyota Tercel with their car windows down, belting out songs by the pop punk band Blink-

182. "But everyone's gone / And I've been here for too long," they sang. "I guess this is growing up."

Music became even more important to Kevin once the Grahams moved to California. Kevin was a junior and didn't know a single person at San Pedro besides Melanie. Jeff had stayed behind in Virginia to prepare for the start of classes at the University of Kentucky, so it was also the first time in Kevin's life that he had been apart from his older brother. "It was like Kev's security blanket was gone," Carol said.

It was a difficult transition for Melanie as well, and the two siblings found themselves spending most of their free time together. Most weekends Kevin would ask his parents if he and Melanie could head to downtown Los Angeles for a punk rock concert. Mark and Carol would always say yes. "Have fun and be safe," Carol would say as Kevin picked up the keys to his mint-green 1989 Honda Accord and headed for the door. He was seventeen and his sister was fifteen.

At the shows Kevin would hand his wallet, glasses, and cell phone to Melanie and then disappear into the mass of shirtless young men bouncing off one another in front of the stage. He'd dance until the show ended, then walk back to his sister, drenched in sweat. Years later, she shook her head at the memory. "It was insane that our parents would let us do this," she said. "I was basically a child, and we were going to these really sketchy clubs. Looking back, it's kind of absurd."

Kevin's love for music helped him gradually find a new social circle at San Pedro. His friendship with David Miller began because they were both into Weezer, an alternative rock band. David was in a punk band called YSL with classmates Jack Svicarevich and Seth Barnes, and Kevin quickly became close with the two of them as well. When YSL got a chance to play the Roxy, a legendary concert hall in Hollywood, Kevin drove down from San Pedro and stood a few feet from the stage, cheering on his friends. "Our own families didn't come to as many of our shows as Kevin did," Jack said.

Music was also a central part of Kevin's relationship with Heather. Shortly after they started dating, the young couple spent an entire evening lying in the open back of her pickup truck and trading favorite lyrics from songs by Blink-182, Reel Big Fish, the Dave Matthews Band, and other groups. Later that summer they spent a happy, drunken day at the Warped Tour, an all-day rock festival, dancing around to Green Day and Weezer.

The other thing that helped Kevin get over his innate shyness was alcohol. He had a fake Ohio driver's license, which meant that he would always be the one charged with buying booze for house parties or nighttime barbeques on the beach. He would bring wine coolers and light beer for Melanie and her friends and Jack Daniel's for himself and his close friends. Carol and Mark wouldn't realize until much later that their son was using alcohol to mask the depression that was casting an increasingly large shadow over his life. "He would drink pretty heavily, so he had definitely begun to build up quite a tolerance," Heather said. "He was so quiet when he was sober, but when he was drinking he would all of a sudden become more boisterous and outgoing. Some people said they barely recognized him."

Kevin didn't drink just when he was out with his friends. One Thanksgiving, Jeff and Grant Breithaupt flew out to California to spend the holiday with the Grahams. Mark and Carol were driving to the mall with Jeff, Kevin, and Grant in the backseat. The three teens had snuck some vodka into a can of Coke and were quietly passing it back and forth. Carol, oblivious, asked for a sip of the Coke. Grant remembers Jeff getting visibly nervous at the thought of his parents discovering the booze, but Kevin quickly thought of a solution.

"Mom, it's not a Diet Coke, so you probably don't want it," he said.

"Okay, honey, you keep it," she replied. "Enjoy."

The three boys finished off the vodka-spiked Coke by the time they reached the mall. Mark and Carol never found out that the can held anything other than soda, and they didn't realize that Kevin had a drinking problem until much later. It wouldn't be the only time that he kept something from his parents, and it wouldn't be the only time they missed a sign that Kevin Graham wasn't the perfect young man he seemed to be.

Carl Shroat returned home one Thanksgiving after a house call, brushing snow off his coat and taking his shoes off by the door before sitting down at the dining room table. Kevin was just five, but the image would stay with him for the rest of his life. "He was wearing a white physician's coat and had a stethoscope around his neck," Kevin wrote nearly fifteen years later in an application for a scholarship sponsored by a local association of military spouses. "From that point on, I knew I wanted to be a doctor."

Kevin aced his math and science courses in high school, and he seemed to have his future mapped out. He would go to the University of Kentucky, major in biology and premed, and spend his summers working in a lab. "I also plan to join the university's reserve officers training course because I have respected my father's service to his country and I too would like to serve my country in the military," he wrote in the application. "After college I hope to go to medical school, after which I would join the army in the medical corps. I have set my goals fairly high, and I don't believe they are impossible."

Kevin won the scholarship, but the essay reflected what Mark and Carol wanted for their son's future as much as it reflected Kevin's own hopes and dreams. He was a gentle young man with an inquisitive, deeply philosophical nature and a genuine revulsion toward bloodshed and violence. His friends couldn't imagine anyone less suited for the army's rigid hierarchy. "He was the person that you could have philosophical debates with on just about anything," Ted said. "He was always asking questions and never taking what he was told at face value. That obviously wasn't the way the military worked."

Alone with Heather, Kevin would confide that he had little interest in joining the military. Many of his closest friends thought he'd be happiest as an academic, teaching literature or philosophy while leading a life of the mind. But his path seemed preordained, and it didn't involve a future as a professor. Kevin had grown up in a household where military service was venerated, and he and his siblings were expected to call Mark "sir" and Carol "ma'am." Jeff, the person Kevin idolized most in the world, had already begun the University of Kentucky's ROTC program. Mark and Carol pointed out that ROTC would allow him to go to college for free, do his four years of military service, and then choose whatever he wanted to do with the rest of his life. "I don't think he ever really wanted to do the military," Melanie said. "I feel like my parents just put this enormous pressure on him to go the ROTC route. It wasn't something they said out loud, but Kevin definitely picked up on it."

Carol was far more explicit when it came to medicine. She venerated her father and told Kevin that she wanted him to follow in Carl's path. He didn't need very much convincing. The memory of his grandfather loomed large, and Kevin seemed to genuinely enjoy the science and math courses he was taking at San Pedro in preparation for an undergraduate premed program. Looking back, Mark and Carol believe that Kevin was trying to find a way of pleasing them by joining the military while staying true to his essentially pacifistic nature by choosing a field that allowed him to heal others rather than seeking to harm them. "Kevin wanted to live up to what he thought we expected of him," Mark said. "He would say what he thought we wanted to hear and do what he thought we wanted him to do."

Those who knew Kevin best also doubted that he really wanted to go to the University of Kentucky. Kevin had spent a summer at Washington University in St. Louis and fallen in love with the school. He told his parents and close friends that he would apply but wasn't sure he would get into the highly competitive school; his friends all assumed that Kevin's sterling academic credentials would make him a virtual lock.

But his top choices were a pair of California schools, UCLA and Berkeley. Heather had been accepted into California Polytechnic State University's physical therapy program, and going to school in California would allow him to stay close to the girl he hoped to one day marry. Ryan Lai, David Miller, and several of his other close friends were planning to start classes at UCLA that fall, which meant that he would have a social circle waiting if he chose to enroll there after finishing at San Pedro. The only person he would know at the University of Kentucky, which had more than twenty thousand undergraduates, was Jeff.

Carol felt conflicted. She thought Kevin would flourish at Washington University, which had a campus studded with ivy-covered Gothic buildings and one of the nation's best premedical programs. Berkeley, she felt, would be a good second choice because it would keep Kevin close to Heather and his friends while allowing him to go to a better school than UCLA and to live in a smaller, safer city than Los Angeles. Jeff saw things very differently. He wanted Kevin to join him at the University of Kentucky, and he called Kevin virtually every day to tout the wonders of Lexington and stress how much fun they'd be able to have there. "Jeff put on the full-court press," Carol said.

Jeff's constant talk about the University of Kentucky gradually won his mother over as well. Mark had just gotten word of a new assignment in Korea, and the family was slated to move to South Korea's Osan Air Base just weeks after Kevin's graduation. That meant Kevin would soon be hundreds of miles away from his brother and thousands of miles away from his other relatives. Carol had a recurring nightmare that Kevin would get into a car accident in Los Angeles and have no one nearby to help. She began telling Kevin that he would be much better off at the University of Kentucky, where he'd be able to live with Jeff and lean on him or Carol's mother and sisters if he ran into any hard times. Melanie had also begun thinking about college, and the University of Kentucky was the only school on her list. Mark and Carol told Kevin that they loved the idea of him, Jeff, and Melanie all going to the same school.

The lobbying campaign paid off. Kevin had always tried to please his family, and picking a college was no exception. Jeff was pressuring him to come to the University of Kentucky, and his parents were subtly making clear that they wanted him to go to school there as well. Kevin started filling out applications for Washington University and Berkeley but never completed them. He knew that his parents would have had to pay his full tuition at the two schools, and he didn't want to be a financial burden to his family. Mark and Carol strongly encouraged their son to enroll in an ROTC program, which would cover the entire cost of his college education, and he eventually agreed. Like his older brother, Kevin applied to only one school, and like his brother he was accepted into the University of Kentucky almost immediately. The school gave him a Chancellor Scholarship for outstanding academic achievement before he even arrived on campus, and its ROTC program gave him a four-year scholarship, making his education completely free. In the wearying years ahead, Mark and Carol would lie awake at night, haunted by the question of how differently Kevin's life might have turned out if they had let him follow his heart and stay back in California. "We have asked ourselves that a million times, along with countless other what-ifs," Carol said.

In his final months in California, Kevin Graham prepared for a future that had been largely determined by other people. Mark and Carol wanted him to be a soldier and they wanted him to be a doctor. Jeff wanted him to come to the University of Kentucky. Kevin had always been interested in medicine, and he had grown up believing that military service was both a duty and an honor. He wasn't sure those were still the paths he wanted to take, but always the dutiful son and brother, he decided to walk them anyway.

CHAPTER 7

Louisville, Kentucky, January 2003

Jeff Graham took out his cell phone, steadied his voice, and called Korea. "Kevin, there's this lady who keeps calling and said she's from the DEA," he told his younger brother. "She said she has some questions about a package you'd ordered, and I don't know what to tell her." Kevin was thousands of miles away at his parents' house in Seoul, but the call hit him hard. A few weeks earlier he had ordered a box of Ritalin from a company in Pakistan that hadn't bothered to ask for a prescription. Kevin realized that the shipment must have arrived at the off-campus apartment he shared with Jeff and Melanie while the three Graham children were away in Korea for Christmas and New Year's. ROTC cadets weren't supposed to take drugs like Ritalin; the fact that he'd purchased the medications without medical approval would only make things worse. Panicked, Kevin decided to lie. "I have absolutely no idea what you're talking about," he told his brother.

Jeff had found the drugs by accident after leaving Korea early to spend more time with Stacey. One afternoon he found a note taped to the front door that said there was a package waiting for Kevin Graham at the post office. Jeff figured he'd do his brother a favor and pick it up. His eyes went wide when he saw that the box had come from Pakistan. They went even wider when he cut it open and saw the neat rows of Ritalin tablets. Stacey, who was studying pharmaceutical science, told Jeff that it was illegal to buy that kind of medication from a website and urged him to throw it away. Jeff decided to have a bit of fun instead. He called Kevin every day to relay messages from the DEA agent and to ask if he should give her Kevin's number in Korea. Kevin quickly caved. He told Mark and Carol all about his Ritalin use and called Jeff to ask for the DEA agent's phone number. Kevin told Jeff that he would call her first thing the next day and confess what he had done. Jeff let the words dangle in the air for a second and then giggled. "Kev, there's no woman," he told his younger brother. "I was just having a bit of fun with you." Jeff had a cruel streak that sometimes went too far. This was one of those times. Kevin, furious at a joke that had hit far too close to home, didn't speak to his brother again for days.

Kevin had been taking Ritalin for months, hoping it would help him concentrate in his science courses and reverse a sudden decline in his grades. He first heard about the ADHD medication from his classmates in the University of Kentucky's premed program, where Ritalin was just as popular as coffee and thought to be just as harmless. It wasn't the only drug he was taking. Kevin had been diagnosed with depression a couple of months earlier and put on antidepressants. He hadn't told his parents or siblings when he began taking the drug, and he kept it secret from his fellow ROTC cadets as well. Kevin was waging a last-ditch battle against the demons that had tormented him since he was a child. The drug was his final means of defense.

In the weeks before Jeff's graduation, Kevin worked himself into the best physical condition of his life. The ROTC program required all of its cadets to do early-morning workouts a few times per week, but Kevin didn't stop there. He went for long daily runs around the University of Kentucky campus, lifted weights in the school gym, and stocked his bedroom with bodybuilding magazines, protein bars, and protein-heavy nutritional supplements. For the first time in his life, Kevin was in better shape than his older brother. Mark and Carol were planning to fly in from Korea for the commencement, and Melanie joked that they wouldn't recognize Kevin when they got to Lexington. Neither she nor Jeff realized that Kevin's newfound physical fitness was a mask; he looked great on the outside, but on the inside he'd never been in worse shape.

Kevin Graham wandered down Bourbon Street, picking necklaces of beads off the ground and waving to anyone he saw in a Kentucky T-shirt. It was the spring semester of his junior year, and Kevin had road-tripped down to New Orleans with Jeff and several of his older brother's closest friends for a long weekend of Kentucky basketball. The Wildcats had made it to that year's Southeastern Conference championship, and the brothers and their friends weren't about to miss out on a chance to see Kentucky battle for the title in person. They spent their days in the Superdome, cheering on the Wildcats, and their evenings partying at the House of Blues and other New Orleans bars. They pulled a drunken all-nighter when Kentucky rallied to beat Mississippi State in the conference finals. "It was basically a weekend of basketball and Bourbon Street," Jon Burns, one of the Grahams' closest friends, recalls.

Kevin had moved into Jeff's apartment at the Royal Lexington the summer before his freshman year and quickly adopted his older brother's obsession with Kentucky basketball. He filled his closet with blue Kentucky T-shirts and camped with his brother outside the school's Rupp Arena for tickets. He even signed off on Jeff's edict banning anyone who wasn't wearing University of Kentucky clothing from entering their apartment.

Kentucky hadn't been Kevin's top choice, and he tried to hold on to as much of his former life in California as possible while he adjusted to Lexington. He saved up money to fly out to Los Angeles every few months to see Ryan Lai and David Miller and tried to catch up with them every few weeks by phone. He worked even harder to maintain his relationship with Heather, who visited Kentucky in the summer of 2000, just weeks after her graduation from San Pedro, to meet Jeff there for the first time. Heather could tell how much the trip meant to her boyfriend, who idolized Jeff and desperately wanted his older brother to approve of their relationship. She was determined to win Jeff over, so she made a point of talking to him about University of Kentucky basketball and Salvador Dalí, his favorite artist. She also tried to impress him by drinking as much beer and whiskey as he did, though she soon realized that she couldn't keep pace. Jeff seemed to appreciate the effort. "This girl is a keeper," he told Kevin.

At first Kevin made sure that Heather knew he felt exactly the same way. They spoke every day by phone or e-mail, sharing gossip about their old friends and details of everyday life in Kentucky and California. Heather told him that she was thinking of transferring to Northeastern University in Boston so they'd be closer to each other. Privately, Kevin told his friends that he was deeply in love with Heather and hoped to one day marry her. Privately, Heather told her friends the same thing about him.

But the relationship didn't last. Whole weeks—and soon whole months—would pass without Kevin calling or e-mailing. Heather tried reaching out to him, but Kevin didn't respond to her phone messages and e-mails. She initially attributed his silence to his building a new life in Kentucky and spending most of his free time with Jeff, but she gradually concluded that he simply didn't want to talk to her. "It was very painful because I felt like he was rejecting me and not telling me why," she said.

Early in her sophomore year, Kevin called Heather and apologized for being so distant. He told her that he was having a hard time adjusting to life without her and that every conversation made him miss her more. He promised to do a better job of staying in touch, but soon he cut off all communications. Kevin would later tell Carol that he had decided that he wasn't good enough for Heather and that she would be better off without him.

"She deserves more," he told his mother. "I'm not worthy of somebody like her."

Melanie had surprised her guidance counselor at the American high school in Osan by applying to only a single school. She had a simple reason for choosing Kentucky: Mark and Carol were staying in Korea, and Melanie desperately wanted to be close to her brothers. Her parents encouraged her to apply for an ROTC scholarship that would cover the costs of her tuition and living expenses, but Kevin was adamantly against the idea and it was never raised again. When she got to Kentucky, Mark and Carol paid for Melanie to have a dorm room, but she moved out and settled in with Kevin and Jeff. It was a small apartment, and Melanie quickly saw how badly Kevin was missing Heather, and how lonely he seemed without her. Jeff and Kevin had taken care of Melanie when she was a kid. Now, as an adult, she felt like it was time to return the favor. She tried to fix Kevin up with some of her friends, but he'd come back from the dates and tell her that none of the girls measured up to Heather. Kevin spoke about her constantly and made no real effort to move on. Heather waited until her junior year to begin another relationship. Kevin never seriously dated anyone else.

He was having similar problems in the classroom. Academics initially seemed to come as easily to Kevin at the University of Kentucky as they had in high school. He got six As during the fall semester of his freshman year and five more during the spring. He finished the year with a 3.78 grade point average and a spot on the dean's list. But the early success didn't endure. Kevin got three Bs the first semester of his sophomore year and two Es—the lowest grades possible—in the second one. His GPA fell to 3.3. Things got even worse during his junior year. He got a

D in organic chemistry, Es in biology and physics, and an incomplete in a class on stem cell research. His GPA for the semester was just 1.27, and his overall GPA slipped to 3. Kevin was earning his lowest grades in precisely the sorts of science classes that would be most important to his medical school applications.

Kevin's entire life was in disarray by the start of his junior year. He had cut ties with Heather but been unable to find a new girlfriend. Jeff was spending virtually all of his free time at Stacey's new apartment, so Kevin was living without his best friend and closest confidant. He was drinking heavily—Kevin downed twenty-one shots of whiskey on the night of his twenty-first birthday, though Jeff had quietly slipped the bartender $100 to water them down—and having a hard time sleeping. His grades were plummeting and medical school seemed out of reach. He went out occasionally with small groups of friends but spent increasing amounts of time alone. Kevin Graham was spiraling down, but no one knew just how far.

On a crisp, sunny day in October 2002, Kevin walked into the University of Kentucky's library and took a short written test designed to identify signs of depression. He screened positive and was assigned to a counselor named Lori Molenaar. She could tell he needed help before their first one-hour session had even ended. Kevin told her that he felt lethargic, unmotivated, and distant from his friends, three of the primary symptoms of a disorder called vegetative depression. "It's what people think of when they think of depression—a person just sitting off by themselves, feeling sad and alone," she said. "They don't want to go anywhere or do anything. And even if they did, they wouldn't have the energy to actually do it."

Lori diagnosed Kevin with the disease and gave him a prescription for Celexa, which immediately improved both his energy level and his mood. In October, Kevin called Carol to tell her that he had depression but had begun taking a medication that seemed to be helping him manage it. He seemed relieved to know that his pervasive sadness had a biological cause.

"Mom, did you know that depression is an actual illness and not just a feeling?" he asked Carol. "Maybe I can be cured."

"Sometimes you need an antibiotic for an infection," Carol agreed, trying to inject a note of cheer into her voice that she didn't actually feel.

Unsure of what else to say or do, she told Kevin that he could overcome his sadness on his own if he would just drink less, exercise more, and focus on eating fish and vegetables rather than pizza and hamburgers. Kevin, always eager to please his mother, promised to do everything she had suggested.

He was also doing everything Lori Molenaar had asked of him. He showed up on time, never canceled an appointment, and was unfailingly polite. Many of the students who sought help at the counseling center showed up disheveled or in ratty, unwashed clothing. Kevin was always clean-shaven and dressed in clothes that looked like they were fresh out of the dryer.

Kevin wasn't a model patient for very long. Lori told him that drinking was making his depression worse and pleaded with him to cut back, but Kevin kept showing up at her office with the sickly sweet smell of alcohol on his breath. His mood was changing rapidly, bouncing from high to low and then back again, sometimes in the same day. "We would get him in a good place and he would be out of the clinic for a couple of months or so, and he would come back and tell me, 'Well, it's back again,'" Lori said.

Kevin returned to Lori's tidy office near the end of 2002 to tell her that he felt the dark clouds returning. She switched him from Celexa to Prozac, and the clouds seemed to lift. Kevin told her that he was beginning to feel like himself again. Lori was struck by something else: For the first time in their months of work together, Kevin seemed excited about the future.

Mark and Carol Graham told themselves that maybe—just maybe—the old Kevin was back for good. The three Graham children had flown to Korea to spend Christmas 2002 at their parents' new house at the Yongsan military base in downtown Seoul. Jeff and Melanie didn't know about Kevin's depression, and Mark and Carol didn't bring it up. It wasn't the first time the Graham children had traveled to Asia. One year earlier, in late 2001, Kevin, Jeff, and Melanie flew to Korea to link up with their parents and then continue on to China for a short vacation. They walked the Great Wall on New Year's Day, bundling themselves in layers of warm clothing because of the strong wind roaring down from the mountains ringing the centuries-old fortification. A few hours into the hike, Mark stopped in front of a lookout post with a clear view of the smooth white wall stretching off into the distance. He told his children that they'd found the perfect spot for a picture. The three Graham children clustered together and smiled for the camera. Jeff is on the left, holding his gloves in his hand. Melanie, her neck wrapped in a scarf, is in the middle. Kevin stands to the side, hands in the pockets of his jacket. A framed copy of the photo was one of the first things Mark and Carol set out in their home in Seoul.

Now, together for the first time in more than half a year, the family played bridge and watched movies in the living room, squeezing onto the couch and eating bowl after bowl of microwave popcorn. Kevin horsed around with Jeff and Melanie and tried to wake up early enough to see Mark before he left for work. "Kev looked great, and I must have convinced myself that he was over it," Carol said.

One afternoon she drove Kevin and Jeff to a tailor in Seoul's main shopping district to pick up a pair of custom-made suits. Kevin had chosen a solid black suit, and he added a solid black tie and a light-green shirt. Jeff bought a navy blue suit and a shirt with white pinstripes because one of his friends at the University of Kentucky had told him that stripes would make him look taller. Carol beamed as she watched her sons try on their outfits. *They are so handsome,* she thought. *They look absolutely perfect.*

Kevin didn't feel perfect. Carol knew that her son could be moody, but he had been so cheerful since arriving in Korea that she was thrown when he abruptly started mumbling short answers to her questions and avoiding eye contact with her and Jeff. When Carol asked him what was wrong, Kevin said that he was feeling stressed out by the weight of the decisions he'd have to make when he returned to Lexington. She assumed he was debating whether to change his major or rethinking his commitment to the ROTC program. Carol smiled at her son and tried to find a way of cheering him up like she'd done so many times before.

"Even with all the problems that you think you have at least you are Kevin Graham and there's nobody else in the world you should ever want to be," she told him.

"Mom, there are so many people I would rather be," he replied.

Kevin's comment sent chills down Carol's spine and would haunt her for years. At the time, though, she largely dismissed it. She and Mark had raised three beautiful, smart, and seemingly well-adjusted children. It seemed impossible to imagine that Kevin actually hated himself so deeply.

Carol flipped open her Bible and sought God's help for her son. Melanie had returned to Kentucky after the holidays and told her mom that Kevin seemed sadder and lonelier than ever before. Carol had the family Bible and a book of daily devotionals in her living room in Korea, and she regularly sought solace in the prayers and parables she'd been reading since she was a child. She also kept a journal, putting down on paper the feelings of fear and shame that she had difficulty expressing to Mark. One night she penned a particularly anguished entry about her younger son. "Dear God," she began, "my heart is so heavy with such a burden for him." She blamed herself for pushing Kevin to choose the University of Kentucky instead of Washington University. Mark and her own mother, Carol wrote, were urging her to leave Kevin alone and give him the space and time to work through his own problems, but Carol worried that her son needed something more. "Please send him an angel," she concluded. "I would gladly die for my children if on my death it would bring them closer to you."

Carol couldn't stop worrying. Kevin had begged his mother not to talk about his depression with anyone in the family, including his siblings, but Carol thought her sister Sandra might be able to help. At Carol's request, Sandra e-mailed her nephew in the spring of 2003 to tell him that she had been given a diagnosis of bipolar disorder in 1993 and understood—better than anyone else in the family—exactly what he was going through. Sandra said that she'd kept the diagnosis secret for years because she was afraid it would alienate her husband and colleagues. In the end medication and counseling had helped her save both her marriage and her career, and Sandra told Kevin they could do the same for him. She closed by telling her nephew that she would be there for him anytime he wanted to talk, by phone or in person. "I know this is really hard," she wrote. "I've been there." Kevin e-mailed back to thank Sandra for caring enough to share such intimate details about her own life, but he didn't acknowledge that he had been diagnosed with depression or indicate any desire to speak to her about his own feelings and fears.

Kevin was just as tight-lipped with his own siblings. He worshipped Jeff and didn't want his older brother to think any less of him, so he didn't tell him or Melanie about the depression or the drugs he was taking to fight it. Although the three siblings shared an apartment, Kevin was so careful about taking his medication in private that Jeff and Melanie didn't find out about his disease until Stacey wandered into Kevin's room one afternoon in the spring of 2003 and found empty containers of Prozac in the garbage can. Jeff and Melanie told themselves it was nothing to worry about. They were proud of their brother for acknowledging his problems and taking concrete steps to fix them.

In early June, a few weeks after Jeff's graduation, Sandra spotted Kevin in the waiting room of a doctor's office in Frankfort. He told her that he was planning to talk to the physician about his depression and to ask what else he could do to fight it. Sandra wanted to believe that her nephew was serious about taking on the disease, but she had her doubts. His breath reeked of alcohol and he looked more disheveled than she'd ever seen him. She felt that he needed regular, intensive sessions with a doctor in Lexington who could see him every day, not a one-off conversation with a physician in distant Frankfort. She later found out that Kevin had returned home without ever talking to the doctor about his depression.

As he lived alone with his disease, Kevin's downward spiral accelerated. He wrote a poem that began, "Sorrow fills my lonely soul today . . . Tell the voices I don't hear 'em / And I'll walk around pretending that I'm sane." He wrote a to-do list, mostly composed of ordinary tasks from everyday life like waking up early, getting allergy shots, and doing the laundry. But the list, which his siblings didn't find until much later, concluded with a deeply alarming line: "Take toaster into bathtub."

My career could be over before it even starts, Kevin thought. *If they find out about the Prozac, I'm done.* It was late spring 2003, and ROTC was the one area of his life where Kevin was still flourishing, in large part because of its strict structure and clear hierarchy. ROTC cadets weren't facing remotely the same challenges that actual serving officers faced, but it was a tough program all the same. Future officers such as Kevin Graham met at Buell several times per week for multihour classes in military history, giving orders to enlisted personnel, and responding to directives from higher-ranking officers. Cadets were held to stringent physical fitness standards and could be kicked out of the program and lose their scholarship at any time if they were caught using drugs, getting publicly intoxicated, or otherwise misbehaving on campus or elsewhere in Lexington. ROTC participants also had to prepare themselves mentally to accept that the army could send them wherever it wanted and was under no obligation to honor their request for service in specific areas like the infantry.

Kevin had no problem with any of that. He was named the University of Kentucky ROTC's battalion commander, the highest honor available to a future officer. He also ranked as one of the top three cadets of his ROTC class because his cumulative GPA remained well above average for the program and his commanders gave him high marks for his physical fitness and willingness to coach other cadets. They saw him as a natural leader.

Kevin was slated to begin the next phase of his military training in June 2003, shortly after Jeff's graduation, with a monthlong training course at Washington's Fort Lewis. Operation Warrior Forge is a program designed to hone cadets' physical conditioning, marksmanship, land navigation skills, and expertise using army-issued radios and communications gear. The centerpiece of the program is a mock deployment to a war zone where cadets live in the field and conduct multiple combat missions per day. Kevin was also tapped to attend a second summer course, the Cadet Leader Training Program, which gives ROTC personnel short apprenticeships with active-duty units. Kentucky had received only a single slot in the highly selective program, and Kevin was the one chosen to fill it. He was slated to leave for a unit in Germany at the end of the summer.

Kevin felt a growing sense of dread as the end of the school year drew closer. He hadn't told any of his ROTC instructors that he was taking Prozac, but he was certain the army would find out when he got to Fort Lewis and was given a urinalysis. Carol, one of the few who knew Kevin was taking the drug, called the army to find out what would happen if an ROTC cadet was found to be taking medication for clinical depression. She was told that he'd lose his scholarship and be deemed "mentally ill and not fit for military duty." Kevin asked Lori if she thought he could safely stop taking the Prozac, and she told him it was too dangerous to even consider.

"That would be a terrible idea," she told Kevin. "Maybe you shouldn't be in the military if it means you can't have your medicine."

Kevin shook his head and stormed out of her office. His low grades had ended his dreams of becoming a military doctor, but he'd committed to the ROTC program and wanted to see it through. A few days later he abruptly threw away his pills. That would have been risky for anyone with clinical depression, but it was a particularly dangerous move for Kevin because of his heavy drinking and extreme mood swings. Kevin hadn't told anyone outside his family that he had begun taking Prozac. When he stopped taking it, he didn't tell a single soul. Lori never saw him again.

In early May, Mark and Carol boarded a plane in Seoul for the long flight home to Kentucky for Jeff's graduation, which they knew would be one of their last chances to see their oldest son before he moved to Fort Knox and began training for a potential deployment to Iraq. Jeff had been named a Distinguished Military Graduate, the highest honor available to an ROTC cadet. On Friday, May 9, Mark, wearing an army dress uniform emblazoned with pins representing all of his military citations, walked onto a stage at the University of Kentucky's Memorial Hall to lead Jeff through the oath recited by all new officers. Mark hugged his son, whose military career formally began as soon as Jeff finished reciting his promise to "support and defend the Constitution against all enemies, foreign and domestic."

The school's engineering department held its graduation ceremony the next day. Jeff, smiling from ear to ear, posed for a picture with Kevin and Melanie after receiving his diploma. Mark and Carol would come to treasure the photo. It was the last picture they would ever take of all three of their children.

A few days after Jeff's graduation, the Graham children drove their parents to the Louisville airport to say good-bye. Carol couldn't shake the feeling that she was abandoning Kevin when he needed her most, but she told herself that his brother and sister would somehow keep him safe. As she approached the security checkpoint, Carol turned around and looked her son in the face.

"You really are okay, right, Kevin?" Carol asked.

Her younger son just nodded.

Mark and Carol navigated through the towering stacks of boxes early one Saturday morning in June 2003. Mark had received orders to return to the United States for his next posting, and he and Carol were racing to pack up their house at Yongsan. The phone rang shortly after nine. It was Kevin, but he didn't sound like himself. He told Carol that he'd just finished a three-day stretch where he'd done nothing but play *The Sims*, a video game that allows players to create animated avatars and then guide them down various career paths. Kevin said that he'd just been promoted to astronaut and then to general, two of the game's highest possible achievements. "It's just not all it's cracked up to be," he told his mother. "I hate the way the world measures success."

He also began quoting from Henry David Thoreau's *Walden*. "The mass of men," Kevin said to his confused mother, "lead lives of quiet desperation." Kevin told Carol that he dreamt of moving to a farm with his father and brother so the three men could spend their days working the land and their evenings reading the Bible together. The comment threw her. Kevin attended church with his family every Sunday, but he had told his friends he was an agnostic. The family had never lived or worked on a farm. The next thing he said rattled her even more. "My brain doesn't work," he said flatly.

Carol later learned that Kevin's decision to quit taking Prozac had allowed his depression to return with full force. But she didn't know any of that yet. Instead, on that suddenly frightening morning in June, she passed the phone to Mark, hoping he'd know how to help their son.

Trying to keep his voice level, Mark urged Kevin to take a leave of absence from the ROTC program so he would have time to get proper help. He offered to reimburse the military for the cost of Kevin's scholarship so his son would be under no further obligation to the army. Kevin immediately rejected the offer. Leaving the ROTC program, he told his father, would mean he was giving up. "That would make me a quitter," Kevin told Mark before saying good-bye and hanging up the phone.

On June 20, Kevin stopped in the Royal Lexington's front office and gave the complex manager a pair of checks for that summer's rent. Dutiful as ever, he wanted to make sure he was fully paid up. The manager noticed that he looked ashen and tried to cheer him up.

"You're so handsome that I bet you have your choice of girlfriends," she told him.

"No," Kevin replied. "I don't have any friends."

That night Kevin walked into Melanie's room and sat down on her bed. She had been listening to Bad Religion, a punk band she and her brother both liked, so she was surprised when Kevin reached over and shut off the music.

"Don't listen to that kind of depressing music anymore," he told her. "And don't drink. Drinking just makes all of it worse."

Melanie had no idea what Kevin was talking about. Her brother was the one who introduced her to Bad Religion, and they'd been drinking together since high school.

"You're really freaking me out," she told him. "Why are you being so serious?"

Kevin didn't answer. Instead, he looked his sister in the eyes and whispered that she should always remember how much potential she had. He left without saying good night. A few hours later Melanie woke up to use the bathroom and noticed that her brother's bedroom door was closed, which was unusual. She made a mental note to ask him about it in the morning and went back to bed.

The following morning Jeff called Melanie and asked her to check in on Kevin and find out why he hadn't shown up for the golf game. She opened her brother's bedroom door and froze when she saw him hanging from the ceiling fan. At first, she assumed Kevin and Jeff were playing some sort of twisted joke. She put her hand on his arm to shake him out of it, but his skin was cold to the touch. A neighbor named Chris Risalvato cut Kevin down and tried to administer CPR, but it was too late. Melanie called Jeff and managed to tell him that his brother was dead before she dropped the phone and began to scream.

CHAPTER 8

Fort Knox, Kentucky, June 2003

Stacey Martinez was relaxing at her mother's house on a lazy, quiet Saturday morning when her phone rang. Jeff had told her that he'd be spending the day golfing with Kevin, so she hadn't been expecting a call. She picked up the receiver and heard a man sobbing so loudly that she couldn't tell who it was or what he was saying. She asked who it was, but the person at the other end couldn't get the words out to answer. She asked again and finally made out the familiar voice.

"Kevin's dead," Jeff said. "He hung himself."

Stacey wasn't sure that was true. Kevin might have tried to kill himself, she reasoned, but that didn't mean he had succeeded. Asphyxiation was a relatively slow way to die, and paramedics could easily have saved his life if they arrived at the apartment quickly. By the time Jeff arrived at her house, Stacey had convinced herself that Kevin was still alive.

"Jeff, he might not be dead," she said. "Maybe the police got there or the ambulance got there and they were able to revive him. He might be okay."

The optimism didn't last. Jeff called Melanie back and asked if she was sure Kevin was dead. Stacey was standing a few feet away but could hear Melanie scream "Yes!" again and again. Jeff went pale and slumped to the floor. He was in such shock that he couldn't remember Mark and Carol's phone number in Korea. Jeff called his aunt Jackie Sue, who answered the phone, kidded him about not knowing his parents' number, and casually asked him how his day was going.

"You mean you don't know?" Jeff asked.

He slammed down the phone and walked away, furious. Stacey's mom picked it up and told Jackie Sue that Kevin had killed himself and that they needed to get Mark and Carol's phone number as quickly as possible. She scrawled the digits down on a sheet of paper and handed it to Jeff. He called his parents from the kitchen, leaning against the counter to keep himself from collapsing again.

Mark and Carol were sound asleep in their sparsely furnished bedroom at Yongsan when the trilling of their phone woke them up. Mark answered, and Carol could hear the muffled voice of her oldest son, though she couldn't make out what he was saying. Mark hung up the phone, hugged Carol close, and softly told her that Kevin had just killed himself. She couldn't think or breathe, and Carol felt herself hyperventilating and beginning to lose consciousness. Her mind went blank as the numbness and shock set in.

Mark reacted very differently, setting aside his own pain and trying to focus on the logistics of getting home. Friends from the close-knit military community at Yongsan did their best to help. One neighbor rushed over to pack Carol's clothes and toiletries, while another forced her to drink a Slimfast shake so she wouldn't pass out from hunger or dehydration. Officers from the base got Mark and Carol tickets for a flight to the United States that was leaving later that same day. Mark didn't have a warm relationship with his boss, General Leon LaPorte, but the commander and his wife flew back from Guam early so they could sit with the Grahams at the airport to make sure they wouldn't wait for the plane alone. A base doctor quickly wrote Carol prescriptions for Ambien and Xanax and made sure she had the drugs with her when she left for the airport. Carol popped one of the Ambiens shortly after taking her seat on the plane and quickly fell into a dreamless, restless sleep. "I would have taken heroin," Carol said. "I would have taken anything that would ease the pain." Mark cried most of the way home, doing his best not to wake his wife.

Sandra picked them up at the airport with Melanie and Jeff in the backseat of her car. Jeff's eyes were so red from crying that Carol couldn't see his pupils. Melanie's eyes looked swollen shut, like she'd been in a fistfight. Carol had never seen her children look so physically and emotionally broken. Jeff, who had become the most devout of the Graham children, was also having trouble deciding whether Kevin would be punished for violating the biblical rules against suicide. "Mom, is Kevin in hell?" he asked. Carol tried to reassure him that his brother had gone to a better place, but part of her also wondered.

Mark and Carol wanted to see their son as soon as possible, so Sandra drove them straight to the Lexington coroner's office. A glass door separated the morgue from a small observation room. A technician let Mark, Carol, Jeff, and Melanie into the mortuary area and slid the shelf holding Kevin's body out of a large refrigerator. A white sheet covered him up to his chin. Jeff pulled it back, giving Mark and Carol their first, and last, look at the mottled, scarlet bruises that ringed Kevin's neck. Carol's legs buckled and she slumped to the cold tiled floor. Melanie sobbed so loudly that Mark worried she'd collapse as well. He put his arms around his daughter and pulled her into a firm embrace. Jeff looked down at his brother and laid his hand on Kevin's bare shoulder.

"Why, Kevin?" he asked through clenched teeth. "Why didn't you call me? Why didn't you tell me?"

Kevin looked so peaceful that Carol briefly imagined that her son was merely resting and could be woken up with a kiss, like in *Sleeping Beauty.* She and Mark gently brushed their fingers against his cheek. Carol hugged Kevin's body and begged him to forgive her for not hearing his calls for help. His skin was hard and cold to the touch. "The Kevin we knew and loved was not there, and no matter how much we loved him, he had left us," Carol said. "It was just Kevin's shell. His soul was some-place else."

Jeff and Melanie said good-bye to their brother and walked out of the mortuary, arms around each other's shoulders. Mark and Carol kissed Kevin on his forehead. Carol reached down and took one of Kevin's hands between her own, clutching it tightly. She held on to Kevin's hand for so long that Mark had to gently pull her out of the mortuary room.

I could see Kevin again, Carol thought. *I could be back with my baby.* It was the night before Kevin's funeral, and Carol was debating how she should take her own life. There was a bridge a short distance from her mother's house that connected the old and new parts of Frankfort. Carol was certain that she'd die if she jumped into the flowing water hundreds of feet below. She had also been given prescriptions for Xanax and Ambien to help her get through each wearying day and sleepless night, and she watched enough TV to know that swallowing all of the pills at the same time would likely cause a fatal overdose. But her mind kept returning to the idea of hanging herself. Her beloved son had taken his own life by fashioning a makeshift noose, winding it around the ceiling fan, and stepping off his bed so his feet could no longer touch the floor. Carol was increasingly certain that she should do the same. One night she found an electrical cord in the closet and twisted it around her neck, planning to squeeze it tight until she was dead. Carol dropped the cord after a few seconds and huddled on the floor of the closet, furious with herself for not being able to go through with it. "I wanted to atone for not being there when Kevin needed me," she said. "I wanted to die the way he died."

Carol and Mark were so consumed by guilt and pain that they could barely eat or sleep. Their son had been calling out to them for help, but they realized, far too late, that they simply hadn't heard him. Mark spent hours alone in a bedroom at Jackie Shroat's house, staring off into space. Carol reacted very differently, putting on what she described as her "CSI hat" and trying to find out as much about her son's final days as she could. Searching through Kevin's belongings, she found a business card for Mary Bolin, the head of the University of Kentucky's counseling program, and a to-do list with a cryptic reference to "call Mary." Carol called on Friday evening, hours after Mary had left her office, but the doctor got her phone message and felt that it would be unconscionable to wait until Monday before responding to a grieving mother. Mary picked up the phone at her house and slowly dialed Carol's number, half expecting Carol to lash out in fury and accuse the university of failing her son. Instead, Carol gently asked if Mary could tell her anything about how Kevin had reached such a point of despair and hopelessness that he chose to take his own life rather than continuing to get help. Carol was crying, and Mary was on the verge of crying as well. Carol, she realized, wasn't angry. She was broken by the tragedy of losing her son and simply looking for anything that could help her better understand why it had happened. Mary had nothing to offer.

"I never had the privilege of knowing your son," she told Carol. "I'm so sorry that you lost your child and that I don't have any information I can give you, but I never knew him."

Lori Molenaar was the only counselor at the university who was in a position to tell Carol about Kevin's last months, but she was just as stunned as the Grahams. She knew that many patients who battled depression their entire lives were able to conceal the severity of their disease, and that those who seemed to be the most stable were sometimes the ones who were most in danger of harming themselves. Still, Lori's last session with Kevin had left her convinced that he had finally gotten his depression under control. He had lost weight and clearly improved his physical conditioning. Kevin talked about entering the military with more excitement than she'd ever seen from him before. He didn't look or act like a man contemplating suicide.

Carol eventually realized that her son had been wearing a mask. He hid his true feelings from his therapist and kept his own pain bottled up to avoid frightening his parents or detracting from the family's joy over Jeff's graduation and commissioning into the U.S. Army. Kevin killed himself just six weeks later, and Carol has never forgiven herself for failing to spot her son's rapidly deteriorating mental condition.

In early May, Kevin had called from Lexington to tell Carol that he was failing his classes and needed to see a psychiatrist. She and Mark were slated to fly home in less than a week for Jeff's graduation, and Carol told her son that she would stay behind when Mark returned to Korea so he wouldn't have to go through treatment by himself. Carol hung up the phone, walked to her bedroom, and began gathering up all of the clothes she'd need for the summer. She had her ticket to Lexington booked, and she wasn't planning on taking the return flight.

Carol's next move was to call TRICARE, the military's health insurance system, to see if Kevin could get a referral to see a psychiatrist in Kentucky. The TRICARE representative asked if Kevin had attempted suicide. When Carol said her son was simply suffering from depression, the official said she couldn't authorize a session with a psychiatrist unless there were "extenuating circumstances."

Carol was still hoping to find a way of somehow beating the system, so she asked Sandra to try to find a psychiatrist in Lexington or Frankfort who was willing to accept TRICARE. Sandra called every psychiatrist in the two cities, but she couldn't find a single one who took the military insurance.

When Mark got home a few hours later, Carol told him that Kevin's phone call had convinced her to stay in the States after Jeff's graduation rather than accompany him back to Seoul. Mark didn't like the idea. He told Carol that he was working long hours in a high-stress job and didn't think that he could finish packing up their house in Yongsan by himself. He also felt that Carol was forgetting that their son was an adult, not a child, and that she was exaggerating the severity of his depression. Carol hadn't held a steady job since her children were born, leaving her with plenty of time to take an unusually hands-on role in their lives. Her three children sometimes accused her of meddling. Mark knew that Carol was acting solely out of her fierce love for them, but he sometimes agreed that she needed to give the kids more space to deal with their problems on their own. "Don't you think Kevin can handle this by himself?" Mark asked her. "Don't you think you're babying him?"

Carol's mother made a similar argument. She felt that Carol was inadvertently making Kevin's depression worse by calling him every day to ask how he was doing rather than giving him the space to work through things on his own. Leaving Mark to handle the move home by himself, Jackie said, would distract him from his work and potentially harm Mark's career. The best thing Carol could do, she added, was set aside her own fears and do her best to be there for Mark.

Carol reluctantly agreed to fly back to Korea after Jeff's commissioning. She didn't tell Kevin about the change of plans, but he figured out that she wasn't going to be staying in the States when he picked her up at the airport and saw that she hadn't brought Wicket, the family's beloved Yorkie. Kevin knew that his mother wouldn't have left the dog in Korea if she'd planned on staying behind in Kentucky. He told Carol that he was fine with her going back after the graduation, but she could tell that he was deeply disappointed. Her son looked like he was in the best shape of his life, though, and Carol persuaded herself that he would be okay without her.

Kevin didn't give Carol any reason to think otherwise during the week the Grahams spent in the United States for Jeff's commissioning. On Mother's Day the three Graham children drove to Frankfort to celebrate with their parents, grandparents, aunts, uncles, nieces, and nephews. The family went to church for Sunday services and then headed back to Sandra's house for a loud, happy supper, complete with fresh-baked cake for all of the mothers in the room. Near the end of the party, Jeff, Kevin, and Melanie gave Carol a University of Kentucky coffee mug and pendant, as well as a Mother's Day card all three had signed and inscribed. Kevin's portion of the card thanked Carol for "rescuing me from rock-bottom and insanity so many times" and "for being there for me when I have nowhere else to turn."

The Graham children drove Mark and Carol to Louisville the next day for the long flight home to Korea. Carol had discovered that Kevin could keep going for counseling at the university's behavioral clinic if he paid a onetime $250 fee. She handed him a check at the airport, but he told her that he didn't want to start over with another therapist. Kevin never cashed it. Six weeks later he took his own life. "I did not think that his words in the card were literal, but now I know he was trying to let me know he was suffering," Carol said. "I never rescued him from anything. I let my son down."

Sandra Shroat Bush also wonders if she could have done more to save her nephew. She took her daughters shopping in Lexington one day in late May and decided to pay a last-minute visit to Kevin's apartment to see how he looked and sounded. She knocked on the door but no one answered. Kevin finally opened the door, blinking in the midafternoon sun. It was after two o'clock, and he had clearly just woken up. Sandra could see the indentation on the couch where he'd been napping and smell the alcohol on his breath. Empty bottles of beer, whiskey, and bourbon littered the apartment. Kevin was red-eyed and disheveled. After his death, coroners would discover that he had a blood-alcohol level of 0.144, nearly double the level that would warrant a drunk driving citation. "I could tell he was self-medicating, but I didn't know how much he was suffering," Sandra said. "I'll always wish I had."

Melanie Graham feels a different kind of regret. In early June, she aced one of her final exams and offered to treat her brother to lunch to celebrate. It was a sunny day, with temperatures in the mid-eighties, and Kevin had his sunroof open. Melanie felt that it was a perfect moment, the type a person dreams of but rarely experiences.

"I love days like this when you just smile for no reason," she told her brother.

"I don't know what that's like," he responded in a flat, cold voice.

After his death, Melanie would look back at the conversation and wonder how she could have missed so clear a sign that her brother felt trapped in a dark tunnel, the light receding farther and farther out of sight. At the time, she thought her brother was simply being moody. Kevin had suffered brief bouts of sadness since they were children, and Melanie had long ago learned not to worry too much about them. His mood would always quickly improve. She assumed he'd bounce back this time as well.

Melanie had a harder time forgiving herself for how she'd treated Kevin after he took her aside one afternoon and confided that he was taking Prozac, begging her not to tell anyone else.

"Are you crazy?" she asked him. "Only crazy people take that kind of stuff."

Her brother's face flushed bright red. The next day Kevin told her that he needed the drug to even get out of bed in the morning.

"Mel, there are days when I wake up and I just don't want to do anything," he told her. "This keeps me from just staying in my room and waiting for the day to end."

Melanie didn't want to hear it. She suggested they jump in the car, put on some music, and go for a long drive around Lexington to clear their heads. Melanie and her brother never talked about his prescription drug use again.

Heather, Kevin's first and only serious girlfriend, didn't find out about Kevin's suicide until the middle of July. She hadn't been checking her school e-mail account that summer but logged in one afternoon and saw a string of weeks-old e-mails from Ryan Lai. The first asked her to call him as soon as possible. The second told her that Kevin had passed away. She initially assumed that he'd been in a car accident or died from alcohol poisoning. "I thought it was the normal thing that could happen to a college student," she said.

Heather realized that she'd missed Kevin's funeral and called Melanie to apologize. Melanie was incredulous when she asked how Kevin had died.

"Oh my God, you haven't heard?" Melanie asked her. "He hanged himself."

Heather threw herself down onto a friend's bed, sobbing. She blamed herself for not reaching out to Kevin after he'd stopped calling or e-mailing and felt that she'd failed to be there for him when he needed her the most. Carol e-mailed her to check in, but Heather ignored the notes and cut off all contact with the Grahams—until a second, equally devastating tragedy struck the Graham family, and Heather realized that she was being selfish by wallowing in her own pain over Kevin's death and not doing more to assuage Mark and Carol's.

Heather poured her feelings of grief and guilt into a poem she wrote in honor of the man she'd loved and once planned to marry:

> Sorrow unseen, unknown troubled soul,
> Hopeless and lonely, shuddering cold.
> Friends unaware of the sadness inside,

Carefully concealed, tactfully he'd hide.

A hand I once held, a heart that touched mine

Lost in a moment, cheated by time.

Kevin Graham was buried on June 24, 2003, three days after he took his own life. Shroat funerals normally took place at Frankfort's First United Methodist Church, but Kevin's memorial service was held at a nondescript two-story funeral home on the outskirts of town because of a sharp debate within the family over how to commemorate someone who had taken his own life. Carol's sister Debbie felt that Kevin didn't deserve the honor of a formal church service because he had violated a central tenet of the family's faith by committing suicide. She argued that he should be buried quietly, in a service limited to his immediate family. "Debbie wondered why they should have a funeral for him, a church funeral," Sandra said. "She felt it should be hidden." Mark and Carol had also been raised to believe that suicide was a sin, and they understood Debbie's thinking. They didn't ultimately agree with it, though. They decided that they simply could not accept the idea that Kevin had violated God's laws by succumbing to demons he had not created and battling an illness he could not control. They were heartbroken by their son's death, but they refused to feel ashamed. In the end, they decided on a compromise: Kevin's funeral would be open to anyone who wanted to attend, but it would be held in a funeral home, not a church.

More than two hundred mourners streamed into the main hall of the Lecompte-Johnson-Taylor Funeral Home for Kevin's memorial service. Most of Kevin's fellow ROTC cadets, resplendent in their green dress uniforms, drove down from Lexington to say good-bye to their classmate. Not all made the trip: Major Dwayne Edwards, one of Kevin and Jeff's primary ROTC instructors, opted not to come because he saw Kevin's suicide as an act of weakness. But Edwards was very much in the minority. Lieutenant Colonel Brian Wade, who ran the University of Kentucky's ROTC program, organized the caravan of cars and trucks that carried the cadets to Frankfort and made clear that he felt Kevin's death was a tragedy, not a personal failing.

Kevin's casket sat on a wooden riser in the front of the room, large pillars of flowers placed near his head and feet. He wore the custom-made black suit, light-green shirt, and solid tie that Carol had ordered in South Korea. Ben Baxter, a close friend of both Kevin's and Jeff's, told the crowd that he struggled to understand how God could have allowed Kevin to die so young and so abruptly.

"An earthly angel was taken from us way too early, but the impact he had on all those around him is timeless," Ben said to the mourners. "We are all better people for knowing him, and I know my life has had an amazing chapter added to it from me knowing Kevin Graham."

Jeff stood next to his brother's casket, reaching down every few minutes to brush lint off Kevin's lapels or straighten his tie. He didn't leave Kevin's side until the casket was closed and placed into the hearse for the short drive to Frankfort's main cemetery.

In the months to come, Mark would begin to have trouble getting out of bed and going to work. He had received orders to deploy back to Fort Sill, the base where he'd begun his military career so many years earlier, and he told Carol that he planned to retire from the army after finishing his assignment there. Mark never talked about Kevin's death, but his close friends could tell how much pain he was feeling and worried that he was harming himself by keeping all of it bottled up. Carol threw herself into support groups for families who lost loved ones to suicide and spoke to everyone she met, including total strangers, about the importance of ensuring that their friends and relatives received help if they needed it. Jeff cut down on his drinking and began attending church every Sunday, quoting biblical passages to his sister, and praying each night before going to sleep. Melanie didn't talk about Kevin's death with many of her friends or classmates, afraid that they would judge her for failing to keep her brother from taking his own life. Her grades plummeted. Melanie never again set foot in the apartment she and Kevin had shared at the Royal Lexington.

On the somber afternoon when Kevin was buried, though, no one in the Graham family was thinking of anything other than the sudden, searing loss of their son and brother. Mark and Carol listened as local ROTC cadets played taps, and numbly accepted a folded American flag. A gentle breeze rustled the leaves of the trees surrounding Kevin's grave as Jeff hugged his sister close. Mark and Carol, eyes red from crying, had no idea how soon they would find themselves back at that exact spot.

CHAPTER 9

Frankfort, Kentucky, June 2003

He didn't have to go. In late June, a few days after Kevin's death, a military chaplain showed up at Jackie Shroat's house on the outskirts of Frankfort to tell Jeff that he could stay at Fort Knox rather than reporting to Fort Riley and a near-certain deployment to the battlefields of Iraq. Carol, Melanie, and Stacey wanted Jeff to stay back. Still in shock, Mark was torn. He had spent many sleepless nights wondering whether he had pressured his young son into pursuing a military career; should he have been quicker to realize that Kevin would have been better off leaving the ROTC program and doing something else entirely? But Mark knew that after a certain point his opinion had no longer mattered. Once Kevin committed to the military training program, Mark was powerless to get his son out of it. It was different with Jeff. Mark was a fast-rising officer with friends and mentors sprinkled throughout the upper reaches of the military. The army was already offering Jeff a chance to sit out the war, at least for a while. It would take a few phone calls, but Mark was confident that he could ensure that staying back didn't harm Jeff's career or his chances of deploying to Iraq down the road. At the same time Mark knew that Jeff loved the army and had long wanted to lead soldiers into combat. Would it be fair, Mark asked himself, to force his son to abandon his dreams?

A short time after Kevin's funeral, Mark and Jeff went for a long evening walk in a hilly park near Jackie's house. Jeff was scheduled to travel to Fort Riley in October to finish his final training before deploying to Iraq. His unit, the 1st Battalion, 34th Armor, would by then be on the ground engaging the enemy, and Jeff hoped to join them as soon as possible. The chaplain had just left, so father and son were free to talk alone as the summer sun slipped behind the copses of trees ringing the park. Major General Terry Tucker, the commander at Fort Knox, had offered to find Jeff a staff job at the base that would keep him far from danger. Mark told his son to seriously consider the offer. There was no shame, he told Jeff, in taking a short break to process the pain and shock of losing Kevin before being thrown into the crucible of Iraq.

"Dad, I have to go," Jeff said. "What about my men?"

"You don't have any men yet," Mark replied.

"But I will, Dad," Jeff replied, looking his father dead in the eye. "I'm going to be a platoon leader, and my men need me."

For Mark, that conversation settled the issue. "As a father, I didn't want Jeff to go," he said. "As a soldier I knew how he felt. I knew that he had to go."

Stacey hated the idea of spending a year apart from Jeff, but she felt oddly confident that he would make it through Iraq unscathed. The Grahams had already lost one son. It seemed inconceivable that they would lose another one.

"I kept thinking that Jeff had this invisible shield around him, that there was absolutely no way that Jeff was going to die at war because God would never do that to a family like the Grahams," she said.

Before leaving Kentucky, Jeff gave Stacey a custom-made teddy bear named Lieutenant Sandifur, who wore a camouflage vest and dog tags emblazoned with a quote from the Old Testament. The bear had a built-in audio recorder, and Jeff left Stacey a message that he hoped would help her through their time apart. "Hey, sweetie, it's me," he said on the recording that would play whenever she pressed the bear's paw. "I just want to say that I'm safe and that I love you very much and I'll see you soon."

Jeff got to Fort Riley in mid-October. Four weeks later he boarded a bus for the long ride to the Baltimore/Washington International Airport in suburban Maryland. The 1st Battalion, 34th Armor, had a sudden need to replace a lieutenant who had been seriously wounded while leading his platoon on patrol, so Jeff was being rushed to Iraq. He had filled out a will and knew the dangers that awaited him. "I leave for war tomorrow," Jeff wrote in the journal he'd been painstakingly maintaining since Kevin's death. "If I do happen to die, at least I'll be with my favorite person in the whole world, but I'm not ready yet. I want kids, a dog, and a long life."

Jeff flew to the Middle East on November 15, 2003. It would have been Kevin's twenty-second birthday.

The letter Iraqi militants nailed to the outside walls of Combat Outpost Killeen was oddly polite. "To the officers and soldiers of occupation force of the United States of America," the note began in spotty but clear English. "Please, please, in order to save your souls and your blood, and in order to be back peasfully to your family and your home, you have to leave this place." The letter was equally clear about what would happen if the troops stayed. "We will use very destroyful weapon against any soldier found in our dear country," the Islamists wrote. "You have to choose between death and life." The letter was signed by the Resistance Forces of Iraq, one of the many insurgent groups killing and maiming American troops throughout the Sunni heartland of central Iraq.

The threats came as no surprise to the weary, battered soldiers of the 1st Battalion, 34th Armor, 1st Brigade Combat Team, 1st Infantry Division, which had been given responsibility for the dangerous stretch of land linking the insurgent strongholds of Ramadi and Fallujah earlier that fall. The unit, nicknamed the "Centurions," had come under attack almost immediately by Sunni militants who fired rocket-propelled grenades at their vehicles, lobbed artillery shells at their outposts, used snipers to pick off individual soldiers, and planted makeshift bombs powerful enough to obliterate armored Humvees. Many of the grenades and rockets were fired from a dusty, overgrown cemetery across the road from the main U.S. base there, adding a touch of the macabre to the daily stresses of fighting guerillas who carried out lethal attacks and then melted away into the surrounding villages and towns. The U.S. forces knew they were surrounded by enemies, but they had no idea where they were. "The insurgents started hitting us literally the first day we arrived, and they never stopped," said retired lieutenant colonel Jeff Swisher, a West Point graduate and Gulf War veteran who commanded the Centurions. "It was the Wild West."

The Centurions operated out of a Spartan compound called Camp Manhattan that had been built on land that was once part of a World War II–era British air base. They were surrounded by ghostly reminders of British troops who'd served there decades earlier, from the crumbling remnants of the colonial-style building that had once housed the base's officers' club to the overgrown cemetery containing the graves of the British forces that had fought and died there. Journalist Bill Murphy Jr. described Manhattan as "spooky, but beautiful in spots," with patches of lush vegetation and giant palm trees lining its roads. The Centurions couldn't help but grumble about how much better their British predecessors had lived. Manhattan had no running water or reliable electricity, and the U.S. soldiers spent their first weeks there eating packaged Meals, Ready-to-Eat and relieving themselves in outdoor latrines. Some Centurions amused themselves by telling dirty jokes with fake British accents.

Safety was their biggest concern. Hours after the unit's arrival at

Manhattan, Sergeant Benjamin Chavez stripped off his sweat-stained helmet and body armor for a short nap. Chavez was half-asleep when he saw a heavily armored Bradley fighting vehicle suddenly roar away down a potholed road. Seconds later a mortar shell crashed down exactly where the vehicle had been parked, kicking up dense clouds of dust and sand. The sound of the blast echoed between the base's buildings like a thunderclap. "That was the 'oh, shit' moment," Chavez said. "It was no longer a training mission. It was the real thing."

A few days later an armored Humvee rolled over a land mine that had been buried in a road Swisher's men had painstakingly searched earlier that week. No one was hurt, but Swisher realized that militants must have found a way of sneaking onto the base. He ordered his men to bulldoze the buildings and trees closest to Manhattan's outer perimeter, making it far more difficult for would-be infiltrators to sneak up to the base's fences. The insurgents responded by stepping up their efforts to hit the Centurions as soon as they left their fortified outposts.

U.S. casualties came quickly. On October 15, 2003, a young lieutenant named Matt Homa received orders to lead a convoy of five Humvees out on patrol, a routine mission for the Centurions. Homa, as the commander, normally rode in the first truck. That morning he decided to move his Humvee to the back of the convoy and allow a different truck to take the lead. Fifteen minutes after leaving Camp Manhattan, Homa spotted a small bottle in the road and ordered his driver to swerve off the road. "Go left!" he screamed, according to Murphy. "Left! Left! Shit!"

The vehicle didn't make it in time. Homa's Humvee disappeared in a flash of flame, dirt, and smoke. One of the unit's medics, Anuar Valdez, ran over to try to help. Homa was delirious and barely conscious. The blast had torn off part of his hand, broken his arm, caused severe burns to his right shoulder and left leg, and opened up a deep gash on his thigh. That wasn't the worst of it. A red-hot piece of shrapnel had slammed into the small part of Homa's torso that wasn't protected by his body armor. The razor-sharp metal fragment ripped open his chest so badly that his horrified soldiers could see his heart and lungs. "It was just this big, gnarly gash," said retired sergeant first class Mike Crane, who'd been the top noncommissioned officer in Homa's platoon. "The shrapnel burst through the side of the door and sliced him from shoulder to shoulder. The crazy thing was that his body had been ripped right open but his armor hadn't even been touched."

Valdez stanched the bleeding as much as he could as the vehicle raced back to Camp Manhattan. Crane didn't think Homa would survive the flight to a larger military medical facility, and the army didn't either. Homa's mother, Lou Ann, was sitting at home in Pennsylvania when an army official called to say that her son had been badly hurt and was likely to die within three days. The dire prediction proved false. The doctor who treated Homa at the military hospital in Fallujah happened to be a heart surgeon by training, so he was able to stabilize the wounded soldier and keep him alive until he could be flown to the Walter Reed military hospital. He underwent dozens of surgeries and a series of skin grafts, but Homa survived the blast.

Two weeks later a lanky young lieutenant named Todd Bryant led his own platoon out of Manhattan for a patrol through the area where Homa had almost lost his life. The two officers had been close friends, in part because each came from a military family. Homa's older brother Tony was an army sergeant who had taken part in the initial invasion and was still deployed to the war zone. Bryant's parents had served in the air force, his older brother, Tim, was a marine officer, and his older sister, Tiffany, was a West Point graduate. Todd Bryant had grown up dreaming of attending Notre Dame and cheering for the Fighting Irish's legendary football team, but changed his mind when he visited Tiffany at West Point and fell in love with the school. He graduated from the elite military academy in the summer of 2002 and was sent to Fort Riley that December. Homa, who had completed an ROTC program in Pennsylvania, arrived at the base roughly one week later. Bryant used to joke that he outranked Homa because he'd arrived at Fort Riley first. Their wives, both named Jen, also became close friends. They played softball together, and Murphy wrote that Bryant and Homa would sit in the bleachers "arguing intently about whose wife had less talent on the field."

On October 31, Bryant's platoon left Manhattan for a patrol through the area where Homa had been wounded. A short time later the gunner standing in the turret of Bryant's Humvee, Sergeant Earle Bundy, spotted two Iraqi men on the side of the road pointing at them. Taylor, the company commander, radioed Bryant to be extra careful, but the warning didn't come in time. Bryant's Humvee rolled over a massive bomb that eviscerated the vehicle, threw it into a ditch, and left a crater more than ten feet deep. Bryant, twenty-three, lost both legs and suffered a serious head wound. His men pulled him out of the flaming wreckage of the Humvee, started CPR, and tried to stanch the bleeding, but it was too late. He died by the side of the road, blood pooling next to the shattered remains of his body. "I'd seen broken arms, I'd seen burns and lacerations from shrapnel, but I'd never seen anything like that," said retired staff sergeant Jon Pennington, one of the medics who'd worked to save Bryant's life. "I watched him die."

Crane concluded that the makeshift IEDs that maimed Homa and killed Bryant had been constructed out of buried artillery shells and tank rounds most likely controlled by nearby militants who watched the roads and waited for Humvees to pass before hitting the triggers. The battalion's commanders were horrified by what happened to Homa, but the severity of his injuries also raised a serious staffing problem. Homa was clearly not going to be returning to Iraq. His platoon needed a new commander, and there was a lieutenant at Fort Riley waiting for a chance to go to war. His name was Jeff Graham.

Jeff's plane slowed down as it reached Baghdad's United States–run airport, banked sharply toward the ground, and then spiraled down to the runway in slow, tight circles, like someone twisting a corkscrew into a bottle of wine. Jeff had arrived in Kuwait the previous morning and flown out to Baghdad less than twelve hours later. The hulking C-130 flew with its cabin lights turned off, a security measure designed to prevent insurgents on the ground in Iraq from spotting the plane and attempting to shoot it down. The C-130's strange and mildly terrifying landing in Baghdad was another precaution. Planes normally land after a long, slow descent that begins some twenty miles from the runway. That was considered too dangerous for Iraq, since it would allow militants anywhere along the flight path to fire a missile or rocket-propelled grenade as the plane passed overhead. The corkscrew approach allowed Jeff's pilots to keep the craft out of missile range until they reached the outskirts of Baghdad's airport and then gently bring the plane down in what amounted to almost a straight line. "Last night's flight on the C-130 was a little nuts," Jeff wrote in his journal.

Jeff arrived in Iraq during a pivotal moment in the war. The Bush administration's prediction that the Iraq War would come to an end after it ousted Saddam Hussein had proven to be stunningly inaccurate. U.S. forces were no longer fighting the Iraqi army. They instead found themselves enmeshed in an increasingly bloody guerilla war against militants who carried out sophisticated ambushes and mined Iraq's roads with thousands of makeshift bombs before disappearing into the civilian population. The bombs were called improvised explosive devices, or IEDs, an antiseptic term for a low-tech weapon that quickly became the single largest killer of U.S. troops. The White House was just beginning to accept the grim reality that the troops who had taken part in the initial March 2003 invasion wouldn't be going home anytime soon. Pentagon leaders told the administration that it needed to send more U.S. ground forces to Iraq to help pacify the growing insurgency. The problem was where to find those reinforcements.

It was also a pivotal moment for the Centurions, which hailed from a unit with a history of military valor. The 1st Infantry Division, the so-called Big Red One, was the oldest division of the U.S. Army and had taken part in every one of America's major wars. In April 1918 the division captured the beleaguered French town of Cantigny, notching the first American victory of World War I. Decades later it landed on Omaha Beach as part of the D-day invasion and helped repel the last-ditch German offensive known as the Battle of the Bulge. The division fought in Vietnam and led the ground invasion of Iraq during the first Gulf War. Its soldiers wore a distinctive shoulder patch—a red 1 against a dark green background—and were schooled in the division's past exploits. The unit wasn't part of the initial invasion of Iraq, and the Hussein regime fell so quickly that it seemed like the Big Red One would finally be able to sit out a large-scale U.S. conflict. As Iraq collapsed, however, the division was told to pack its bags for Iraq. The Big Red One would fight in America's newest major war after all.

Centurion commanders were scrambling to make their final preparations when they abruptly received news that left them stunned and fuming. The 1st Battalion, 34th Armor, had spent years learning how to fight with Abrams tanks, some of the most powerful ground vehicles in the U.S. Army. Now they were being told to leave their tanks at home. Top Pentagon officials said that it would take too long to ship the seventy-ton vehicles to Iraq. They also argued that the giant vehicles were ill suited to Iraq's narrow streets and risked frightening Iraqi civilians. The men of the 1st Battalion, 34th Armor, were told that they would instead fight as a light infantry unit, riding Humvees on patrol and then dismounting to conduct raids on foot. The changes rankled the unit. Tankers derided infantry soldiers as "crunchies" because that was the sound they'd hear when an opposing fighter fell beneath their treads (ground troops, in turn, mocked tankers as "DATs," or dumb-ass tankers). They had also been taught to live by the unofficial motto of "Death before dismount," which held that a tank crew should never abandon its vehicle. Now they were being ordered to do just that. "To put it mildly, we were very, very unhappy," said Lieutenant Colonel Mike Taylor, Jeff's commander in Iraq. "You're suddenly telling soldiers who may have been on tanks for fifteen years that they're going to fight as infantrymen. It didn't make sense to any of us, and we couldn't get a straight answer why."

Swisher, the Centurions' commander, and his boss, Colonel Buck Connor, lobbied for the order to be reversed, but the directive stood. They were grudgingly allowed to bring over roughly a dozen tanks, as well as a handful of Bradley fighting vehicles and other lightly armored trucks, but that was it. Most of the battalion would instead be sent to Iraq with soft-sided Humvees whose cloth doors couldn't even stop a bullet. The Centurion leadership was given less than six weeks to train their men on how to conduct foot patrols, raid buildings, and set ambushes— skills that infantry troops are normally given months to learn. The training was perfunctory at best. The troops did so-called glass-house exercises, where more experienced soldiers used tape to mark off the outline of a room and tried to show the confused Centurions the proper ways of entering and securing the space. In their spare time, some members of the 1st Battalion, 34th Armor, practiced the maneuvers on their own, meeting up with colleagues and conducting mock raids of their offices and apartments.

The Centurions also received virtually no training in how to recognize and disarm IEDs, which were rapidly becoming the insurgents' weapon of choice in their guerilla war against the United States. The unit got its first and only lesson about the roadside bombs during a brief lecture at an auditorium at Fort Riley. The instructors showed photos of Humvees that had been destroyed by the makeshift bombs and used

PowerPoint slides to illustrate the backpacks, plastic bags, jugs, and bottles that were often the telltale sign of a buried mine. Many of the soldiers slept through the class; others later described it as largely worthless. Swisher said the lecture was the best the army could put together given that IEDs were just beginning to come into wide use. Still, he said, "the class in the theater was not adequate."

The challenges continued when the Centurions arrived in Iraq that September. The battalion didn't have enough night-vision goggles, radios, or M4 assault rifles, and the equipment didn't arrive until March 2004, more than half a year after the troops had started fighting in one of the most dangerous parts of Iraq. The Centurions were sent to Iraq without the right training or equipment, and they paid a heavy price. Twenty-three members of the unit died in Iraq, an exceptionally high number for a single battalion, and dozens more would be wounded. Of the seventy-six soldiers in Taylor's company, eighteen would receive the Purple Heart.

"Hey, LT, where are your stilts?" It was 4:30 A.M. on November 24, 2003, and a young sergeant from the 1st Battalion, 34th Armor, was giving Jeff an unofficial welcome to Iraq. Jeff's Chinook had just landed at the Al Taqaddum air base, or TQ, a bustling facility directly across the road from Camp Manhattan that served as a staging area for the units moving toward Fallujah and Ramadi. Jeff was barely five foot six, and his height quickly became an endless source of amusement to the men around him. He wasn't put off by the gentle mockery. In his letters and e-mails home, Jeff proudly referred to himself as an Oompa Loompa.

Jeff's first day in Iraq flew by in a disorienting rush. A newly arriving officer would normally be given a week or two to get to know his men, adjust to the unfamiliar terrain, and learn the ins and outs of his commander's overall strategy for fighting the insurgency. Jeff wasn't given time for any of that. Matt Homa's unit—2nd Platoon, Charlie Company—had been rudderless since the young officer's injury, and Swisher needed to get it back into the fight. Jeff led his first mission, a foot patrol through a cemetery in the nearby town of Khaldiyah, just hours after landing at TQ. Insurgents had been sneaking into the cemetery at night to fire rocket-propelled grenades and crude mortar shells at Camp Manhattan, which was just a few hundred yards away. Jeff didn't find any of the militants, and he thought that slowly making his way around the piles of dirt that marked each individual grave was "scary as hell." Khaldiyah itself was almost entirely deserted. It looked, Jeff thought, "like a Hollywood set of a ghost town."

Jeff had his first meeting with Swisher on November 25, Thanksgiving Day. The battalion commander wasted little time with small talk when they sat down in Swisher's tidy office. He told Jeff that the Centurions were getting hit multiple times per day and had just lost two popular lieutenants, including Jeff's predecessor. The unit was fighting in one of the most dangerous parts of Iraq, and Swisher wanted Jeff to know exactly what was waiting for him each time he left the fortified walls of Combat Outpost Killeen, the tiny base that housed his platoon.

"This is what you're stepping into," Swisher told him. "The enemy is aggressive right now. Get your head screwed on straight if it's not on straight already."

Jeff spent his first days trying to get to know Crane, his unit's top enlisted man, and the other soldiers of his platoon. He was deeply shaken by what he found. The men were struggling to recover from the shock of Homa's injury and were openly fearful of getting blown up by an invisible IED or shot by an unseen sniper. "You're not human if you don't get scared, and we had reason to be scared," Chavez, one of Jeff's soldiers, said later.

As time went on, Chavez added, many of the men from his platoon began to question why they were in Iraq and how they could possibly win a war with no front lines or clear objectives. Soldiers were being killed and wounded virtually every day, and many of the Centurions concluded that further losses were inevitable.

"The morale here is low," Jeff wrote on Thanksgiving Day. "Guys try, but they all think they're going to die."

Jeff quickly got a sense of why his men were so afraid. On December 1, his platoon was designated as the battalion's quick response force, or QRF, which meant they would be the first troops called in if other Centurions came under attack. Just after 11 A.M., Jeff's radio suddenly crackled to life. A convoy of U.S. Humvees had been surrounded by insurgents armed with machine guns and rocket-propelled grenades while the vehicles were passing through the rough, tense town of Habbaniyah. The Humvees were coming under fire from multiple directions, and one soldier, Sergeant Uday Singh, had already been seriously wounded. Take your men, Jeff was told, and get out there as fast as you can.

Jeff's platoon jumped into their trucks and roared out of Camp Manhattan. They reached the ambush site ten minutes later, just as an army medical evacuation helicopter was setting down to pick up Singh's motionless body. Jeff ordered his gunners to lay down covering fire for the chopper by pounding away at the unseen militants with the powerful .50-caliber machine guns mounted to the roof of each Humvee. He and Mike Crane ran out to link up with some of the other men from Singh's unit, firing their M4s as they ran. The news was grim. A bullet had ripped through the young soldier's helmet, passing through his forehead and then out the other side. Singh never regained consciousness and was declared dead during the short flight to a military hospital in Fallujah.

The death hit Jeff hard. He had gone on three patrols with Singh and remembered that the young soldier always seemed to be smiling. Singh, twenty-one, had been born in India to a family with a long history of military service. His grandfather joined the nascent Indian air force in the

1930s and fought Japanese forces in Burma during World War II. Singh's father, Preet, spent twenty-five years in the Indian army as a tank commander and took part in the war against Pakistan in 1971. Uday had been accepted into the University of Illinois but chose to enlist in the army in the summer of 2000 instead of beginning college. He died just days after receiving his U.S. citizenship.

"Tough day, tough day," Jeff wrote in his journal that night, describing a raid that ended with his soldiers arresting four Iraqis. "I thought my guys were going to kill 'em."

The violence continued. On December 14, the day after U.S. forces captured Saddam Hussein, an enormous car bomb demolished an Iraqi police station in Khalidiya, killing twenty Iraqi cops. Jeff had been in the station more than half a dozen times and knew some of the dead men. Two days later he was getting ready to go to Camp Manhattan when his radio squawked. "Cobra X-ray, Apache," a panicked voice said. "We've been hit." Jeff escorted the unit medics out to the site of the blast. An IED had blown up a U.S. Humvee, severely wounding two of the Centurions inside. Jeff watched, horrified, as one of the soldiers readjusted the blood-soaked bandages covering his head and sent half the skin on his face sloughing off, exposing the bone below.

"I finally have seen combat. War. Hell," Jeff wrote. "It's not pretty. I wish I wouldn't have to see it again."

Jeff woke up and fell asleep to the sound of distant explosions. He began to have vivid, unsettling nightmares. In one dream Kevin walked up to him at a party, visibly drunk, and began choking so badly that Jeff could see the veins of his face turn blue. In another, Kevin told his brother that he was still alive and had simply taken a nap. Jeff woke up with a start after each nightmare and couldn't fall back asleep.

U.S. troops continued to die, seemingly by the day. On January 9, insurgents shot down a Black Hawk helicopter near Fallujah, killing all nine of the soldiers aboard. On January 24 a suicide bomber in a Toyota Land

Cruiser detonated his explosives outside the gates of a small American outpost, killing two soldiers instantly. A third died while he was being flown out to a military hospital. Jeff and Mike Taylor spent the following day at the blast site, picking body parts and scraps of blackened flesh out of the crater gouged by the bomb. They wanted the families of the fallen soldiers to have something to bury, no matter how small, and they were determined not to leave the remains of a pair of American soldiers to rot in the sun. Three days later an IED went off less than six hundred meters from Combat Outpost Killeen, killing three of the four soldiers in a passing Humvee, including a company commander and a senior non-commissioned officer (the fourth soldier soon died from his wounds). Jeff and his men began to feel an overpowering sense of bloodlust and fury. They imposed a midnight curfew in K-Town and talked about killing any Iraqi they saw on the streets. Jeff seemed almost excited by the prospect of retribution.

"This job is tough, but losing 6 guys in 4 days . . . ," he wrote in his journal. "It's time for payback and all the guys are ready."

Not all of Jeff's time in Iraq was so grim. He retained his obsession with Kentucky basketball, unfurled a large University of Kentucky banner near his bed, and was happy to talk trash with fans of other schools. He played football and video games with the soldiers from his platoon to build unit cohesion and try to keep morale as high as possible. He was quick with a joke and never seemed to take himself too seriously. On Christmas, Colonel Swisher walked over to Jeff's table and handed him a plastic toy that had been mailed in from a McDonald's back home. "Here," he told Jeff. "You forgot the toy from your Happy Meal." Jeff was sitting with his platoon, and there was a moment of nervous silence as the soldiers waited to see how their commander would react to so public a joke about his height. There was an audible gasp of relief when Jeff took the toy, proudly placed it on the edge of his tray of food, and then burst out laughing.

Still, Iraq was changing him. It hardened and conditioned him to withstand exposure to carnage that he would have found unimaginable just months earlier. He began sprinkling his letters home with repeated references to "hojies," a racial epithet of sorts about Iraqis. He made casual reference to letting his men rough up Iraqis, run them off the road, or even shoot them. Like veterans of other conflicts, Jeff felt transformed by his exposure to war. The world, in a fundamental way, was beginning to feel different to him.

"Most of the time it's like being in a dream," he wrote in a letter to Melanie. "Neither good nor bad. Just a dream."

Jeff's lodestar was Stacey. In the three years since their engagement, Jeff had never seemed to be in much of a hurry to pick a wedding date or start planning the ceremony. Many of his friends in Kentucky half expected him to end the relationship entirely when he came back from Iraq because they didn't think he was ready to settle down. Once Jeff got to Iraq, however, he began drawing strength from the knowledge that Stacey was waiting for him at home, counting down the days until he returned. "I don't mention how much Stacey means to me enough," he wrote. "She is my life now. I can't wait to get home and spend it with her." The first step would be to get married, and it was suddenly all that Jeff wanted to talk about.

"How's the wedding going?" Jeff wrote in a letter to Stacey from Iraq. "We still on?"

Stacey struggled to adjust to Jeff's absence. She told her friends that it was like marking time in dog years: Each week that Jeff was away felt like a month to her. She spent each day on edge, fearing for his safety and wishing he could call to let her know that he was all right. The days when CNN carried news of casualties from Fallujah or Ramadi, the cities closest to where Jeff was serving, were always especially hard. Stacey would hold her breath each time she got word that another American had died there and pray that it wasn't Jeff. When she didn't hear from Mark and Carol, she would always assume that he was okay. Still, she had no way of knowing for sure.

As the days stretched into weeks, and weeks into months, Stacey tried to distract herself by planning their wedding and shared future. Jeff's tour was supposed to end in September 2004, and Stacey wanted to get married before he could get deployed again. She picked November 6 and sent a check to their church to reserve the date.

"You better be there!" she wrote to Jeff in December. "Tell your company commander *now* so he can make sure you get leave then. I don't want to have to get married via teleconference."

Stacey closed the letter on an unusually racy note for such a buttoned-up young woman. "I can't wait to get married to you," she wrote, "and I'm *really* excited about our honeymoon."

She chose her wedding dress in early January, e-mailing photos of it to Carol and Melanie after they promised not to forward the picture to Jeff. Stacey even picked the names of their future children: Daine Jeffrey Graham, Coy Alan Graham, and Hope Mattie Graham.

"Hey, sexy," he wrote to her on February 13, the day before Valentine's Day. "Lord, I want you. You have no idea. Just touching you would drive me nuts."

He mailed his last letter home on the evening of February 18. Jeff had been ordered to lead his unit out on an unusually long six-kilometer foot patrol the following morning, and he wanted to make sure that he and his soldiers got enough sleep to stay sharp.

"Happy V-Day again," Jeff wrote to his fiancée. "I miss you so much. I'll call again when I get the chance."

A few hours later, Jeff Graham walked out of the sandbagged gates of Combat Outpost Killeen for the final time.

CHAPTER 10

Khaldiyah, Iraq, February 19, 2004

Jeff Graham yawned and tried to rub the sleep from his eyes. It was just after 5:30 A.M., and a cold wind was howling over the sandbagged fortifications surrounding Combat Outpost Killeen as he stood in the early-morning darkness to brief his men on that day's mission. He had been in command of 2nd Platoon, Charlie Company, for four months, and his men had come to genuinely like and respect the young officer. Jeff made coffee for the soldiers on late-night guard duty, joked around with his men about sports and girls, led his platoon in pickup football games against other units, and spent his free time talking with enlisted troops and sergeants rather than just other officers. He made his soldiers laugh, and he was able to laugh at himself. Jeff told his men that being short would come in handy during a firefight. "It makes it easy for me to keep my head down," he said one winter evening, cracking up the soldiers shivering around him.

On the morning of February 19, though, Jeff was all business. He told his men that they'd be setting out at daybreak to look for any IEDs that might have been buried along Route Michigan, a potholed, four-lane highway that connected Ramadi to Baghdad. American commanders believed it was vitally important to keep insurgents from making the road so dangerous that ordinary Iraqis would be afraid to use it, and the Centurions had been given the tough job of keeping it safe. Jeff told his troops that their specific task would be to make their way down Michigan to Khaldiyah, the small town just outside the gates of Camp Manhattan. Once they got there, they'd walk across the aging bridge that connected Khaldiyah to a small necklace of towns on the opposite side of the Euphrates, check it for bombs, and then head back to Killeen.

Many of Jeff's men audibly groaned when he finished talking. They hated route-clearance operations, the military's antiseptic term for patrols designed to find IEDs before they could be used against U.S. forces or vehicles. It was dangerous, grueling work that turned the troops into human mine detectors. The soldiers would slowly make their way down a road, stopping anytime they spotted something suspicious, such as a backpack, a plastic jug, or an unusual indentation in the dirt. They'd then retreat to a safe distance and call in a specialized explosive ordnance disposal team, like the unit featured in *The Hurt Locker,* which would attempt to disable the bomb before it could be detonated. If the route-clearance troops missed an IED, or triggered it by accident, they would almost certainly be the first to die.

"Our feeling, every time we rode out the gates, was 'Hey, we could get blown up today,'" said Jon Pennington, the platoon medic. "We'd try not to think about it, but it was impossible not to. I mean, that was the reality."

The mission Jeff outlined seemed risky even by the standards of the platoon's normal patrols through the militant-haunted roads and towns of central Iraq. The Centurions tried to vary their routes so the insurgents would have a harder time predicting when and where to plant an IED or conduct an ambush. This time they'd be taking the exact same way back to Killeen that they'd taken when they left the base. The soldiers, all former members of tank crews, preferred to patrol from inside

Humvees rather than on foot. This time they'd be walking. The Centurions conducted roughly half their missions under the cover of darkness, when night-vision goggles allowed them to hunt their foes while the insurgents were effectively blind. This time, the unit's schedule had them going out during the day. "We're tankers, and we belong on a tank," said Ray Navarrette, now an army master sergeant. "We aren't infantry. Being out on the road, walking for hours—it just didn't feel right. It wasn't what we were meant to do, and it wasn't what we were trained to do."

To top it off, the mission meant that they'd be spending most of the day on Route Michigan, the blood-soaked road where the 1st Battalion, 34th Armor, had suffered some of its worst losses. Matt Homa's chest had been ripped open by a makeshift bomb there. Captain Matthew August and the three other soldiers inside his Humvee had been killed when a bomb hidden near the median detonated as his truck rumbled past. Dozens of other soldiers had been wounded, some severely, on Route Michigan. "This patrol was going to be one of the longest and most vulnerable patrols we had ever conducted," said retired specialist Richard Wagner, who served as Jeff's driver and spent most of his waking hours with him.

The members of Jeff's platoon immediately understood the mission's dangers, but they were also struck by the unusual notes of doubt that they heard in their lieutenant's voice. Jeff had grown up fast during his months in Iraq, and he was no longer the green officer he'd been when he arrived in the country the previous November. His commands were clear and precise, and he always seemed to know exactly which route to take and which house to search. Jeff was a cheerful, confident officer who was capable of pushing his men forward even when they were physically exhausted. He never appeared flustered or uncertain. This time around, he did. "Graham expressed some of his many concerns about the upcoming mission to us," Wagner said. "There was something different about him that morning. He was still positive, still resolute, but knowing him as I did, I could see it was forced."

Jeff folded up the laminated map he'd use to chart the day's route and told his men to make sure they were carrying enough water and ammunition. They'd be walking along a dangerous road for several miles in the midday heat, and Jeff wanted to make sure the men of the 2nd Platoon would have everything they needed for the long and risky day ahead. He himself had gone to sleep early the previous night to make sure that he would be mentally sharp when his unit left Combat Outpost Killeen. Lying on his cot and using a flashlight to write in the darkness, Jeff finished a letter to Stacey and then pulled out his spiral-bound journal to detail the next day's mission.

"Should be fun," he wrote in the last entry of his journal. "I'll keep in touch."

Jeff and his men had arrived at Combat Outpost Killeen two days earlier and were scheduled to return to the relative safety of Camp Manhattan just over twenty-four hours later. Killeen was built on the grounds of a small compound that had once belonged to the Fedayeen Saddam, a feared paramilitary unit under the direct control of the Iraqi dictator. The complex held a pair of buildings—a two-story office building and a one-story structure that resembled a shack—separated by a dirt parking lot. The taller building looked out over a nearby grove of palm trees and a grassy hill that sloped down toward the muddy brown waters of the Euphrates. "It was kind of pretty, to be honest," said Sergeant First Class James Spiker, one of the top noncommissioned officers in Jeff's platoon. The buildings themselves had been gutted in the chaotic early days after Saddam's ouster, with looters smashing down the doors and windows and lugging away any furniture they could carry. They'd torn the toilets and sinks out of the bathrooms and stripped the copper electrical wiring out of the walls and ceilings.

The Centurions lived in the shells of the ruined buildings. Killeen had no running water or electricity, so the soldiers showered with bottles of water and used flashlights to play cards or read tattered paperbacks at night. They subsisted on Meals, Ready to Eat, high-calorie rations that included chicken, pasta, or beef entrées along with trail mix, candy, or pastries. When the temperatures dropped at night, they'd pull on army-issued fleece jackets, hats, and gloves and crawl into the sleeping bags many had purchased at Fort Riley and brought to Iraq. They used an armored M113 personnel carrier as a makeshift command center, squeezing into the back of the truck to plan missions and radio back and forth with Jeff Swisher and the other senior officers at Camp Manhattan.

The Centurions spent most of their time fortifying Killeen against insurgent attack. They surrounded the compound with barbed wire and walls of Hesco barriers, open-topped mesh containers that the soldiers filled with dirt and rocks and arrayed next to one another to form bullet-proof barricades. They built sandbagged fighting positions on the roof of each building that allowed soldiers to monitor the area around the base and open fire on anything that approached its outer perimeter. They also put speed bumps and Hesco barriers on the narrow road leading to Killeen's main gate, which forced cars to slow down and made it easier for soldiers to stop any suspicious vehicles before they could reach the base's outer walls.

The soldiers rotating through Killeen had reason to be wary. The towns and villages surrounding the outpost had prospered under Saddam Hussein, and local residents had never been particularly friendly to the Americans. Still, the relationship between the Iraqis and the Centurions had gotten noticeably worse in recent weeks. U.S. patrols were ambushed or hit by IEDs virtually every day, sending the unit's casualty count soaring. The attacks brought a quick and violent U.S. response. American troops began speeding down the center lanes of Route Michigan and other highways, sometimes firing on cars or trucks that came too close to their convoys. They set up impromptu roadblocks to search cars for weaponry and explosives, causing massive traffic jams. And they began raiding Iraqi homes at night in search of suspected militants, kicking in the front doors, tearing up floorboards, and destroying furniture as they looked for fighters and weapons.

The raids sparked widespread public fury. Iraqis complained that U.S. troops were indiscriminately arresting men of fighting age, slapping plastic handcuffs around their wrists, and taking them into custody without ever specifying the charges. Iraqi troops working alongside the Americans regularly beat the detainees before returning them to their families, sometimes badly enough to leave them crippled or blinded. Dozens of Iraqis gathered outside Camp Manhattan in late October to protest the new policies and accuse the United States of orchestrating a car bombing at a local Iraqi police station. A second demonstration broke out on February 6 in response to the large number of Iraqis that had been arrested by the Centurions after seven American troops were killed during a single week in late January. At least three hundred people took part in the protest, many waving Iraqi flags or handwritten signs denouncing the United States. Swisher walked outside the walls to meet with the organizers of the protest, a small group that he and his commanders had dubbed "the Young Khaldiyans." "My message was that local citizens needed to do their part in providing security for the area," he said. "If they stopped the attacks, we would have no need to detain anyone."

Swisher and his commanders had no way of knowing, but another deadly attack was just hours away, and it was approaching fast.

Jeff wasn't supposed to go out on the patrol. Clearance operations on Route Michigan were normally led by sergeants, not officers, and Ray Navarrette had been slated to oversee the mission. Early that morning, however, the men at Killeen received some surprising news. Lieutenant Colonel Mike Taylor, Jeff's commander, wanted to join the platoon for part of the foot patrol. Taylor knew that his men hated route clearance missions, and he thought it was important to show them that he was prepared to assume the same risks they were taking. "I had told my guys up front, 'I'm not going to tell you to do anything that I'm not willing to do myself,'" Taylor said.

Navarrette woke Jeff at 5 A.M. to tell him that Taylor would be coming along on the mission. Jeff didn't think it would be right for a higher-ranking officer to head out on patrol while he stayed back, so he told Navarrette that he'd lead the mission himself. An hour later Jeff gathered his men just inside Killeen's main gate and had them do a final check of their weapons and body armor. The plan was to finish the loop to Camp Manhattan and then stop back at Killeen to pick up Taylor. Taylor had initially planned to walk alongside Jeff and the platoon's radio operator, Roger Ling, a young Chinese American soldier whom the platoon had nicknamed "Panda," but Jeff persuaded him that it would be too dangerous for the two officers to be out on patrol together. A single bomb, Jeff argued, would wipe out the leadership of both the platoon and the overall company, leaving the units rudderless. Taylor agreed to travel with a different part of the platoon. At the time he didn't think much about it. Later Taylor would realize that that short conversation probably saved his life.

The Centurions left the base just after sunrise and began making their way to Habbaniyah, the small town next to Camp Manhattan. They didn't notice anything out of the ordinary on Route Michigan and were relieved to see locals walking along Habbaniyah's potholed streets and milling outside the modest little stores, cafés, and falafel stands. The Iraqis glared at the passing soldiers when the troops waved at them or tried to beckon them over to talk. Still, the Centurions had the odd feeling that they were safe. The troops knew that the Iraqis functioned as a de facto early warning system. Locals often got advance word of impending insurgent attacks and would abruptly vanish from sight just before the ambushes started or the IEDs went off. Seeing the Iraqis outside, as unfriendly as they were, put the Americans somewhat at ease.

The troops walked to the edge of the town, stopping when they could see the armored M113 truck parked outside the western gate of Camp Manhattan, and then started on the long walk back to Killeen. The temperature had soared to well over 100 degrees Fahrenheit, and the platoon was exhausted from walking under the unforgiving sun for nearly three hours in their bulky body armor and helmets. They were supposed to stop back at Killeen to pick up Mike Taylor and then continue on toward the bridge linking Khaldiyah to the towns on the other side of the Euphrates. Spiker, one of the unit's top enlisted soldiers, worried that some of his men might collapse from heatstroke or dehydration and asked Jeff to delay the second half of the patrol until that evening or early the following morning. Jeff, anxious to complete the mission, said no. The bridge was less than fifteen hundred yards from the walls of Killeen, and it had been a quiet day so far. "We're almost done," he told Spiker. "Let's finish what's left and then call it a day."

Jeff had divided his platoon into two squads of about six soldiers each so one group could advance a few hundred meters while the second team watched their backs and kept their eyes peeled for any signs of an impending ambush. The two teams would then switch missions, with the second squad moving forward while the first guarded their flank. Wagner, Jeff's driver, walked out in front of the rest of the platoon as the troops approached a concrete overpass leading onto the bridge. His mission was to spot enemy fighters or bombs before they could hurt other Centurions. The men were feeling confident; that portion of Route Michigan had been cleared days earlier and was so close to Killeen that the Centurions thought militants would be unable to bury an IED without being spotted and killed. Iraqis were walking across the bridge and driving along the highway and overpass, giving the troops more reason to believe that the area was safe. Still, Spiker saw something strange that gave him a momentary feeling of unease. Squinting in the midafternoon haze, he spotted four Iraqis sitting motionless at a wooden table on the side of the road. At first he thought his eyes were playing tricks on him. As he drew closer to the overpass, however, Spiker realized that the men were not figments of his imagination. There was a small, silver-colored teakettle on the table, but it was otherwise bare. "I can still remember the faces," Spiker said. "They just watched us. No movements, no words, nothing."

The Centurions continued their slow walk to the overpass, a concrete road lined with a metallic guardrail. Their M4 assault rifles hung slack in their arms, their heads were pitched forward, and many of the soldiers were having so much trouble lifting their feet off the ground that they lost their footing and barely managed to avoid tumbling down onto the pavement. The men looked back longingly at Killeen, just a few hundred meters away. They couldn't wait to strip off their body armor, chug down bottles of water, and pass out on the cots they'd laid out in the shady recesses of the shattered buildings.

The soldiers snapped back to attention as they neared the overpass, well aware that it would be a perfect place for an IED or ambush. Wagner brought his rifle up and used the scope to check out an abandoned two-story house a short distance from the bridge. He didn't see any signs that militants had hidden themselves in the structure. He proceeded slowly along the overpass and then abruptly stopped. There was an unusually flat spot in a patch of dirt alongside one of the paved portions of the road. He'd never have spotted it when the Centurions first arrived in Iraq. This many months in, however, Wagner automatically registered it as a potential threat. Insurgents routinely buried IEDs under the dirt, smoothing out the ground to make them invisible to the naked eye, and Wagner worried that the side of the road had been booby-trapped. He held up a closed fist so the rest of the platoon would stop in its tracks and then made his way, alone, toward the indentation. He knelt down and began gently brushing away the sand with his gloved hand, exposing a flat piece of metal that glinted in the midday sun. Wagner's mind went blank with fear. "My pulse was pounding," he recalled. "I was thinking about what the hell I was going to do if this thing turned out to be an IED. Running would be pointless; there was no good cover nearby, not good enough against an IED. It was too late to do anything but continue to brush off the sand and hope for the best."

A few seconds later Wagner finished cleaning the dirt off the thin slab of metal. It was the same size and color as the four-inch-wide posts of the guardrail lining the overpass, and he took a deep breath as he realized that it was probably just a piece of metal that had broken off and been gradually covered by dirt. He called over another soldier, Jeremy Kerr, for a second opinion. Kerr compared the guardrail to the loose piece of metal and quickly agreed with Wagner's assessment that it was no cause for alarm. "There's nothing here," he yelled back to Jeff, turning around to motion Taylor and the rest of the platoon forward.

Jeff walked up to the patch of dirt and realized, too late, that Wagner had been wrong. He made a split-second decision to order his men to stop in their tracks. "Wait up," he radioed back to Mike Taylor. "I think I got something."

The bomb exploded seconds later in a sudden roar of flame and smoke that sent clumps of dirt and chunks of concrete raining down on the platoon and triggered a thunderclap that echoed all the way back to Combat Outpost Killeen. The blast sent Wagner flying through the air and knocked Kerr onto his back with wounds to his head, torso, and legs. Wagner, in shock from the explosion, was briefly transfixed by the sight of the dirt, sand, and smoke swirling above the bridge. Then he realized, with a sudden flash of horrifying clarity, that Jeff and Ling seemed to have disappeared.

Taylor was standing less than a hundred meters away with Valdez, the platoon medic, and the two men sprinted toward the stretch of the overpass where the bomb had gone off. Sam, an Iraqi interpreter who'd been walking with the two Centurions, was still alive, but barely. He was missing both legs and one arm; the other had been slashed by so many pieces of shrapnel that it was barely recognizable as a human limb. Sam muttered to himself in Arabic and then stopped moving. The fourth man in the stricken group, a young Iraqi police officer, had taken the brunt of the blast and could only be identified by the shredded remnants of his blue-and-white uniform.

One squad of soldiers from the platoon set up a defensive perimeter near the overpass in case militants tried to follow the IED with an ambush, and a second team scoured the road for Jeff and Ling. The radio operator was found first. The force of the blast had killed Ling immediately and thrown what was left of his body into one of the palm trees that lined the overpass. He had been carrying mounds of cash to buy CDs and magazines at Camp Manhattan, and the bloodstained $20 and $50 bills rained down like snowflakes onto the Centurions tasked with pulling pieces of his body down from the tree and placing the remains into a black body bag. Weeks later Ling's father, Wai, a Vietnam veteran, stood at Arlington National Cemetery to watch the burial of his only son. He would be too incapacitated by grief to say a single word.

Jeff was still alive when his soldiers found him a few yards away from where the blast had gone off. The explosion had sheared off both of his legs at the thigh, blood pouring out of the blackened stumps, and sliced off one of his hands. It had also savaged his head and face so completely that many of his colleagues couldn't recognize him. "Jeff didn't have a face," Taylor said. "I knew it was him because of his haircut, because he'd just gotten a fricking buzz cut. But I was looking down at him and there was just nothing left."

The platoon's quick reaction force had raced out from Killeen in a makeshift ambulance as soon as they heard the blast and arrived at the overpass less than three minutes later. Ray Navarrette, who was leading the reinforcements, had a brief moment of hope when he was told that Jeff was still alive. "I knew it would be bad, real bad, but I also knew of guys who'd survived being blown apart into little pieces," Navarrette said. "I was holding on to that as I ran toward him. I thought maybe we could save him."

Navarrette's hopes evaporated when he saw the shattered remains of Jeff's body. Jeff was still conscious and talking when he reached him, but his breathing was ragged and the sergeant knew Jeff wasn't going to make it. Navarrette, crouching on the bloodstained ground, leaned forward to hear what he knew were going to be his friend's final words.

"Tell my entire family I love them," Jeff wheezed. "Tell them I love them."

"Yes sir, I will," Navarrette told him. "I promise I will."

Jeff was dead before the medics were able to load him into the armored ambulance. Kerr suffered a range of injuries, but he made a full recovery, and no one else from the platoon was hurt or killed. Jeff had managed to stop them from walking onto the overpass just in time. If he hadn't ordered them back, the IED would have claimed even more American lives. Mark and Carol would later learn that Jeff ended most of his journal entries with a prayer that God give him the wisdom and strength to bring his men back home safely. In the end, Jeff managed to do just that. "Jeff was a hero, pure and simple," Swisher said. "He died keeping his men safe."

Taylor believes that the bomb was triggered by a militant who had been sitting at the edge of the bridge and waiting for a large cluster of troops to gather by the hidden bomb. He had ordered his men to scour the area right after the blast in the hopes of finding the insurgent, but the Centurions returned empty-handed. "It was a needle in a haystack at that point," he said.

Spiker, for his part, believes that the four Iraqis he'd seen at the wooden table at the edge of the road were linked to the attack, though he never got the chance to find out. They jumped into a white Toyota shortly after the blast and sped away down a back road that linked up with Route Michigan. They were never seen again.

Wagner left the army in 2006, hobbled by PTSD and haunted by his failure to spot the IED that killed Jeff Graham. He would distance himself from his friends and family and try to numb himself to a world that had come to seem capricious and unfair. "I knew I should feel something—fear, anger, grief—but there was nothing there," he said. "I felt that this world expanding around us was some sick, cruel, evil, painful place and the only way to survive it was to not feel it, any of it."

Ray Navarrette was still in the army in 2014. He did five tours in Iraq and Afghanistan, spending more than half a decade overseas. He thinks of Jeff daily and struggles to overcome his overpowering feelings of guilt about surviving the blast that killed his friend. "If things could have been different, I would rather it be me gone than Jeff," he said. "Sometimes I just feel like I had lived my life. Why did Jeff have to go?"

When the military returned Jeff's personal effects, Mark and Carol were surprised to find Kevin's driver's license. He had carried it with him wherever he went, and it had been in his pocket on that final patrol.

CHAPTER 11

Fort Sill, Oklahoma, February 2004

Major General Dave Valcourt was desperately trying to avoid Mark Graham. Valcourt was the commanding general of Fort Sill, and Mark, a colonel, was his chief of staff. The two men spoke more than a dozen times per day and lived in neighboring houses on a tree-lined street paved when the base was founded in the late 1800s. Valcourt respected Mark's professional competence and quiet, modest nature, a rarity among fast-rising officers who seemed bound for greater glory. He and his wife, Diane, had also come to genuinely like Mark and Carol, who had helped them move into their cavernous official residence and regularly joined them for Sunday dinners and late-night games of bridge. Those were precisely the reasons that Valcourt was hiding from his chief of staff. The general had just received some of the worst news imaginable, and he couldn't share it with Mark just yet.

The telephone had rung just after 2:30 A.M., waking the two Valcourts. Dave knew it was something bad; generals weren't woken up if it wasn't. He expected to learn that one of his soldiers had been involved in a bad car accident or been arrested for drunk driving, rape, or another serious crime. Instead, he heard the weary voice of one of his closest friends, Major General Dennis Hardy, the commander of Fort Riley.

"Dave, this isn't an official notification," Hardy told him. "That will come later. But I just got off the phone with one of my brigade commanders in Iraq, and he told me that an hour and a half ago Second Lieutenant Jeffrey Graham was killed by an IED while he was on patrol in Khaldiyah. I thought you should know."

Valcourt shot out of bed, startling Diane. One of Hardy's aides e-mailed Valcourt a short time later with more details. The IED had been hidden in a guardrail near the on-ramp to a bridge, and the platoon's point man had walked past it without spotting the bomb. Jeff, he wrote, saw the buried bomb and managed to radio a warning back to Taylor just before it detonated. Valcourt understood that Jeff's quick actions likely saved the lives of much of his platoon. Still, the news hit Valcourt hard. He knew that Mark had already lost one son, and he couldn't imagine the pain his friend would feel when he learned that he had lost another. But Hardy's call also left Valcourt in a serious bind. Military regulations forbade him from telling Mark until the Department of the Army had confirmed Jeff's death and formally notified his next of kin. Valcourt and Mark spent many of their waking hours together. The general knew that he couldn't tell his chief of staff what had happened, but he cared about Mark too much to deliberately keep him in the dark. The only solution, Valcourt realized, was to hide from Mark until he'd been cleared to let him know about Jeff. The question was how to do it.

Senator James Inhofe had no idea what he was being dragged into. The Oklahoma Republican was a regular visitor to Fort Sill, the largest employer in his entire state. He drove to the base that morning to see a demonstration of an advanced new training system and then to fly with Valcourt to California for meetings at the Institute for Creative Technologies, a research organization that was receiving military funding to develop ways of remotely diagnosing PTSD. Valcourt was leading Inhofe through the building when he gently took the senator aside and pointed to Mark, who was standing a good distance away with his back to the two men.

"Senator, do you see the colonel over there?" Valcourt asked. "Colonel Graham's my chief of staff. He doesn't know it yet, but he lost a son in Iraq this morning and I haven't gotten permission to tell him. It's going to be a rough day, and I'll be needed here. I'm sorry, but I just can't go with you to California."

Valcourt walked Inhofe out of the facility and then snuck away as soon as the senator climbed into his waiting SUV. Mark assumed his boss was on a plane to California, but Valcourt had actually gone home to lobby friends throughout the army for permission to let the Grahams know about Jeff's death sooner than usual. The leadership of Fort Sill was a small, close-knit group of officers, and both news and gossip traveled fast. Valcourt was terrified that Mark would learn about the loss of his only surviving son prematurely, forcing him and Carol to scramble for details before the army was willing or able to formally provide them.

"The reality of it was that I was hiding from my own chief of staff," Valcourt said. "I had to play hide-and-go-seek and stay away from the headquarters building. Nobody knew that I was home with my wife, waiting. I hadn't even told my secretary."

Shortly before noon the army finally cleared Valcourt to tell Mark the news. Mark walked out of his office and was startled to see his boss standing in the hallway. Valcourt had told him that he'd be spending the day in California with Inhofe. How, Mark wondered, could he have made it back to Oklahoma so quickly?

"Sir, what are you doing here?" he asked. "You're not supposed to be here."

"Mark, I am here, and I need to talk to you," Valcourt said, motioning Mark toward his office.

"Just a second, sir," Mark said, immediately assuming that Valcourt wanted to give him a new set of orders. "Let me just grab a piece of paper and a pencil."

"Mark, you don't need a pencil or paper," Valcourt replied, his voice softening. "It's not that kind of conversation. It's about Jeffrey."

It took Mark barely a second to process what his boss was telling him.

"No," Mark said, his voice breaking. "Please tell me it's not my son."

Valcourt didn't say anything else. He didn't need to. The general pulled his chief of staff into a hug and held him there, listening to Colonel Mark Graham quietly begin to sob. Years later Valcourt would remember the moment as the most painful of his four decades in the army. On that grim February morning the general tried to quickly pull himself together. Valcourt had another mission to fulfill, one that he had been dreading since receiving the news of Jeff's death nine hours earlier. He had to help Mark tell his wife that she had lost her oldest son.

Carol Graham had been scouring the Web for news about Iraq earlier that morning when she saw the article that would yet again mark the abrupt end of one phase of her life and the beginning of another. She'd woken up at five, roughly three hours after the Valcourts had learned about Jeff's death, and been unable to fall back asleep. She padded downstairs to a small office next to the kitchen, poured a cup of coffee, and turned on her computer. She was on AOL's home page when she saw a breaking news alert from Iraq. Two American soldiers, it said, had been blown up by a roadside bomb in Khaldiyah. Six months earlier Carol wouldn't have had any idea where Khaldiyah was. Now she recognized the name immediately, though she wished that she didn't have to. She knew it was the nasty little town where her son and his men were fighting their piece of the Iraq War, and she was well aware of its dangers. Rationally, she knew that there were hundreds of soldiers deployed to the area around the town, which meant that Jeff was probably fine. But she couldn't shake the feeling that something horrible had just happened to her son.

Carol walked back upstairs and knocked on the door of the bathroom. Mark was inside shaving, and he could immediately tell that his wife was terrified. She told him about the article, and her fears that Jeff was among the dead.

"Mark, would we know by now if it was Jeffrey?" she asked.

"No, not yet," he told her. "But I'm sure he's fine."

Mark was trying to calm his own nerves as much as Carol's. He had been in the army for nearly twenty-five years and knew that it could take the military bureaucracy hours—if not days—to make the final identification of a fallen soldier's remains and then arrange for military personnel to tell the next of kin that their spouse, parent, or child wouldn't be coming home. That he and Carol hadn't heard anything from the army didn't mean Jeff was okay. His son could well have died in the blast, and Mark knew it. In his heart, though, he felt certain that Jeff hadn't been hurt. He and Carol had already buried one son. It was inconceivable to him that they would have to bury another.

Mark finished getting dressed and headed to work. It was shaping up to be a busy day. Inhofe was slated to spend most of the morning at the base before flying to California with Valcourt. Once the general left, Mark would temporarily be in charge of running the entire base.

Carol waited for Mark to leave for his office, and then she and her Yorkshire terrier walked to the Old Post Chapel, a Fort Sill landmark that was built in 1875 and had been in continuous service ever since. The base was just waking up, so Carol had the building to herself. She made her way to the front of the church and knelt at the altar beneath a carved statue of Jesus Christ that hung from a rafter directly above the church's unadorned, dark wood altar. Sunlight streamed through the trio of stained glass windows in the limestone wall behind the altar, casting a kaleidoscope of colors onto Carol's prayer book and giving her a momentary feeling of serenity and comfort. *I'm worrying for nothing,* she told herself. *Jeffrey's fine. Jeffrey has to be fine.*

Carol spent nearly two hours sitting in a pew at the church, singing old hymns from her childhood while praying for the safety of Jeff and his men, before heading home. Shortly after noon she heard the front door of her house swing open. She saw Mark standing with Valcourt, tears streaming down his face.

"It's Jeffrey, isn't it?" Carol asked, knowing the answer before she had even finished the question.

She stumbled out of the room and slowly walked around the house collecting pictures of Jeff and Kevin. She placed the framed photos side by side on the coffee table in her living room, a shrine of sorts to her dead sons.

"Our boys are together again," she told Mark. "Wherever they are, they're not alone anymore."

Mark was thrown by the flat tone of Carol's voice and the vacant, distant look in his wife's eyes. The family friends who began streaming into the house as soon as the news of Jeff's death spread throughout the base were equally surprised to watch Carol bustle around the house, taking their coats and asking if they wanted any coffee. In a house full of sobbing people, Carol Graham was the only one whose eyes were dry. None of them realized that she had gone into shock as soon as she heard about Jeff's death. She had been expecting the worst for months. When it finally came, she was too numb to react.

Hundreds of miles away, Stacey Martinez finished up her clinical rotation duties at the University of Louisville hospital, where she was continuing her pharmaceutical studies, and smiled as she stepped out into the early-afternoon sunshine. It had been unseasonably cold and over-cast all month, but February 19 looked and felt like a perfect spring day. It was warm enough that she could walk around without a coat and bright enough that she put on sunglasses as she walked back to her car. She settled in for the forty-five-minute drive to her mother's house in Eliza-bethtown, turned on the radio, and wondered what Jeff was doing at that exact moment.

It was a question Stacey asked herself every day. She knew that Jeff had been sent to one of the bloodiest areas of Iraq, and she was con-stantly getting new reminders of the dangers facing her fiancé and his men. Shortly after he deployed, Stacey learned that Second Lieutenant Todd Bryant had been killed a short distance from Jeff's new home and that Jeff's immediate predecessor, Second Lieutenant Matt Homa, had been sent back to the States after suffering gruesome wounds in an IED explosion. Jeff's letters home began to detail a seemingly endless series of firefights and explosions, several of which killed soldiers he knew and liked. The news reports from other parts of Iraq that she read online or saw on TV were just as demoralizing, with names being added to the grim roster of U.S. war dead seemingly every day.

One evening in January, Jeff called home from Camp Manhattan and told Stacey that his unit was on quick reaction duty, which meant that they'd be able to hang out around the base unless another unit came under attack. She went to a computer to check her e-mail a short time later and saw a breaking news alert about four American soldiers dying in a pair of ambushes near Habbaniyah. The article said two of the fallen soldiers were killed outright, while the other two were part of a quick reaction force that had arrived at the scene a short time after the initial attack and then been hit themselves. Stacey ran outside to a parking lot and frantically called her mom, terrified that Jeff might be among the dead. She didn't find out that he was okay until he was able to call home again the next day. "The worst part was the waiting," she said. "I was having a freak-out moment, but it wasn't like I could just pick up the phone and call Iraq. I had to stay calm until I heard from him, and that was really hard."

Still, Stacey's panic about the Habbaniyah attack was unusual. She had been pouring herself into planning the wedding and honeymoon, confident that Jeff would make it through his yearlong tour without any physical, psychological, or emotional wounds. "I thought that Kevin's death had given Jeff a free pass through Iraq," she said.

She was completely unprepared for the dire news that was waiting for her in Elizabethtown. Her parents had gotten divorced years earlier and rarely saw each other. The only thing keeping them from severing all contact was their shared love for Stacey and her younger sister, Allison. The family would reunite for the girls' birthdays and for major milestones like Stacey's graduation from the University of Kentucky, but her parents otherwise kept their distance from each other. Stacey did a double take when she saw her father and her mother, Janesa, sitting at the kitchen table, their eyes puffy and red. Stacey's first thought was that something horrible had happened to her sister. The possibility that her parents were waiting to talk to her about Jeff never crossed her mind.

"What's wrong with Allie?" Stacey screamed. "What happened to Allie?"

Her mother gently took Stacey's hand and told her that Allison was fine.

"It's Jeff," she said. "He was in an accident today, a bad one."

"But he's okay, right?" Stacey replied. "When can I talk to him?"

"You can't, honey," her mother said softly. "He's dead."

Stacey's legs buckled, and her mother barely managed to catch her before she hit her head on the floor. Stacey asked her parents to drive her to the family church so she could pray for Jeff and the rest of the Grahams, but she collapsed on the way to the car and lay down in the garage, sobbing so hard that her entire body shook, before they were finally able to make their way there. Stacey and her parents returned home from the church a few hours later, flipped on the TV, and numbly watched episodes of *Friends*, *The Apprentice*, and *ER* to briefly escape from the waves of grief and shock that had been crashing over them since they'd learned about Jeff's death. Shortly before midnight, Stacey crawled into her mother's bed and quickly fell asleep. She woke up the next morning shaken by a vivid nightmare of Jeff dying in Iraq. It took her a few seconds to remember that it wasn't a dream. "It felt like someone had just punched me in the face," she said. "Realizing that it was all real, that Jeff was actually gone, was the worst moment of my life. I would never have thought that it was possible to feel that much pain."

In the days after Jeff's death, Stacey picked up the teddy bear he had given her shortly before leaving for Iraq and played the recording of her fiancé's voice each night before going to sleep. It was the start of a tradition she maintained for years to come. Her final letters to Jeff—one sent on Valentine's Day, one the day before his final mission—were returned a short time later with the word *deceased* scrawled on the front of the envelopes.

Jeff Graham's journey home began with a memorial service in an empty warehouse at Camp Manhattan, a short drive away from the patch of road where he and Roger Ling had been killed. The building had recently been converted into a crude gym, so the soldiers walked past dusty rows of dumbbells and barbells as they made their way to the front of the cavernous, windowless structure. The first thing they saw was a battle-field cross that the men of Charlie Company had built in Jeff's honor by sticking his M4 rifle into a wooden stand, helmet on top and dog tags dangling from the trigger, and then placing the weapon behind a pair of sand-colored boots. The soldiers had built an identical memorial for Ling. The crosses had a simple purpose: to allow the soldiers who had fought alongside Jeff and Ling to pay their respects to the two fallen troops before their remains were flown back to the United States.

First Sergeant Steve Krivitsky, the top noncommissioned officer in Charlie Company, stood in front of the makeshift memorials, ordered the men to come to attention, and began calling the roll in alphabetical order. He yelled out the name of a Centurion, and the soldier immediately shouted back "Here, First Sergeant!" Krivitsky yelled out another name, and a second soldier shouted back "Here, First Sergeant!" He repeated the call-and-response with one more soldier and then paused. The room was silent; all of the men knew what was coming next.

"Lieutenant Graham," Krivitsky called out.

"Lieutenant Jeff Graham," he repeated, this time with a much louder and stronger voice.

"Lieutenant Jeffrey C. Graham," Krivitsky said for a third and final time, the words echoing off the walls of the massive building.

First Lieutenant Brian Horvath walked to the front of the room and looked out over the assembled soldiers, all of whom had known Jeff, many of whom had fought at his side, and several of whom were still alive because he had spotted the hidden bomb and warned them away in time. Horvath outranked Jeff, but he had considered him a close friend. Jeff's death had hit him hard.

"I have lost a sounding board and a peer," Horvath said to the group. "I have lost someone I could laugh with over the confounding situations young officers frequently encounter. In a business that often builds competition over cooperation, I have lost a friend that was a constant pleasure to work with. He was willing to assist me with anything. And I was willing to do the same for him."

Jeff's death, Horvath continued, had torn a hole in the entire unit.

"If a company is a foundation that draws stability from its officers, then Charlie Company is once again unbalanced. A part is missing that can never be replaced," he said. "The army's suffering over the loss of an outstanding officer is not mitigated by Lieutenant Graham's abbreviated service. The loss of Lieutenant Graham is a far greater woe because of the vast potential that will now go unrealized."

Horvath closed the eulogy on a lighter note, one that Jeff's friends and family back home would have appreciated.

"The Cats won again," he said, referring to Jeff's beloved Kentucky Wildcats. "They look to be in great shape for March Madness. I hope in heaven there are comfortable chairs in front of the big-screen TV and that the damn satellite doesn't ever go out."

The remains of Jeff Graham and Roger Ling were loaded onto a C-17 cargo plane a few hours later for the long flight to the Dover Air Force Base in suburban Delaware, the main transit point for the nation's war dead. A familiar face was already there, waiting for Jeff's body to arrive back on American soil.

Retired colonel Michael Thompson, who had entered the army with Mark and served with him in Germany, had been sitting in a business meeting in Washington two days earlier when his cell phone buzzed with a familiar number. "Cheryl," Carol Graham said. "I need to tell you something." Thompson realized that Carol had been trying to reach his wife and dialed his number accidentally. "Hey, Carol baby," he joked. "What's up?" When there was no response from the other end of the phone, Thompson, suddenly concerned, asked Carol what had happened. "The news isn't good," she told him. "Jeffrey was killed today."

Thompson had stayed in touch with Mark long after the two men had gone their separate ways as they ascended the army hierarchy. They updated each other on new jobs and traded friendly gossip about other officers they'd known or served with. But they mainly talked about their boys, who had grown up together in Germany and become close friends because of their shared love of sports and the outdoors. Thompson's son

Michael, universally known as M2, was Jeff's age and treated Kevin like a younger brother. Most of their classmates in Germany spent their free time watching TV or playing video games, but the three boys preferred to play baseball, basketball, and golf. They also loved their Rollerblades, and the three boys would regularly invite Thompson to skate with them up and down the hills surrounding Baumholder, wind whipping in their faces as they picked up speed. Thompson had played semipro hockey in his youth, but he could barely keep up. "They'd remind me that I wasn't on the ice anymore each and every time they shot past me on those blades," he said.

Kevin's suicide less than a year earlier had rocked the entire Thompson family. The Kevin they remembered from Germany was a goofy, cheerful kid who treasured his older brother and seemed happy to take part in any prank Jeff cooked up. Thompson had often thought that Kevin combined the best qualities of each of his parents, mixing Mark's intelligence and modesty with Carol's warmth and gentleness. It was hard for him to believe that Kevin could have ever felt so hopeless that he saw no choice but to take his own life. "This was a young man who was always just smiling and laughing," Thompson said.

Thompson had learned about Kevin's death just hours before his funeral was supposed to begin. Mark called at 8:30 A.M., but his friend had already left for his new job at a defense contractor in suburban Virginia. Cheryl knew something was terribly wrong when she heard Mark's voice. She called her husband at work with a blunt message: We need to go to Kentucky. Thompson was running a business conference and couldn't make the trip to Kentucky, but he quickly booked flights for Cheryl and M2. They raced to Frankfort as soon as they landed and managed to make it to the cemetery in time for the end of the funeral.

Thompson had never quite forgiven himself for missing Kevin's memorial service and failing to be there for Mark and Carol when they needed him the most. Jeff's death offered a way to make things right. This time around, Thompson told himself, he would find a way of doing more for his old friends. He would personally escort Jeff Graham home.

The C-17 carrying Jeff's remains touched down at Dover on a rainy, overcast afternoon. Thompson had arrived at the base hours earlier in a green army dress uniform that he hadn't taken out of his closet since retiring the previous year. Waiting for Jeff's body, he was struck by how many flag-draped caskets were being unloaded from the plane. Thompson watched enough TV to know that the war in Iraq was going poorly, but seeing the human toll up close was jarring all the same. When the plane was empty, Thompson was led to a mortuary affairs building near the runway to identify Jeff's body before it was transferred into a steel casket for the journey to Kentucky. There wasn't much for him to see. Jeff was wrapped up like a mummy, with only one hand fully visible. A military mortician at Dover pulled back the covering by a few inches so Thompson could take a quick glance at Jeff's remains. Thompson gasped when he saw how little of the body was left. "There was very little revealed, but it was more than enough," Thompson said. "I could easily imagine what was under there and what kind of damage I'd see if everything had been taken off."

Thompson was brought to a small waiting area while Dover personnel took Jeff's corpse to a rear fitting room, dressed it in an army uniform specially tailored to hide his missing and mangled limbs, and carefully arrayed rows of multicolored ribbons and medals on his chest to signify the commendations Jeff had earned during his brief military career, including copies of the Bronze Star and the Purple Heart awarded after his death. They placed Jeff's casket into a waiting hearse for the short drive to the Philadelphia airport. Thompson stood on the tarmac there and saluted crisply as Jeff's remains were loaded onto a Kentucky-bound plane.

When the flight landed in Louisville, the captain announced that the plane was carrying the remains of a fallen soldier and asked passengers to remain in their seats so Thompson could make his way down to the runway in time to see the flag-draped casket unloaded. The ground crew did its work in silence, with several taking off their hats as Jeff's remains were loaded into a second hearse. Thompson saluted again, pressing the sides of his fingertips tightly to his forehead, as the doors closed.

Jeff Graham was laid to rest on February 28, just over a week after he was killed. A few hours before the funeral, Stacey Martinez sat with her parents and sister in a hotel room in Frankfort, trying to find the strength to make it through the service without breaking down under the weight of her pain and grief. Allison suggested that her older sister take a Xanax tablet. Stacey shook her head.

"Not today," she told her sister. "I don't want to gloss over this. I want to feel the hurt."

The public response to Jeff's death was completely different from the response to Kevin's, something that would cause Mark and Carol immense pain in the months and years ahead. They were besieged by interview requests from local journalists anxious to speak to the parents of such a heroic young soldier. Kentucky's House of Representatives passed a formal resolution noting that Jeff's death "has left a void that cannot be filled, and he is mourned across the length and breadth of the Commonwealth." Tens of thousands of fans burst into applause when Jeff's photo was flashed on a large monitor at Kentucky's Rupp Arena during a game between his beloved Wildcats and the University of Tennessee Volunteers. Jeff would have been thrilled by the result: Kentucky won by thirty-two points.

The final moments before Jeff's memorial service were difficult for both Stacey and the Grahams, who had to make a painful decision about whether to have Jeff's casket open or closed during the public church service scheduled for later that day. Thompson was the only person to have seen Jeff's remains. He took Mark aside at the funeral home where Jeff's casket had been brought after the flight from Dover and told his friend that it would be better to keep the casket closed.

"Mark, I don't think this is the way you'll want to remember your son," Thompson told him. "It's not the final image you'll want to carry with you."

Mark agreed. He told Carol that seeing the ravaged remains of their son would simply be too much for them to bear. It would be far better, Mark argued, for the family to remember Jeff's smiling face instead. Stacey felt the exact opposite. She wanted to see her fiancé and hold his hand one last time, even if only for a moment. She told the Grahams that it would be the only way for her to fully say good-bye and accept the reality of his death. At the time, Carol agreed with Mark. Looking back, she believes she should have sided with Stacey and insisted on seeing her son one final time. "It somehow didn't seem as real because we never saw his body," she said. "The image in my mind of him all blown up with a leg, hand, and part of his head missing is so horrible that seeing his body in the new uniform with his head bandaged doesn't seem worse."

Hundreds of people lined the streets of Frankfort, waving American flags, as the hearse bearing Jeff's casket left the funeral home and slowly made its way to the First United Methodist Church. A band from the 1st Squadron of the 16th Armor Regiment began to play marching music when Jeff's casket arrived at the church where Mark and Carol had gotten married decades earlier. More than six hundred people had jammed into the main sanctuary of First United, including a hundred young officers from Fort Knox, filling the church so completely that church officials had to set up video cameras and broadcast the service into an adjacent over-flow room. The contrast with the aftermath of Kevin's death couldn't have been starker. Many of Mark and Carol's friends and colleagues hadn't known what to say to them about Kevin's decision to take his own life and often simply avoided bringing it up. Strangers told them that Kevin's suicide had been a sin in the eyes of God, something Carol, a deeply religious woman, often worried about as well. Melanie sometimes chose not to tell her friends or classmates about Kevin's life or death, effectively pretending that he hadn't existed, because she was so afraid that they'd blame her and her parents for failing to get him the help he needed. Kevin's death didn't attract much public notice, and his funeral didn't attract many people. Jeff was mourned by hundreds of total strangers, and his death was front-page news across the state of Kentucky.

During the loneliest moments of Jeff's deployment, Stacey had consoled herself by imagining every detail of her upcoming wedding. She pictured herself walking down the center aisle of First United with a bouquet of white lilies in her hands. She imagined a sanctuary filled with her relatives and friends. In her mind's eye she saw Jeff smiling at her from the front of the sanctuary, waiting to take her hand and bind himself to her for the rest of his life. First United was packed on February 28, but it was full of people who had come to say good-bye to Jeff, not to celebrate his wedding. Stacey made her way down the aisle of First United on the saddest day of her life, not the happiest. She walked unsteadily behind Jeff's flag-draped casket, the teddy bear he had given her months before clutched firmly between her trembling hands.

Ben Baxter gave the eulogy at Jeff's funeral, just as he had done at Kevin's. He was a close friend of the two brothers and shared their love of Kentucky sports. God, he joked, would have a hard time figuring out how to handle them.

"I think God needed help with Kevin, but now he has to deal with them both," Baxter told the crowd. "And I know Saint Peter can't be too happy, because I can see them trying to scheme a way to let all the U.K. fans in, and keep all of the Louisville fans out."

The Iraq War was increasingly unpopular, and Baxter said that he knew many of the mourners were opposed to it. Still, he said that he hoped everyone there could understand—and respect—the sense of duty that led soldiers like Jeff to give their lives for their country.

"Regardless of our own political feelings about the war, I know that Jeff and all the other soldiers fighting for us have our love and support," Baxter told the crowd. "They don't ask questions; they have a job to do, and they go and do it."

Mark saluted his son's casket as it was carried out of the church by members of an eleven-man military honor guard and loaded into a black hearse for the drive out to the Frankfort cemetery. During a brief grave-side ceremony, Army Major Terrance Walsh, a chaplain, mentioned the bear that Jeff had given Stacey and acknowledged how painful it was to hear Jeff's voice confidently saying that he was safe just a few months before his death. Walsh encouraged Jeff's friends and relatives to under-stand those words in a profoundly different way.

"Jeff is safe," he told the crowd of mourners. "Jeff is where he will never be threatened, he will never be hungry, he will never be tired, and he will never be fearful."

Three members of the honor guard fired their rifles into the air seven times, each round echoing through the trees like a thunderclap. A lone bugler played taps as Jeff's casket was lowered into the ground.

Valcourt got down on one knee and presented both Carol and Stacey with a folded American flag, the military's traditional way of offering its condolences to the loved ones of a fallen service member. He gave Mark and Melanie the Purple Heart and Bronze Star that had been awarded to Jeff after his death in Iraq. Mark struggled to maintain his composure; Melanie looked shell-shocked. Kevin's suicide had hit her hard, but Jeff's death knocked her over the edge. Her grades fell further, and Melanie stopped going to classes in May. She tried to return to the University of Kentucky that fall but dropped out for good in October. It would be more than a year before she transferred to a school nearly a thousand miles away to resume her classes and finish her degree.

Stacey grasped onto Jeff's casket and kissed it as she said a final good-bye to her fiancé. Carol stood next to her would-be daughter-in-law, stroking Stacey's hair and trying to set aside her own sadness so she could comfort the woman her son had loved and hoped to marry. She, Stacey, and Melanie gently laid roses on Jeff's casket as the family slowly made their way to a waiting black limousine.

Jeff was buried next to his brother on a grassy knoll overlooking the Kentucky River. A few days after the funeral Mark and Carol noticed that a handwritten sign had been left by the two headstones; it read LAND OF THE FREE BECAUSE OF THE BRAVE. To this day, the Grahams don't know who placed it there.

CHAPTER 12

Fort Sill, Oklahoma, March 2004

Mark Graham had made up his mind: It was time to leave the military. He was barely hanging on after Jeff's death, doing his best to stay strong for Carol and Melanie while keeping his own grief bottled up and hidden away. Carol had come home one night and found him alone in the garage, cradling one of Kevin's old golf clubs. His close friends could tell how much sadness Mark was feeling, but they knew he was also grappling with overpowering feelings of guilt and regret. It wasn't simply that he had lost a second son, though that was devastating enough. It was that Jeff had been killed in action, at the start of an army career modeled on that of his father. Mark was haunted by the thought that Jeff might still be alive if he had chosen a different profession. The army had taken so much from him and Carol. How, Mark wondered, would he be able to put on his uniform each morning and salute the flag as if nothing had happened? He had loved every moment of his service in the army, but it was time to move on.

Mark and Carol arrived back at Fort Sill on March 10 and returned to a house full of ghosts. They had spent their first year at the base mourning one son and praying for the safety of the other, only to lose him as well. The framed pictures of Kevin and Jeff stabbed at Carol like daggers, painful reminders of a family that no longer existed. *My boys are gone,* she told herself. *My precious boys are gone.* She didn't know how she would stifle her own thoughts of suicide, let alone continue as an army wife. She and Mark worried about Melanie and pleaded with her to leave the University of Kentucky and join them in Oklahoma, but their daughter wouldn't step foot in a house whose walls were lined with photos of her two dead brothers. Melanie told her parents that being around them simply made her too sad.

"You got to live forty-seven years of your lives in this perfect world where nothing bad ever happened," she told them. "My world basically fell apart when I was eighteen. I have to somehow find a way to live the rest of my life."

The only surviving Graham child wasn't sure she could. Melanie never told her parents, but Jeff's death left her actively considering whether to take her own life. The only thing that kept her from committing suicide was the thought that she simply couldn't cause her parents any more pain. "I have to keep going until my parents are either old or dead before I kill myself," she remembered thinking. "Nobody will care then."

Mark barely slept the night of March 10 and woke up early the following morning ready to put in his retirement papers. He had prepared a new résumé; the moment had come to send it out to potential employers in the civilian world. Groggy, he made his way downstairs and stepped into the kitchen for a cup of coffee. Carol was already up, sitting at the kitchen table with an eighty-five-year-old book of biblically inspired stories called *Streams in the Desert.* She read from it every day, seeking the type of solace that she had just about abandoned hope of finding. Mark sat down next to his wife and was startled by how fiercely she was crying. "The expression on her face completely threw me," he recalled.

Carol pulled herself together and began to read out loud from that day's chapter, a parable written by James Russell Miller, a Presbyterian minister and teacher who came of age during the Civil War and never forgot its carnage.

"Yesterday you experienced a great sorrow and now your home seems empty. Your impulse is to give up amid your dashed hopes," Carol read. "Yet, you must defy that temptation for you are at the front line of battle and the crisis is at hand. . . . You must not linger at this point even to indulge your grief."

Carol looked Mark in the eye as she began reading the next section, a story about a Civil War general leading an important assault who glanced down and saw his son lying dead on the ground. The general, Miller wrote, set aside the impulse to mourn by his son's body and instead pressed on with the assault, putting duty to others ahead of his personal grief:

> Weeping inconsolably forever beside a grave will never bring back the treasure of a lost one. We never completely recover from our greatest griefs and are never quite the same after having passed through them. Yet sorrow that is endured in the right spirit impacts our growth favorably and brings us a greater sense of compassion for others. Sitting down and continuously brooding over our sorrow deepens the darkness surrounding us, allowing it to creep into our heart, and soon our strength has changed to weakness. But if we will turn from the gloom and remain faithful, the light will shine again and we will grow stronger.

Mark understood that Carol was telling him that they, too, needed to put duty to others ahead of their own grief. The wars in Iraq and Afghanistan were getting steadily bloodier, with hundreds of soldiers like Jeff losing their lives and thousands of others returning to the United States maimed, burned, or injured. Perhaps, Mark thought, he and

Carol would be able to find ways of ensuring that wounded soldiers of all kinds got the care they needed and that the families of all fallen troops were treated with the same compassion and respect they'd received after Jeff's death. Remaining in the military would give them the most—and best—opportunities to help. "I knew right then that I was meant to stay," Mark said.

Mark threw away his retirement paperwork and decided to finish out his remaining time as chief of staff to the commanding general of Fort Sill. He was slated to relinquish that post in the fall of 2005, and he told Carol that he would retire as soon as his replacement was in place. His military career had begun at Fort Sill decades earlier; it seemed somehow fitting that it should end there as well.

"Congratulations, Mark," Major General Dave Valcourt said into the phone. "You're on the list for brigadier general."

It was September 22, 2004, and Mark was at a military conference at Georgia's Fort Benning, one of the largest bases in the entire American military. It took him a few seconds to process what Valcourt had said. Mark had assumed that when he retired in twelve months he would go out as a colonel, a highly competitive rank attained by only a small fraction of army officers. He hadn't led soldiers into combat or served in Afghanistan or Iraq, and he didn't have personal relationships with many of the three- and four-star generals who determined which colonels would make the jump to general. Years earlier, Brigadier General Creighton Abrams had said that Mark had "General Officer potential." It turned out, much to Mark's surprise, that Abrams had been right.

When the initial shock passed, Mark felt like it was no coincidence that he'd gotten the good news on that particular day, and while he was visiting that particular base. Kevin had spent the summer between his sophomore and junior years attending Fort Benning's famed airborne course, a grueling three-week course reserved for the most promising ROTC cadets in the country. He earned his jump wings—a military badge showing a parachute surrounded by a pair of feathered wings—after safely finishing five jumps out the side doors of a military plane flying roughly twelve hundred feet above the ground. Being at the base where Kevin had spent some of the proudest moments of his life left Mark feeling unusually close to his lost son. September 22, meanwhile, was Jeff's birthday. He would have been twenty-five. "At that moment in time at that exact place I knew I was where I was supposed to be and that there was a mission for me to continue in the army," Mark said. "It seemed like my boys were standing right next to me, one on my right and one on my left."

At Mark's promotion ceremony a few months later, Valcourt proudly pinned a silver star to each of his friend's shoulder epaulets. Jeffrey's name was engraved under one of the stars, Kevin's under the other. "Your sons will always be with you," Valcourt told Mark.

Seven months earlier, Valcourt had handed Carol a folded American flag during Jeff's funeral, one of the lowest points of her life. Now he was personally welcoming her husband into the top ranks of the United States Army, a professional accomplishment for Mark that stood as one of the highlights of her life as well. Carol allowed herself to smile, a rare occurrence since the boys' death. She also thought back to a conversation she'd had with Mark during a particularly hard day in Kentucky. A short time before Jeff was laid to rest, Carol and Mark had sat down with a funeral director in Frankfort to discuss the final details of their son's memorial service. On the drive back to her mother's house, Carol turned to her husband and bluntly told him that she didn't think they would ever be happy again. Mark surprised her with his response. "We can let losing the boys be two tragic chapters in the book of our lives, or we can let it be the whole book," he told her at the time. Watching Mark pin on his general's stars for the first time, Carol started to see what he meant. She and Mark had wanted to figure out a way of using their personal losses to help others. Being a general would give Mark the power, and the prominence, to begin doing so.

A few weeks later Mark began preparing in earnest for his new job as assistant commandant of Fort Sill's field artillery school—which teaches troops how to use howitzers, mortars, and other powerful weapons to find and destroy distant enemy targets—and the deputy commanding general of the base itself. Mark inherited an office with a secretary and an aide-de-camp but no other staffers. His top priority was to find a captain who could serve as his executive officer, a key post charged with keeping a general from being overwhelmed by paperwork and ensuring that his orders were precisely carried out. Mark interviewed an array of candidates but was particularly impressed by a young captain named Michael Pelkey, who had gone through Fort Sill's artillery training a few years earlier and just returned from a combat tour in Iraq. Pelkey had received sterling performance reviews at every stage of his young career. He was clearly intelligent, but he wasn't cocky or arrogant in his interview with Mark. Instead, he was soft-spoken and modest about his accomplishments. Pelkey, in a real sense, reminded Mark of himself at a younger age. Mark offered him the job, and Pelkey accepted it. He seemed excited to start work. "Mike was grounded," Mark said. "He had his head screwed on straight."

But Pelkey had another side, one that he was desperate to hide from his new boss. Like Kevin Graham, he was an overachiever who seemed destined for a long and successful military career. And like Kevin, Captain Michael Jon Pelkey was battling demons only he could see.

Captain Stefanie Pelkey could barely recognize her husband when he returned from Iraq in the summer of 2004. They had met in Germany four years earlier, a pair of young officers stationed abroad for the first time. Mike, a burly giant of a man with a surprisingly gentle demeanor and a passionate love for music and dogs, and Stefanie Gomez, a rabid football fan who loved John Cusack movies and reruns of *Saturday Night Live,* had followed similar paths to the military. Stefanie's father enlisted in the army during the Vietnam War; Mike's father served as a Navy Sea-bee, working military construction jobs at posts across the United States. Growing up, Mike had no desire to follow his father into the navy, which seemed like it would keep him too far from the action. He would instead spend hours in the woods hiding from imaginary enemies and thinking about creative ways of ambushing his foes. "Being a soldier was the only thing he ever wanted to do," Stefanie said. Mike went through the University of Connecticut's ROTC program and was commissioned as a second lieutenant in the army's artillery branch. His college friends, awed by how much he could drink without any discernible impact, began to jokingly call Mike "Jackalope," and the name stuck. Stefanie had wanted to enlist, but her father suggested that she at least try college. She went to New Mexico State, finished ROTC, and was also tapped for the artillery.

They became close friends at one of the most difficult moments of Stefanie's life. She had been assigned to the small, remote town of Idar-Oberstein to join up with the 1st Battalion, 94th Field Artillery Regiment, a World War II–era unit known as "Deep Steel." Stefanie was the only woman on the base and had trouble finding friends; even Mike told his father that he didn't think a female soldier belonged in the unit. She was far away from her parents for the first time in her life and felt homesick. Mike listened sympathetically and tried to cheer her up with day trips to places like Trier, the oldest city in Germany, and Baden-Baden, a town in the Black Forest famed for its ancient Roman bathhouses. They explored the old city of Munich and listened to a friend play the saxophone at a smoke-filled jazz club in Heidelberg. Gradually, with neither one really noticing, Mike and Stefanie fell in love. "He was my best friend," Stefanie said. Soon he was also her boyfriend.

Mike called Stefanie on September 8, 2001, just three days before the terrorist attacks that would forever change their lives, and asked if he could come over to her apartment. "I have something I need to tell you," he said. She assumed it was bad news, like orders for him to immediately redeploy to the Middle East, and told herself not to cry. Stefanie breathed a sigh of relief when Mike opened the door with a huge, goofy grin on his face and slid a bottle of chilled Dom Pérignon out of his backpack.

"Do you remember when I said we'd open this for something special?" he asked.

"Oh my God," she joked. "Are you pregnant?"

She stopped laughing when Mike got down on one knee, diamond ring in hand.

A justice of the peace married Mike and Stefanie in front of a small courthouse just outside her hometown of Houston on November 2, 2001. They flew back to Texas the following summer for an outdoor ceremony at Shady Oaks, a parklike wedding venue outside Austin whose six grassy acres were bounded by a white picket fence. Stefanie wore a strapless white wedding dress with a diaphanous lace veil; Mike wore his army dress uniform, complete with red lapels and gold braid on the shoulders. They posed for photos with unlit cigars in their mouths, smiling broadly.

Stefanie got pregnant almost immediately, but the timing couldn't have been much worse. The Bush administration spent much of the fall and winter of 2002 building up its forces throughout the Middle East for what looked like an inevitable war with Iraq. The Pentagon knew that Saddam Hussein's military possessed large numbers of tanks, armored vehicles, and heavily fortified military bases. Destroying them would require experienced artillery officers such as Mike and Stefanie Pelkey. Mike was told that he would be deploying to the Middle East in early 2003. Stefanie, who was due to give birth in March, was told that she'd be given four weeks to look after her baby and find relatives who could take

care of the infant when she returned overseas. The young couple prepared for war and parenthood simultaneously. Some days required trips
to a small military human resources building to complete their wills or
sign paperwork to send their new baby back to the United States after
they deployed. Others days were spent in Idar-Oberstein buying a crib,
changing table, and stroller. "Everything just happened so fast," Stefanie
recalled. "It was one big blur."

Mike left for Iraq at the end of March, less than two weeks after the
birth of his son, Benjamin. He soon had a pair of close calls. The first happened when an Iraqi man grabbed him by his body armor and tried to
yank him out of the window of his Humvee. Mike was certain he was
going to be dragged away and killed, but he managed to shove his M16
into the Iraqi's face and force him back until the truck was able to rumble
away. "I was never so close to ending another person's life," Mike wrote in
a journal entry addressed to his infant son. "I was so close: round in the
chamber, weapon on fire, and finger on trigger. It was pointed right in his
face. Thank God I didn't have to pull the trigger."

A few weeks later Mike was standing near a British soldier when an
unseen sniper opened fire, hitting the Brit in the head. The dead soldier's
blood and brain matter splattered onto Mike's uniform and boots, a horror he was never able to forget. Mike didn't tell Stefanie a word about it.

Mike returned to Germany in July. He didn't laugh anymore, and he
didn't seem interested in having sex with his wife. He had a hard time
eating or sleeping and would yell at Stefanie for no reason. Mike knew
that he needed help and did his best to get it. He had completed a written
mental health assessment when he got back to Germany and was strikingly blunt about what he was feeling. He had constantly been afraid of
being killed in Iraq, Mike wrote, and had personally seen the killings of
both coalition troops and Iraqi civilians. He noted that he was jumpy and
afraid of crowds. He wrote that he regularly felt depressed, hopeless, and
unsure of why he should keep on living. Mike visited the base's primary

care physician on July 28 and told her he was beginning to pick fights with both Stefanie and his close friends. She referred him to a counselor, but the base of several thousand soldiers had only two psychiatrists on staff and Mike couldn't get an appointment before he, Stefanie, and Benjamin boarded a plane for the long flight to Oklahoma.

The problems only got worse at Fort Sill. Mike had purchased a Sig Sauer 9-millimeter handgun during a trip to Germany and drove into Lawton one afternoon to buy a Heckler & Koch handgun, an expensive, technologically advanced weapon used by elite special operations personnel the world over. He kept the guns in his closet at first but soon began sleeping with at least one of the weapons tucked neatly underneath his pillow. Stefanie woke up one morning and saw the barrel of a gun pointing right at her face.

He also began to have vivid nightmares about being shot. One night Mike and Stefanie went to sleep after watching an episode of the Discovery Channel's *Mystery Diagnosis,* a show about people with unusual illnesses. Stefanie woke up to hear her husband screaming. "Blood!" he yelled. "There's blood everywhere!" He bolted out of bed, frantically running his hands over his face and chest while he searched for a bullet wound. He calmed down after several minutes and smiled sheepishly at his wife. "Just a dream," he said, crawling back into bed. Stefanie cradled him like a baby and tried to rock him to sleep, but she could still feel his heart pounding in his chest.

Mike again sought help from the military's medical system, and he was again rebuffed. He went to the offices of Fort Sill's mental health counselors but was told that it would be at least a month before he could get an appointment. Fort Sill, like Mike's base in Germany, had far too few psychologists and psychiatrists to deal with the flood of Iraq and Afghanistan war veterans with PTSD and depression.

Stefanie decided to take matters into her own hands. More than a year earlier, Carol had called TRICARE, the military's health insurance program, seeking help for Kevin. Stefanie was now doing the same thing for Mike. The TRICARE representative directed her to a family counselor in Lawton named Joanni Sailor. Sailor met with Stefanie and Mike on October 11, 2004, and told them that she wanted to see them individually as soon as possible. Later that month the Pelkeys went to the house of John Molina, a Catholic chaplain at Fort Sill who'd become a close family friend, for a small Halloween party. Mike told Stefanie that he was going to sell his guns because parenthood meant that they could use any extra money they could find. Stefanie told her husband that she knew how much he loved the guns and didn't want him to ever blame her for making him sell them. She suggested that he put them in the attic, safely out of reach. Stefanie didn't realize until it was too late that he wanted her to sell the guns to make sure they were entirely out of their house. "I will regret that for the rest of my life," she said.

A few days later Mike found out that he been selected to be Mark Graham's executive officer. "I can't wait for you to meet him," he told Stefanie. "He's lost both of his sons, but he's just this amazing, kind man. He's the first person who really wants to get to know me."

The last week of Mike Pelkey's life began on a high note. He saw Sailor, his counselor, again on Monday, November 1. She told him that he had a full-blown case of PTSD, and that there was medication that could help. Stefanie had never heard of PTSD, and later wondered why the military hadn't told her or other military spouses to be on the lookout for signs that their husband or wife had returned from the war zones with the disorder. At the time, though, all Stefanie cared about was that there seemed to be a reason for her husband's problems—and, potentially, a cure. She hadn't seen Mike so happy since before he'd left for Iraq a year earlier. "I'm not crazy," he told Stefanie. "There's a light at the end of the tunnel." Sailor told Mike to see his primary care physician so he could get a prescription for Lexapro, an antidepressant, but Mike never made an appointment with the doctor or got the prescription filled.

Stefanie's parents were visiting for the weekend, and on Friday, November 5, she and her mother woke up early to drive to Oklahoma City for a prayer session and luncheon at a Catholic church there. Mike was still asleep, and Stefanie briefly lay down next to him before she left. She had a sudden premonition of something bad happening to her husband, though she didn't know where it came from. "Mike is a great dad," she told her mom. "If something happened, I could at least say that he had been a good dad."

When Stefanie got to Fort Sill's chapel, the first stop on the trip to Oklahoma City, she realized that she'd left her Bible and rosary at home and called Mike to ask him to bring them to her. She hugged him in the parking lot of the chapel and apologized for having been rushing around so much that morning. He smiled and pulled her into his strong arms for a hug. "I love you," Mike said. She never saw him alive again.

Stefanie had taken Benjamin with her for the trip to Oklahoma City, so Mike returned from the chapel to an empty house. He called his wife to check in, and they made plans to go out with her parents that night for steaks and martinis. Sailor's office phoned Mike later that morning to confirm that he'd see her again on Monday, and he assured them that he'd be there. In hindsight, however, something was obviously very wrong. Friday was supposed to be his first day at work in Mark Graham's office, but he never showed up. Mike had spent weeks telling Stefanie how he couldn't wait to start his new job as Mark's executive officer. When the moment finally arrived, Mike was nowhere to be found.

Stefanie's father returned from a day of golf that afternoon and found Mike's body on the couch of their living room, a single red blossom spreading slowly from a single gunshot wound in his son-in-law's chest. Pelkey, twenty-nine, had killed himself less than a week after he had been diagnosed with PTSD and just three days after his third wedding anniversary. Mike's father-in-law kissed him on the forehead and then called Stefanie's mother on her cell phone. Stefanie saw her mother go pale and knew before she even opened her mouth that something horrible had happened to Mike. She sobbed for the entire ninety-minute drive back to Fort Sill.

Stefanie Pelkey didn't return to her house for almost a week. She spent her first night as a widow in the Fort Sill hospital under heavy sedation because of fears that she would kill herself. On November 6, Stefanie's doctors moved her to Chaplain Molina's house so she wouldn't have to be alone in her own home, haunted by the memories of what had just taken place there. The next day she heard a knock at the door and saw a pair of unfamiliar faces. Mark and Carol had been on an official visit to Fort Leavenworth, in Kansas, but rushed back to Fort Sill as soon as they heard about Mike's death. Mark couldn't believe that the energetic, smiling young man he'd tabbed as his executive officer just weeks earlier had taken his own life. He blamed himself for not spotting signs of Mike's distress or making sure that he got the help he so desperately needed, and asked himself over and over again whether he had done or said something that could have put additional stress on Mike and inadvertently pushed him over the edge. "I just could not get my mind around how I could have not seen something or heard something in Mike's voice that might have allowed me to intervene," Mark said. "Like Kevin, Mike had a mask that I could not see past."

Mark also had a more practical concern. Mike's suicide had widowed Stefanie and left Benjamin, who was just beginning to walk, fatherless. He felt a level of responsibility to the two survivors and wanted to find ways of helping them. The first was to use the story of Kevin's suicide to reassure Stefanie that her husband's decision to take his own life hadn't been her fault. On November 7 he and Carol walked into the living room of Chaplain Molina's house and introduced themselves, Mark still in shock, Carol's eyes red from crying. Stefanie, who hadn't eaten or slept in days, wondered how Mark and Carol could care so deeply about someone they'd barely known. She knew that they had lost both of their sons, but she didn't know that one of them had committed suicide.

"We've been through what you're going through, and we know what you're feeling," Carol said during that first meeting, hugging Stefanie tight. "Just remember that it's not your fault."

Mark told Stefanie how much he had respected her husband and how excited he had been for the two of them to work together. He was devastated when Stefanie told him how hard Mike had worked to get the help he so desperately needed. Fort Sill, Mark told her, had failed Mike Pelkey. He promised to find out why the base dropped the ball when Mike came forward to ask for assistance and to improve how the post identified and treated those with severe cases of PTSD or who seemed to be most at risk of taking their own lives.

That proved easier said than done. The base's behavioral health clinic was located in a separate building from its hospital, which meant that soldiers taking one of Fort Sill's internal buses could immediately see which of their colleagues were on their way to a regular doctor's appointment and which were heading off to see a shrink. Mark pushed for the clinic to be moved inside the hospital so soldiers seeking counseling wouldn't need to worry about being spotted—and potentially mocked—by their peers. "The idea was to get rid of a concrete manifestation of the stigma that was keeping people from seeking help," Mark said. His boss supported the change, but nothing happened. Nine years later the clinic and the hospital remain in separate buildings, and Fort Sill officials say they have no plans to combine them. It was the first time Mark saw the army's internal bureaucracy stifle a simple, potentially powerful new way of keeping troubled soldiers from taking their own lives. It wouldn't be the last.

Stefanie, for her part, had had enough of the military. She resigned her commission as an officer shortly after Mike's death and formally left the army. Initially Stefanie had a hard time accepting that her husband had committed suicide and not accidentally shot himself while trying to clean out his handgun. Within months, though, she emerged as one of the nation's most eloquent commentators on the growing scourge of military suicide, sharing Mike's story with both family members of troops who had taken their own lives and lawmakers in Washington.

"Although he was a brave veteran of Operation Iraqi Freedom, he did not die in battle, at least not in Iraq," she testified at a congressional hearing. "He died in a battle of his heart and mind."

Stefanie urged the lawmakers to press the military to improve its handling of PTSD and the other invisible wounds that had led to her husband's death. She spoke of the pervasive stigma within the armed forces that prevented troubled soldiers from seeking help because they worried about being passed over for promotion or being looked down upon by their colleagues. She said severe shortages of mental health professionals meant that soldiers like her husband, who set aside fears for their careers and sought help, couldn't receive it in time. And she faulted the army for refusing to acknowledge that combat veterans, even if physically unhurt, often returned with life-threatening wounds all the same. "The war does not end when they come home," she testified.

The memorial service for Captain Michael Pelkey was held on November 10 in a packed chapel at Fort Sill. Stefanie's memories from the day are blurry and bittersweet. She's not clear about who spoke or what they said, but she remembers being surprised by how many of her friends either left early or didn't show up at all. There's one other thing that she remembers clearly nearly a decade later: Mark and Carol Graham, whom she barely knew, came on time, made a point of spending the memorial service huddled with her and her family, and didn't walk out of the sanctuary until the ceremony had ended.

Mark took Stefanie aside after the service and asked if she was getting all of the help she needed during the most painful and wearying days of her life. "Is there anything at all that I can do for you?" he asked.

Stefanie told Mark that the army was keeping her in its Individual Ready Reserve, or IRR, which meant that she was at risk of abruptly being called back to active duty and shipped off to Iraq or Afghanistan. That would have been difficult enough even if Mike was still alive. As a widow and a single mother, she told him, being forced to move overseas and leave her only son behind would simply be too much for her to bear. Mark nodded his head; he understood that she was indirectly telling him that she might kill herself if forced to say good-bye to Benjamin. "I'm not going to let that happen," he assured her. "Don't worry."

A few days later Stefanie received an e-mail from the army letting her know that she'd been removed from the IRR, effective immediately. She's never asked him directly, but Stefanie is certain that Mark was the one who managed to get her out of reserve duty so she could focus on rebuilding her shattered life. Mark Graham, she believes, knew exactly what she was going through, and he kept his promise to help.

CHAPTER 13

New Orleans, Louisiana, August 2005

Brigadier General Mark Graham's Black Hawk helicopter swooped low over the brackish waters covering New Orleans, the sound of its powerful rotors echoing off the empty, ruined buildings below. The doors had been left open, and Mark tried to stop himself from gagging at the putrid smells of burning gasoline and raw sewage that wafted up from the submerged city. It was pitch black, and Mark couldn't spot a single light in any of the apartment buildings, office towers, or houses below. *This is a major American city,* he thought, *and it's absolutely dark.* He had never seen anything like it.

Mark's destination was the Superdome, a football stadium that had become an emergency refuge for tens of thousands of desperate New Orleans residents who fled their homes but failed to make it out of New Orleans before floodwaters destroyed many of the city's roads and bridges. The refugees had been trapped in the stadium for days and were rapidly running out of food and water. Television crews were broadcasting harrowing images of young mothers holding their babies up to the cameras and begging for help. Reports from inside the stadium talked about robberies, rapes, even murders. The situation at the Superdome was turning into a humanitarian disaster and a national embarrassment. Something had to be done, and President George W. Bush decided to send in the army. Mark Graham, who had just been promoted from colonel to brigadier general, was put in charge of evacuating the stadium, and then the rest of the city. He knew it was going to be a tough job, but the magnitude of the challenge didn't come into sharp focus until Mark's chopper landed in a helipad in a parking lot behind the stadium. A colonel walked out of the darkness and saluted. "Welcome to New Orleans," he said.

Mark told the officer that he had heard about how bad things were inside the Superdome but needed to see it for himself. He walked to the upper deck of the stadium, flanked by the colonel and a pair of armed National Guard soldiers, and looked out at the Superdome for the first time. He saw that the stadium's domed ceiling had been perforated with debris, leaving a constellation of large, ragged holes. Forecasters were beginning to warn that another major storm might soon bear down on the region, and Mark realized that a hurricane even remotely as strong as Katrina would bring down the roof and flood the stadium. Amazingly, that was the least of the Superdome's problems. The stadium was using emergency generators that were rapidly running out of fuel. Its bathrooms had stopped working days earlier, leaving the toilets and sinks fetid and overflowing. Mark looked down at the bedraggled refugees who filled the lower half of the stadium and realized that there was no way to evacuate the building by helicopter. A Black Hawk could carry out five or six people at a time, a Chinook around twenty. At that pace, it would take weeks to clear the stadium.

Mark was mentally running through other evacuation options when the soldiers' radios squawked with reports of shots being fired elsewhere in the stadium. The National Guardsmen lifted Mark up by his elbows and rushed him out of the Superdome. Standing outside in the cool early-morning air, Mark spotted a pedestrian bridge connecting the stadium to a nearby Marriott Hotel. He and his escorts crossed the bridge, made their way down to the hotel's waterlogged lobby, and opened the sliding doors that led to the street outside the building. Mark had just made a discovery that would allow the military to evacuate the Superdome faster and more safely than had been deemed possible. Walking back to his Black Hawk, he obsessed about the sweaty, desperate people he'd seen inside the stadium. He felt ashamed that they'd been left there to suffer and determined to do something about it. A refugee tapped him on the shoulder, pulling him out of his reverie, and begged Mark to fly him out on the waiting helicopter. Mark reluctantly shook his head. The helicopter had only a couple of spare seats, and Mark worried that pulling one man aboard while so many others were waiting for a way out would trigger a riot. "It wouldn't be fair to take you and not any of these other people," he told the refugee. "But I promise that we're going to get all of you out of here as fast as we can." Mark Graham meant what he said. The only question was how to do it.

Mark had been shaking hands at a reception in his honor two days earlier when the levees protecting New Orleans failed during the storm, sending water sluicing through the city. He and Carol had just arrived at San Antonio's Fort Sam Houston so he could take on a new job as the deputy commanding general of Army North, the military unit responsible for helping federal and state governments respond to large-scale terror attacks and natural catastrophes such as Katrina. Lieutenant General Robert Clark, the overall commander of Army North, was hosting a formal ceremony welcoming the Grahams to the base, and Mark was in the middle of a receiving line when he noticed Clark motioning him toward a quiet corner. "Have you been watching TV?" the general asked. "You're needed in Louisiana. Get a team together and head down there as fast as you can." Mark grabbed the first twenty officers and noncommissioned troops he saw and told them to rent some Suburbans and pack enough clothing for an indefinite stay in the disaster area. They set out for Louisiana in a convoy of sport-utility vehicles early the following morning, encountering virtually no traffic. The highways were jammed with cars trying to escape the Gulf Coast; few people were trying to make their way in.

Mark arrived in Baton Rouge that afternoon and headed straight to Louisiana's crowded emergency operations center, the locus of the expanding relief efforts. He spotted his new boss, Lieutenant General Russel Honoré, the charismatic, cigar-chomping Louisiana native who commanded Joint Task Force Katrina, a makeshift military unit that had been given de facto authority over the Gulf Coast after state and local authorities buckled under the strain of trying to deal with one of the worst natural disasters in American history. Honoré was in the middle of a heated conversation with Louisiana governor Kathleen Blanco and the officer in charge of the state's National Guard troops when Mark walked over and saluted.

"Mark Graham reporting for duty, sir," he said.

"Good to see you, brother," Honoré said. "Let's talk."

Honoré led Mark into a small room overlooking the operations center. Blanco and Honoré had spent the morning in New Orleans and looked shaken by what they'd seen. Clark had told Mark that his primary duties in Louisiana would be to represent the military in high-level meetings and work to repair the army's frosty relationship with the Federal Emergency Management Agency. Honoré threw those assignments out the window and gave Mark a different, and far more challenging, pair of missions.

"Mark, go evacuate the city of New Orleans," he told the stunned new arrival. "When that's done, go evacuate the greater New Orleans area."

Mark and his team set up shop in a small storage room in the back of the building. It had no windows and so few desks that some members of his team had to work standing up. They had computers, satellite phones, and intermittent Internet access, but their BlackBerries rarely worked and their cell phones were essentially useless. Bleary-eyed from the long trip to Louisiana, the soldiers guzzled coffee and Diet Coke to stay awake. They knew the stakes: Hundreds of people were already dead, and the tally was poised to rise in the days ahead as stranded refugees ran out of food and water. There would be time for sleep later.

Mark made his fateful trip to the Superdome at two o'clock the next morning and came back to Baton Rouge shortly before dawn, unable to forget the putrid smell of the stagnant floodwaters and the unsettling sight of a completely darkened American city. He told his team that the enormous numbers of refugees at the Superdome meant that evacuating them with helicopters was out of the question. The fastest way to get them all out safely, he continued, was with buses. The Superdome held approximately twenty-six thousand people. Each bus could carry forty or fifty people, double or quintuple the number that could be ferried out by helicopter. The U.S. military had the most sophisticated aircraft in the world at its fingertips, and there was nothing glamorous about relying on decidedly low-tech vehicles like the yellow school buses that have ferried kids to school for generations, but Mark insisted that there was no better option.

The next step was to win over FEMA. The military had the manpower, but the disaster relief agency had the money Mark would need to put his evacuation plan into effect. Clearing out the Superdome forty people at a time would require at least 650 buses, possibly more. "I can't do this with a dozen buses," Mark told FEMA's top transportation official in Baton Rouge. "I need hundreds of them." The FEMA official, to Mark's enormous relief, picked up his phone and began calling dozens of Gulf Coast school districts and commercial touring companies. Within days FEMA had contracted for a veritable armada of school buses and white and black luxury vehicles from companies that normally shuttled well-heeled tourists to New Orleans's famed French Quarter and the casinos and resorts of the Gulf Coast. Now Mark needed to figure out the best way of using the buses.

Mark was walking through the operations center in Baton Rouge a short time later when he saw a handful of men in civilian clothes passing around high-resolution satellite photos of New Orleans. He asked if their images could provide an estimate of how deep the floodwaters were near the Superdome. One of the men, a professor from Louisiana State University, said the street closest to the stadium itself appeared to be covered by at least a foot of water, way too high for a bus to drive through, but that the water in front of the hotel looked a bit shallower. Mark radioed one of his aides at the Superdome and told him to walk across the footbridge to the Marriott lobby and measure the depth of the water on the street there. The officer radioed back in a few minutes: The water covering the street in front of the hotel was about seven inches deep. FEMA's top transportation official was standing nearby, and Mark motioned him over.

"That kind of water, can a bus make it through?' Mark asked. "Is it still too high?'

"That close to a foot of water is really pushing it," the official replied, pausing as he chose his next words carefully. "But in an emergency like this a good driver can probably make it work."

There was no question that the situation at the Superdome was an emergency. Unless it was handled discreetly, Mark worried that the arrival of the buses could set off a riot as desperate refugees jostled with one another for seats. Other crowds might block the buses and refuse to budge unless they were allowed to squeeze onboard. It was even possible that armed refugees would simply try to force—or shoot—their way on. "I didn't want it to be a 'last helicopter out of Saigon' moment," Mark said.

Operating on pure adrenaline, Mark decided to take a page from the military's handbook. Soldiers waiting at army airfields for combat missions or flights to other bases are divided into "chalks," groupings of twelve to twenty troops who are assigned to a specific inbound helicopter or airplane. That allows the troops to board as soon as an aircraft touches down because they know exactly which plane or chopper they're meant to use. Mark put a similar system in place at the Superdome. He ordered the police officers and National Guard personnel at the ruined stadium to divide each group of four hundred refugees into ten sets of about forty people each, and then had FEMA send a convoy of ten buses at a time toward the Marriott. When they arrived at the stadium, armed soldiers made sure that each set of refugees boarded its designated bus as quickly as possible and sped away. The *Times-Picayune* estimated that 828 buses ultimately made their way to and from the stadium over the next two days, evacuating forty-one thousand refugees who had either spent the storm at the Superdome or begun streaming there when they saw the rescue vehicles begin to arrive. No one died or was seriously injured.

Mark's discovery of an alternate route out of the Superdome was one of the most important early victories in the frantic effort to evacuate stranded refugees from New Orleans before crime or disease pushed the storm's death toll even higher. Honoré was the face of the recovery effort and received well-deserved public acclaim for imposing a sense of order and cutting through red tape to free up as many military and civilian aid resources as possible. Mark operated in the shadows, but Honoré and other top officials involved in the rescue say that Mark's role was vital to the city's salvation. He and his team also organized the evacuation of the Ernest N. Morial Convention Center, where five thousand more refugees had been stranded for days without food or water, diabetics had collapsed because of a lack of insulin, and the corpses of several dead women had been left to rot in the sun. Mark also arranged for the thousands of people who'd taken shelter at the Louis Armstrong New Orleans International Airport—sleeping on conveyor belts and raiding fast-food restaurants for supplies—to be moved to formal evacuation sites.

By Sunday, September 4, the Superdome, convention center, and airport had all been emptied out, and Mark began taking some time to walk the streets of New Orleans and see Katrina's devastation for himself. He had read dozens of briefing papers, stayed in daily contact with army troops on the ground, and examined detailed satellite imagery of the city. Still, nothing fully prepared him for what he saw on those trips: a massive fishing boat carried by the floodwaters more than a mile inland before being unceremoniously dumped; a multistory house sheared clean off its cement foundation and sent careening into a row of other buildings before coming to rest several blocks away; abandoned police cars and ambulances bobbing in the water like bathtub toys, some with their sirens still blaring. "I kept reminding myself that this wasn't Iraq and this wasn't Afghanistan," Mark said. "It was America, and that was a very hard thing to wrap my arms around."

Seeing the human toll of the storm up close was even harder. Mark watched rescue workers carry black bags holding the remains of New Orleanians who had drowned or been crushed to death. He walked past homes that had *x*'s scrawled on their doors—to indicate that the structures had been searched—and hand-drawn numbers indicating the number of corpses found inside. "People had lived there with their families, and all that was left of them was that *x* and that number," Mark said.

The National Hurricane Center later estimated that Katrina killed more than eighteen hundred people along the Gulf Coast, mainly in and around New Orleans, and caused an estimated $108 billion of damage. It was the costliest storm in American history and one of the deadliest natural disasters in decades. Honoré said more people would have died if Mark hadn't figured out how to safely evacuate the Superdome, convention center, and airport, the three most visible symbols of the federal, state, and city governments' inept initial response to the storm. Clark, the Army North commander, said his deputy was "the unsung hero of Katrina."

"He jumped right into all of the chaos at the Superdome and began to set things right," Clark said. "There were a thousand things he did to manage that situation there and reassure people that they were going to be taken care of. He figured out how to empty the building, but giving a psychological boost to the people of New Orleans at that exact moment was just as important."

Mark returned to San Antonio in the fall of 2005 after nearly three months in southern Louisiana. Carol had undertaken a mission of her own while he was away. Fort Sam Houston housed the Brooke Army Medical Center, or BAMC, the military's primary hospital for treating troops with severe, life-threatening burns. Many patients returned from Iraq or Afghanistan disfigured so badly that they were unrecognizable to their loved ones and to themselves. The wounded troops often needed dozens of operations and skin grafts. Their spouses, parents, and children visited Brooke as often as possible, but most lived far from Texas and couldn't be there for all of the surgeries. That meant the war-shattered troops had no one at their side as they underwent countless operations and tried to adjust to their new bodies. Carol visited Brooke one afternoon and couldn't get the images of the burned and maimed young men out of her mind. Many of them had been wounded by the same kind of roadside bomb that killed Jeff. The thought that her son could have been lying in that same hospital, alone and in pain, broke her heart. Carol began visiting the hospital a few times per week to check in on the soldiers and try to console their relatives and friends. She was soon there nearly every day, often arriving early in the morning and staying late into the night. Mark joined her whenever he could, slipping a sterile gown over his military uniform so he could spend time talking to the soldiers in the intensive care unit who were able to have a conversation or silently pray alongside those who were comatose and barely clinging to life. "Carol basically just moved into that hospital," said Carol Triesch, another regular visitor to Brooke. "She immersed herself in these soldiers' pain to help with her own. Carol seemed to believe that doing that kind of work would bring her close to Kevin and Jeff again."

The two Carols formed close friendships with a pair of young troops who had suffered unusually gruesome wounds, even for Brooke. Army sergeant Kevin Downs was a member of the Tennessee National Guard who had been a track star in high school. Earlier that year his Humvee had been on a routine patrol in northeastern Iraq when it struck a powerful IED. The three other soldiers inside the Humvee—all close friends and fellow members of the Tennessee Guard—died instantly. Downs survived, but barely. He lost both legs and the use of one arm and one hand. The fire sparked by the blast seared away most of the skin on his face and left him with burns over 60 percent of his body. The military doctors who treated him in Iraq and Germany didn't expect Downs, then twenty years old, to make it, and they told his family to prepare for the worst. But the young man proved them wrong, fighting his way through dozens of excruciating surgeries and skin grafts. The two Carols took turns spending hours in his room when Downs's own parents weren't able to make the trip to San Antonio for one of the operations. "We didn't want that young boy to be in there alone," Carol Graham said. Downs would eventually recover enough that he could move back to his native Tennessee, find a job, and get married.

The two women also began spending long stretches of time with Marine Sergeant Merlin German, an outgoing New Yorker who dreamed of returning home from Iraq and either modeling or joining the FBI. On February 21, 2005, German was standing in the turret of his Humvee when an IED went off, hurling him from the vehicle with his body on fire. German suffered severe burns over 97 percent of his body before other marines managed to stamp out the flames. German, like Downs, hadn't been expected to make it, but he eventually regained the ability to talk, walk, and even dance. The young marine had the same birthday as Kevin Graham, and Mark and Melanie made a point of visiting him whenever

Mark and Carol in the main sanctuary of First United Methodist Church in Frankfort, Kentucky, on their wedding day, August 13, 1977.

Photo courtesy of Mark and Carol Graham

The Grahams at Fort Sill in September 1984. Melanie (left) and Kevin (right) were each born at the sprawling Oklahoma base.

Photo courtesy of Mark and Carol Graham

Mark and Carol in Augsburg, Germany, in December 1990. Mark would deploy to the Middle East for the Gulf War less than two weeks later.

Photo courtesy of Mark and Carol Graham

Melanie, Jeff, and Kevin in Baumholder, Germany, in spring 1992. The three Graham children were extraordinarily close as they grew up, a bond that helped them deal with the challenges of constantly having to make new friends whenever the family moved to a new army base.

Photo courtesy of Mark and Carol Graham

Jeff, Melanie, and Kevin at the Great Wall of China on New Year's 2001. The three Graham children lived together at the University of Kentucky, a testament to the bond between them. This picture is one of the last Mark and Carol have of their children together. *Photo courtesy of Mark and Carol Graham*

The Grahams at First United Methodist Church, May 11, 2003. Kevin, Melanie, and Jeff (back row) are standing with Bill Conrad, Mark's stepfather, while Mark stands next to his mother, Pat, and Carol's mother, Jackie Shroat. *Photo courtesy of Mark and Carol Graham*

Mark and Carol at Colorado's Fort Carson in early 2009 holding the folded flags they received after the deaths of their two sons. They are among the family's most cherished possessions. *Matt Slaby*

The Grahams at Jeff's burial in Frankfort, Kentucky, on February 28, 2004. His fiancée, Stacey Martinez (center), clutches a custom-made teddy bear Jeff had given her before deploying. It played a recording of his voice: "I just want to say that I'm safe and that I love you very much and I'll see you soon." *Mark Cornelison*/Herald-Leader

Melanie's wedding to Joe Quinn at West Point's Cadet Chapel on July 9, 2011. Mark thanked everyone there for being with them "during some of our bumpiest times." *Photo courtesy of Mark and Carol Graham*

Stefanie and Mike Pelkey on their wedding day in Shady Oaks, Texas, in the summer of 2002. Mark had chosen Mike to be his executive officer, but the young army captain—haunted by nightmares from his time in Iraq—killed himself days before he was supposed to start the job. *Photo courtesy of Stefanie Pelkey*

Benjamin Pelkey, the only son of Mike and Stefanie Pelkey, kissing his father's headstone in Wolcott, Connecticut, in July 2008. It was the first time Benjamin, now eleven, had visited his grave. *Photo courtesy of Stefanie Pelkey*

Then defense secretary Bob Gates and then chairman of the Joint Chiefs of Staff Admiral Mike Mullen at the Pentagon on September 23, 2010. The two men worked to make it easier for troubled soldiers to seek and receive help. In an interview for this book, Gates said that he feared the military's suicide problem would get worse in the years ahead. *Jim Garamone*

Then army general Pete Chiarelli at a memorial service in Indianapolis, Indiana, on May 27, 2011. When one of Chiarelli's men killed himself in Iraq, the general left the soldier's name off of a unit memorial wall. Years later he described himself as a "Neanderthal" when it came to military mental health and helped lead the army's efforts to reduce stigma and prevent soldiers from taking their own lives. *Sergeant John Crosby*

Then colonel Randy George in the eastern Afghanistan province of Nangarhar on October 11, 2009. A battle-hardened combat veteran, George would become one of Mark's closest allies in his push to bring Fort Carson's sky-high suicide rate under control and develop new ways of honoring troops who killed themselves. *Private First Class Elizabeth Raney*

The graves of Kevin and Jeff Graham, who were buried next to each other in a cemetery in Frankfort, Kentucky. Carol's mother visits the site every few days to tidy up and think about the lives—and deaths—of her grandsons. "I have to re-mind myself that they're not really here," she said after one trip. "But it comforts me to know that they're together again." *Photo courtesy of Mark and Carol Graham*

they could. Carol helped organize his twenty-first birthday party and began to grow worried when German was close to an hour late. He finally came into the room, smiling broadly. "Where's the beer?" he joked. German survived more than one hundred operations but eventually died from a seemingly minor infection in his lip. Carol flew to San Antonio the day after his death to comfort German's parents and siblings. "I loved him so much that I felt like I was losing a third son," she said.

When she wasn't at Brooke, Carol hired a trio of handymen to hang pictures in the new family home at Fort Sam Houston, set up the TV and stereo, and rearrange the furniture until everything was in its correct place. It was fairly expensive, but Carol considered it to be money well spent. She wanted to make sure the new family home was completely furnished and decorated before her husband returned from Louisiana and walked through the front door for the first time. "I wanted him to come back to a home, not just a strange house full of boxes everywhere," she said.

Mark's service during Katrina earned him the Humanitarian Service Medal, one of the military's top honors, and put him on the fast track for another promotion. The water that had submerged New Orleans in the summer of 2005 had finally receded, paving the way for reconstruction and renewal. The dark waves that were about to wash over the army were just beginning to gather strength.

Jennifer Wright was terrified. It was January 2002, and her husband, a Special Forces soldier named William "Bill" Wright, had done one tour in Afghanistan, the scene of the nation's newest war, and was preparing to deploy again. The Wrights' marriage was on the rocks, and Jennifer had quietly started a new relationship with the choir director of her church. She started to receive threatening letters and phone calls warning her to stay away from her new love interest. They were all anonymous, but

Jennifer told friends that she thought they'd come from Bill. A short time later she was at home when her burglar alarms started blaring. Jennifer looked outside and saw someone prowling through her backyard in the darkness. She called the police, but they couldn't find any evidence of an attempted break-in. Two months later, in March 2002, Bill Wright left for Afghanistan. Friends thought that Jennifer, thirty-two, looked happier than she had in years.

Bill returned in late May a changed man. He had deployed to the war zone as a shy, even-keeled soldier who largely stayed away from alcohol. He came back to Fort Bragg, the headquarters of the army's elite Special Forces and Ranger units, as a heavy drinker who erupted into sudden bouts of rage. Before he left, Bill had told Jennifer that he wanted a divorce. When he came home, he began pleading with her to stay with him. It was too late. Jennifer had packed up all of Bill's clothes during his deployment and carried them into the garage. In late June, according to a detailed account in *Vanity Fair,* Jennifer presented her husband with separation papers. She had just days to live.

On June 29, Bill unlocked the back door of his house and walked into the master bedroom he'd once shared with his wife. They began arguing about the divorce, and Bill felt a sudden flash of white-hot fury. He grabbed a baseball bat and smashed Jennifer in the head. When she fell to the ground, he strangled her to death, rolled her body into a parachute kit bag, and buried her in a wooded area near Fort Bragg where he and his friends had occasionally hunted squirrels. Bill reported Jennifer missing on July 1. On July 19, shortly after the police asked him to take a polygraph test, he confessed to killing his wife and took the police to the spot in the forest where he'd hidden her.

Lieutenant Sam Pennica of the Cumberland County Sheriff's Department was waiting in the forest for a coroner to come pick up Jennifer's body that evening when his cell phone rang. Pennica, according to *Vanity Fair,* turned to his colleagues. "We got another one," he said.

Local police had just found the bodies of Sergeant First Class Brandon Floyd, a commando from the army's secretive Delta Force who had recently returned from Afghanistan, and his wife, Andrea. Coroners concluded that Brandon had shot Andrea, the mother of his three children, before putting the gun to his own temple and pulling the trigger. The Floyd murder-suicide came just six weeks after another Special Forces veteran, army sergeant Rigoberto Nieves, shot his wife, Teresa, in the bedroom of their brand-new home and then took his own life. Like Wright and Floyd, Nieves had completed a stint in Afghanistan just weeks earlier.

The Fort Bragg killings were early harbingers of the suicide epidemic that would erupt when the Iraq War began in 2003 and then gain strength as that war and the war in Afghanistan dragged on. In the decades after Vietnam, senior Pentagon officials prided themselves on overseeing a force of soldiers who were better adjusted, mentally and psychologically, than their civilian counterparts. The nation's top military officials were particularly proud of the army's suicide rate, which was significantly lower than the national average. In 2001, the year al-Qaida brought down the World Trade Center and set the nation on a path toward war, the national suicide rate for civilian men between the ages of eighteen and twenty-four—the demographic segment that most closely mirrors the composition of the military—was 19.64 per 100,000. The military rate was just 9.0 per 100,000 soldiers—the lowest the army had seen since it began tracking suicide two decades earlier. It was a period of calm before the storm, and it wouldn't last much longer.

Joseph Suell was a small-town boy from tiny Lufkin, Texas, who loved three things in life: his wife, his young daughters, and the U.S. Army. Suell had enlisted right out of high school, a decision that angered his mother and stunned the rest of the family. He was the son of a minister and a deeply devout Christian who believed that hell was real and that suicide was a sin. He was also a gentle and romantic young man who drew hearts on the letters he sent home to his wife and told her that he was counting down the days until he'd be able to return.

Suell left for Iraq in April 2003, just weeks after U.S. forces stormed into the country, and almost immediately felt a desperate need to return to his family. "This place is not for me," Suell wrote in a letter home. He asked his wife to contact his commanding officer to see if she could persuade him to send Suell back early. Rebecca Suell told her husband's boss about how difficult it was for her to raise their daughters while simultaneously attending nursing school and working at Walmart. Her husband, she said, had missed the birth of his youngest daughter and barely knew her sister. All he wanted, Rebecca told the officer, was to be home with his family for Christmas. He'd return to Iraq right after. Suell's commander told her that he would try to get her husband home for the holiday but couldn't make any promises.

"The commander said, 'We'll do everything that we can to get your husband home, it'll take a while'—they ignored it," Rebecca Suell told the *Washington Post* at the time. "If he just had some time with his family, he'd still be here."

A few weeks later, on Father's Day, Suell swallowed an entire bottle of Tylenol at his base in Iraq and died a short time after. The army classified his death as a suicide and ruled that he had intentionally overdosed. There were reasons to doubt that conclusion. Suell hadn't been taking Lariam, a controversial antimalarial drug that had been linked to a spate of suicides. He hadn't given his family any indication that he was depressed enough to take his own life. In his letters home, he still sounded like the religious young man who'd headed off to war just weeks earlier armed with an unshakable Christian faith. "Over here you never know what's going to happen next," he wrote to his mother-in-law. "So I just keep faith in Jesus and keep my eyes open." Suell had no history of mental illness and had been making concrete plans for his future. He and Rebecca had gotten married by a justice of the peace in a sterile room at the Lufkin City Hall. When he returned, Suell promised his wife, they would do a full church wedding, with all of the pomp and ceremony. They never got the chance.

Suell, twenty-five, was one of the first U.S. soldiers to kill himself in Iraq, but he was far from the only one. Private First Class Corey Small arrived in Iraq in May 2003 and was deployed to an abandoned hospital in Baghdad that had no running water or electricity. Outside temperatures soared to more than 120 degrees Fahrenheit during the day, and Small, a Pennsylvania native, had a hard time writing letters home because his hand kept sticking to the paper. "I sweat constantly, even when I am sitting still," he wrote in a June 15 letter to his grandmother. On July 2, less than three weeks later, Small was on the phone with his wife when other soldiers suddenly heard him start yelling at her about money. Seconds later, he dropped the receiver, placed a gun to his head, and pulled the trigger. Amanda Small heard a gunshot and then the sound of something heavy hitting the floor.

The suicides in Iraq began piling up, one tragedy following another. On September 15, an army interrogator named Alyssa Peterson shot herself after telling friends that she felt U.S. troops were torturing Iraqi prisoners. Two weeks later a young soldier named Dustin McGaugh shot himself at the Balad Air Base, one of the largest U.S. bases in Iraq. Their deaths, like those of Suell and Small, were largely lost in the waves of press coverage about the military's inability to find weapons of mass destruction in Iraq and the beginnings of the country's descent into civil war. Still, there were warning signs of what lay ahead. In October the military-affiliated newspaper *Stars and Stripes* reported that half of the troops surveyed in Iraq said their unit's morale was low and that roughly a third characterized the war as adding little to no value to the national security of the United States. Thirteen soldiers and marines had taken their own lives in Iraq at the time the survey was published, mostly by shooting themselves with their military-issued weapons. Two months later, the tally had climbed to twenty.

Senior Pentagon officials were slow to acknowledge the suicide problem and quick to underestimate its severity. On February 25, 2004, Dr. William Winkenwerder, the Pentagon's assistant secretary of defense for health affairs, told a House Armed Services Committee panel that 21 soldiers had taken their own lives since the start of the Iraq War, putting the military's suicide rate for the conflict at 15.8 per 100,000 soldiers. Between 1995 and 2002, the military's average rate was just 11.9 suicides per 100,000 soldiers. Still, Winkenwerder said, the high numbers from the new war weren't indicative of a broader problem. "While every suicide is a tragic loss, the suicide rate for soldiers deployed to [Iraq] is not significantly different from the range of recent annual army suicide rates," Winkenwerder testified.

The numbers quickly became hard to ignore. In 2004, 67 soldiers took their own lives. In 2005, the year Mark Graham led the evacuation of New Orleans, 87 soldiers committed suicide, more than quadruple the number of suicides in 2003. Those figures would increase sharply every year of the two wars. By 2012, more soldiers were dying by their own hand than in combat. Suicide effectively became the army's third war, and it was a conflict the military was singularly ill prepared to fight. Decades of chronic underfunding meant that the Pentagon had thousands of unfilled slots for psychologists and psychiatrists when the conflicts in Iraq and Afghanistan began. Those shortages forced some returning soldiers to wait months for an appointment, an eternity for those wrestling with the demons of depression, PTSD, and traumatic brain injury, or TBI, which is caused when the brain is injured by an external force like an impact or explosion. Military mental health professionals, meanwhile, started quitting in droves because they couldn't handle the constant strain of trying to treat so many troops with so few resources. That made the waiting times even longer. In several cases, troops who'd sought help were given such long waits that they killed themselves in the interim. Mark would sometimes stay awake at night haunted by his failure to spot Mike Pelkey's deterioration or use his powers as a general to help Mike bypass Fort Sill's backlog and get help in time. "We were not prepared for the flood of PTS and TBI cases," retired admiral Mike Mullen, the former chairman of the Joint Chiefs of Staff, said in an interview for this book. "We were, and remain, badly understaffed in mental health professionals."

The soldiers who even bothered to reach out for help were very much the exception. Many troubled troops, no matter how severe their PTSD, tried to hide the symptoms from their fellow soldiers. The primary message they absorbed in basic training, ROTC, and military academies such as West Point was that mental illness was a sign of weakness, and that weak soldiers had no place in the army. Those beliefs were so widely held throughout the army that roughly 75 percent of the troops surveyed by groups such as the American Psychiatric Association told pollsters that they wouldn't seek help because they were afraid it would make their colleagues think less of them, harm their chances for promotion, or bring their military careers to a premature end. They were right to worry: hundreds of soldiers were hazed or drummed out of the army after others found out they had sought assistance or begun taking psychiatric medication. Kevin Graham could easily have been one of them. He would almost certainly have been kicked out of ROTC if anyone had discovered that he was on antidepressants, and the risks to his career would have increased if Kevin had managed to finish the program and enter the army. The pervasive stigma surrounding mental health issues made a bad problem worse. Growing numbers of troubled soldiers killed themselves in Iraq or came home and committed suicide in front of their loved ones. Sometimes, like at Fort Bragg, they killed their wives or children first. Many of those soldiers had known they needed help, but they were too afraid to ask for it. The military's toughest adversary as the suicide numbers started spiking was its own macho culture.

CHAPTER 14

Fort Carson, Colorado, May 2006

Private Tyler Jennings was ready to die. A burly former football player, Jennings had spent a year battling Sunni militants at a small outpost near where Jeff Graham was killed. He watched friends get killed and maimed by the same types of hidden bombs that had taken Jeff's life just two years earlier. One soldier from Jennings's unit was decapitated and cut in half by a bomb that tore through the young man's Humvee; the force of the blast threw another soldier into the steering wheel of the armored truck with such force that it left his corpse crumpled like a piece of paper. A close friend, Private First Class Samuel Lee, shot himself in the head at an army barracks in Iraq. Jennings returned home tormented by memories of the carnage he'd seen and by nightmares so vivid that he rolled over in bed some nights, put his hands around his wife's neck, and started squeezing down until she woke him up. On a cool night in May he decided to end his suffering. Jennings, then twenty-three, tied an orange extension cord around his neck, opened the window of his apartment, and stepped out onto the ledge. He chugged a bottle of vodka to calm his nerves and looked down at the pavement below, ready to jump.

Jennings's path to the ledge began with the horrors of Iraq, but it didn't end with them. Five months earlier, Jennings had visited Fort Carson's medical center seeking help with his nightmares and flashbacks. A hospital staffer wrote that Jennings had reported bouts of "crying spells, hopelessness, helplessness, worthlessness," all textbook symptoms of PTSD. The diagnosis didn't win him any sympathy from his bosses or fellow soldiers. Sergeants from Jennings's unit ordered him to spend twenty-four straight hours at Fort Carson in what one of his noncommissioned officers described to National Public Radio, which did several detailed reports about Jennings's case, as a "dunce's corner." They promised to get him kicked out of the military. Jennings had won a Purple Heart in Iraq, but lower-ranking soldiers accused him of faking his symptoms to avoid being sent back to war. They ignored him when he walked by and called him a "shitbag" to his face. "He's an outcast now," Corey Davis, who served with Jennings in Iraq, said at the time. "He's not even looked at. I mean no one looks at him, no one talks to him, no one said hi to him. He's not there. He's invisible."

The threats and bullying so rattled Jennings that he decided to take his own life. In the end, he was too drunk to carry through with it. He walked back into the apartment, shut the window, and promptly passed out. "You know, there were many times I've told my wife—in just a state of panic, and just being so upset—that I really wished I just died [in Iraq]," he told NPR. " 'Cause if you just die over there, everyone writes you off as a hero."

At Fort Carson, by contrast, Jennings was seen as a weakling unworthy of wearing the army's uniform. When he woke up the morning after he'd stepped out onto his apartment ledge, Jennings phoned one of his sergeants to say that he'd come close to killing himself and needed to skip that day's formation so he could check himself into the base's psychiatric ward. That was exactly what the army said that it wants suicidal soldiers to do, but Jennings's commanders instead tried to have him arrested for missing the drill. A civilian doctor said Jennings was suffering from

severe PTSD, but the military rejected that diagnosis. And when a urinalysis came back positive—Jennings's doctor said he'd begun drinking
and taking drugs to help deal with the PTSD and depression he'd carried
back from Iraq—the army had all it needed to get rid of him. Jennings
was discharged for "patterns of misconduct," which left him ineligible
for free military-provided medical care for life, a pension, or the benefits
offered by the GI Bill. The army said such discharges can also "result in
substantial prejudice in your civilian life," effectively making it harder
for soldiers like Jennings to find private-sector jobs to replace the military ones they lost.

Other soldiers from Jennings's unit had also sought help, and they
were punished in much the same way. Private Alex Orum began drinking heavily, suffering from horrific nightmares, and lashing out at his
wife almost immediately after returning to Fort Carson in August 2005.
In Iraq his fellow soldiers said he was one of the toughest and most com-
petent men in their unit; at home his wife said he had changed so much
that she couldn't bear living with him and wanted a divorce. Orum visited the mental health ward at Fort Carson's hospital and told staffers
there that he was having trouble sleeping and couldn't hear loud noises
without immediately flashing back to his time in Ramadi and diving to
the floor in a defense crouch. He was diagnosed with chronic PTSD. When
one of Orum's sergeants found out about the visit, he quietly passed the
information around to others in the unit. Orum's fellow soldiers, in turn,
began mocking him to his face as a "psycho" and a "coward." They dinged
him for relatively minor infractions such as missing formations, failing to
carry a pen and notebook, coming to work disheveled, missing rent pay-
ments, and otherwise mishandling his personal finances. Each of those
failings could easily be traced to his PTSD, but the army instead booted
Orum out for "patterns of misconduct," just as it did with Jennings. One
of Orum's sergeants, Nathan Towsley, told NPR that he had simply grown
tired of trying to help Orum deal with what he termed daily "personal

problems." "I think some people are just weak," Towsley said of Orum. "You know, you just have to buck up and be a man and face it."

Orum said at the time that Towsley's views were widely shared in his unit and made him realize that troops suffering from PTSD faced a clear choice: Avoid getting help and risk exacerbating their PTSD, or seek treatment and risk missing out on chances for promotion or being drummed out of the military altogether. "You really don't want to be that guy going up to mental health when you're trying to be a career soldier," William Morris, another soldier from the unit, said at the time. "You don't want to be that guy because as soon as you are, you're done."

For decades, many in the military derided the soldiers who claimed to be suffering from PTSD as fakers and cowards. Those kinds of troops, skeptics felt, were simply trying to find excuses for their own personal failings or fears about being sent off to war. Real warriors kept their problems to themselves or found ways of fighting through them on their own. The troops who couldn't or wouldn't do so weren't worthy of promotion, the respect of their peers, or the privilege of serving in the United States Army. That belief system wasn't unique to Fort Carson, or to veterans of the wars in Iraq and Afghanistan. It was called stigma, and it would become the enemy that Mark and Carol Graham would fight the hardest to defeat.

The sounds of the cannon blast echoed between the redbrick buildings of the Walter Reed Army Medical Center, the military's flagship hospital. It was 2005, and the century-old medical facility was struggling to keep pace with the thousands of veterans who had begun returning from Iraq and Afghanistan with PTSD or other emotional and psychological problems. Most of them were extraordinarily sensitive to loud noises, so the cannon blasts that marked the formal start of each new day at Walter Reed triggered unsettling memories of the explosions, ambushes, or carnage that had hospitalized them in the first place. The hospital's medical staff pleaded with Walter Reed's top military officials to silence the cannon, but they got nowhere. The base's commanders argued that Walter Reed, like any army post, needed to abide by the military protocols mandating that each morning begin with soldiers raising the American flag, snapping to attention, and standing in formation until the cannon blast sounded. Dr. John Bradley, a retired army colonel who was the head of Walter Reed's psychiatry program at the time, said that the hospital's top military doctor repeatedly petitioned its military commander to end the practice, only to be rebuffed each time. At a certain point the medical staff decided to take matters into their own hands. "Our hospital commander actually disabled the cannon so it couldn't fire," he said.

The fight at Walter Reed was emblematic of a broader vicious circle within the military. Troubled soldiers were encouraged to admit that they had PTSD and seek help. Those who did, however, were forced to confront a system run by officers and sergeants who were either insensitive to them or openly hostile. Many of the troops were denied promotions and encouraged to leave the army voluntarily as soon as their time was up. Research by military and civilian medical personnel suggests that more than 150,000 Iraq and Afghanistan veterans who were diagnosed with PTSD have refused to ask for counseling because they decided that it was simply too dangerous for them to admit they had a problem.

Stigma wasn't a new problem for the military. A 1998 Department of Defense survey found that 80 percent of active-duty army troops believed that seeking mental health counseling would harm their careers. The army investigative team that had been sent to Fort Bragg after the 2002 murder-suicides found that many soldiers there believed that seeking treatment through the military mental health system would be "detrimental, and often terminal" to their chances for promotion. Desperate soldiers, the report notes, felt that the only safe way of getting help was by "going downtown," army slang for leaving the base and speaking with civilian doctors rather than military ones. Later studies found that troops who were given complete anonymity were two to four times more likely to admit to depression, PTSD, or suicidal thoughts in written questionnaires than troops who were required to use their real names.

The military has spent years trying to persuade soldiers that they could seek help without risking their careers, but those efforts have yielded only mixed results. An army survey in 2003, for instance, found that 49 percent of the soldiers who screened positive for PTSD worried that they'd lose the confidence of their peers if they sought mental health counseling. The military spent tens of millions of dollars on new anti-stigma training for all of its troops, which brought the numbers down slightly. Seven years later, however, 41.8 percent of its at-risk soldiers still had that fear. Retired admiral Mike Mullen said in an interview for this book that stigma was "embedded" deep within the culture of the military itself. Troubled soldiers, Mullen said, have long feared both personal and professional consequences if they admit they have problems and seek assistance. "The career concern is a huge one in the military, where the perceived threat is that we could lose our security clearance—a professional death sentence," he said.

That wasn't an irrational fear. Question 21 on the military's security clearance form explicitly asked troops if they had consulted with mental health professionals or sought help for a mental health–related condition at any point over the previous seven years. Mullen and then defense secretary Bob Gates worried that troubled soldiers were refusing to seek help because they were afraid they'd lose their clearances if they answered question 21 honestly. They began lobbying to eliminate it. "I thought at the start, 'Well, we're just not going to use that question anymore,'" Gates said today. "I was very naïve."

When Bob Gates was a college student in the early 1960s, he and his friends had little sympathy for those suffering from mental or psychological illness. A Kansan by birth, the future secretary of defense went to the College of William and Mary in Virginia, the second-oldest school in the country. Virginia's Eastern State Hospital, one of the state's primary facilities for the treatment of mental illness, was located a few blocks from the campus. When visitors stopped and asked for directions to the school, Gates and his friends would jokingly direct them to the hospital instead. Gates, like most Americans of his generation, referred to it as an insane asylum. "Growing up, you were either crazy or you weren't," Gates said in an interview for this book. "It was kind of black and white."

Gates developed a more nuanced view of mental health when he took over the Pentagon in December 2006. It was the height of the Iraq War, and the situation on the ground in Afghanistan was steadily deteriorating. Hundreds of Americans were dying in the two war zones—more than one thousand were killed in Gates's first year on the job alone—and tens of thousands were suffering horrific physical and psychological wounds. Pete Chiarelli, Gates's top military advisor at the time, alerted him to the military's growing suicide problem. Digging into the issue, Gates concluded that question 21 was keeping some suicidal troops from seeking help before it was too late. It needed to go, but getting rid of it proved to be much harder than Gates had expected. The defense chief hadn't initially realized that question 21 was used across the entire federal government, not just the military, which meant that getting rid of it—or even modifying the language—required him to win over a broad swath of other senior officials. The fiercest pushback came from the Central Intelligence Agency, an organization that Gates had led in the early 1990s, and the rest of the intelligence community. The agencies argued that the provision was necessary to prevent individuals with lingering psychological problems—particularly those taking prescription medications that could theoretically impair their judgment—from having access to classified materials.

President Bush eventually weighed in on behalf of Gates and Mullen, and the two men struck a compromise with the CIA and the nation's other intelligence agencies. In May 2008, after nearly a year of intensive lobbying, Gates publicly announced that what he described as the "infamous question 21" would remain in place, but with a significant change: Troops would no longer have to disclose prior mental health treatment unless it had been court-ordered or involved past episodes of violence. That meant that soldiers who had sought counseling after their wartime service in Iraq or Afghanistan no longer had to worry that acknowledging it on the form would threaten their careers.

Other policies, however, continue to give troops reasons to think twice before openly seeking help. The air force bars pilots with PTSD from flying, so being diagnosed with the disorder can end or derail careers. The policy applies to both men and women, but male pilots rarely experience the kind of physical or emotional trauma that can lead to PTSD because they fly high above the battlefields and don't see the carnage below. Female pilots, by contrast, routinely develop PTSD after being raped or sexually assaulted. That means they are effectively harmed twice over, once by the initial assault and once by the subsequent loss of their ability to fly. The air force does allow pilots who have been symptom-free for six months to apply for an "aeromedical waiver" and return to flight status, but PTSD is an unpredictable injury whose manifestations can recur at any time.

Seeking help for PTSD can have other, more insidious ways of threatening a soldier's professional future. Mark Graham routinely heard senior military officers say that soldiers were faking the invisible wound so they could get out of the army or avoid being sent back to Iraq and Afghanistan. Some of Mark's colleagues told him that they'd intentionally tried to get soldiers who'd been diagnosed with PTSD transferred out of their units and replaced with what the officers saw as healthier and tougher troops.

Carol, for her part, was waiting in line at a behavioral health clinic at Fort Sill once when a drill sergeant ordered a handful of young soldiers to stand up and give her a seat. "You're all a bunch of fakers and crybabies anyway," he shouted.

Carol couldn't quite believe what she was hearing. Noncommissioned officers such as the drill sergeant were the backbone of the army and the ones who did the most to shape young men and women into soldiers. If troops at the very start of their careers were taught that seeking help was a sign of weakness, she wondered, how would they ever learn to think about mental health any differently? She reached into her purse, pulled out photos of Kevin and Jeff, and angrily told the drill sergeant that he had no way of knowing whether any of his soldiers needed counseling or other forms of assistance. Years later, she remains shaken by the entire experience. The drill sergeant, she said today, was delivering "the wrong message to the wrong audience."

Some senior officers convey an even more damaging message through what they choose to keep quiet, not what they choose to say. The military has been at war for more than thirteen years, but virtually no generals or admirals were willing to admit that they'd suffered the same kinds of PTSD and depression as their troops. In a rank-conscious organization such as the military, that sent a simple and dangerous message: If you want to get promoted, keep your mouth shut. "In order to make strides in eliminating stigma, leadership must step forward and acknowledge their own [post-traumatic stress] while setting the example by visibly seeking help," Mullen said. "Some officers have done this, but far too few."

Gates was one of the senior officials who remained silent. Obama had asked Gates to stay on through the end of his second term, but the defense chief said no. He was haunted by the nearly three thousand condolence letters he'd written and by memories of the thousands of young soldiers and marines he'd visited in military hospitals around the world as they recovered from losing limbs or suffering hideous burns on the battlefields of Iraq and Afghanistan. The emotional toll was so heavy, Gates worried that he had suffered invisible wounds of his own.

"I think that there's a form of post-traumatic stress for those who are not directly involved in the battle but who see the consequences of the battle," he said in an interview two years after leaving the Pentagon. "I began to wonder, frankly, toward the end of my time, whether I had some measure of it myself."

It was supposed to be his last mission. David Blackledge, then a one-star general charged with overseeing army civil affairs programs throughout Iraq, was on his way to a meeting with local tribal leaders in Iskandariyah, an ancient city south of Baghdad, when militants hiding alongside the road began firing on his three-vehicle convoy from several directions. Blackledge and his men had chosen to make the trip in Ford Explorers, which were far less conspicuous than military Humvees but carried no armor plating. The bullets punched through the doors of the SUVs, shattering the windows and windshields and sending shards of glass ricocheting through the truck like miniature razor blades. Blackledge, who was sitting in the front passenger seat, grabbed his assault rifle and twisted around to return fire through the wreckage of the back window. He was sure that he was about to die, and he wanted to go down fighting.

Blackledge's driver had a different goal in mind. He wanted to get the general and the other men in the truck out of the insurgent kill zone as quickly as possible, so he floored the accelerator and sent the Explorer rocketing down the road. The driver made it less than five hundred yards before losing control of the truck and sending it flipping through the air. The Explorer came to rest on the other side of the highway, its roof collapsed and its engine smoking. The two men who'd been sitting in the back of the truck—army captain John Smathers and an Iraqi translator named Salah—were lying motionless on the pavement. Salah had been shot through the back of his head and killed instantly. Blackledge assumed Smathers was dead as well but suddenly heard a weak, raspy voice. "Get me out of here," Smathers said. The crash had broken his arms and torn the ligaments and cartilage in his knees, but the young officer was very much alive. Blackledge and his soldiers shoved Smathers into an undamaged Explorer and raced toward the safety of a nearby Polish base.

Blackledge hadn't suffered any visible wounds in the attack, but he felt searing pain up and down his back and could barely move. A military doctor did a CAT scan and found that the general had crushed his lower vertebrae and broken several ribs. They put him into a body cast and flew him to Germany, then on to Walter Reed. He did eleven months of grueling physical therapy at the hospital; by the time it was done, he could walk without pain or a limp. Still, Blackledge was struggling. He had trouble sleeping and couldn't stop replaying the ambush in his head. He would hear the slapping sound the bullets made when they hit the side of his truck and see the distant flashes of the insurgents' guns. Worst of all, Blackledge would remember the feeling that he and his men were about to die.

He also experienced sudden flashes of rage. His wife, Iwona, was an air force nurse, and they commuted to Walter Reed from their home near a large air force base in Florida. Pilots there weren't supposed to practice flying at supersonic speeds until they were out over the ocean, far from populated areas, but a few fighters streaked over their house one day and broke the sound barrier, rattling Blackledge's entire house. Blackledge remembers wanting to track down the pilots and strangle them to death.

Blackledge's doctor at Walter Reed diagnosed him with PTSD but told him that he would leave it out of the general's official record to avoid harming his future in the army. "I understand you're a general officer, so I'll make sure to put this in your file in a vague enough way that it won't hurt your career or security clearance," the doctor said.

The general was discharged from the hospital in January 2005 and sent back to Iraq. In November, Blackledge flew to Amman, Jordan, for a series of meetings and a bit of much-needed R & R. Baghdad was a city of concrete walls, potholed roads, and frequent power outages. Amman looked and felt like a Western city, complete with McDonald's, Pizza Hut, and upscale shopping malls. Blackledge felt safe there. One evening he walked into the lobby of the Grand Hyatt hotel and passed a nondescript Arab man in a business suit. The man sat down in the hotel's coffee shop, ordered a glass of orange juice, and calmly depressed a trigger in his hand. The resulting explosion sent jagged pieces of metal tearing through the lobby, killing nine people, maiming dozens of others, and littering the floor with body parts and pools of blood.

Blackledge was hurtled backward by the blast and suffered whiplash injuries to his neck and shoulder, but his psychological wounds again went far deeper. He had always seen Amman as a refuge of sorts from the war, but now the war had followed him across the border. He heard the screams of wounded Jordanians and watched emergency workers carry out the dead and injured. He had grown accustomed to seeing those horrors in Iraq. Seeing them in Amman was far more jarring, and far scarier. "I'd seen dead civilians and soldiers in Iraq, and that was traumatic enough, but it was a war zone and I sort of knew what to expect," he said. "When you're in a big modern city which is not at war, and it happens there too—well, it just totally took away my peace of mind. I was never the same."

Back home in the States, Blackledge had trouble concentrating at work and couldn't focus on any one task for very long. He had always been an extrovert but suddenly found himself terrified of crowds. One New Year's Eve the Blackledges were at a party at a packed church when he suddenly had a premonition of danger. Everyone around him was dancing and laughing, but David Blackledge was sweating, hyperventilating, and frantically searching for the nearest exit. He wasn't able to calm himself down until he was standing outside the church, alone in the cold night air. He also continued to experience moments of blind fury. One afternoon he was driving home from work and saw a woman in a Cadillac open her window and throw an entire bag of trash onto the road. "I just wanted to kill this woman," he remembered. "If we hadn't been pinned in by traffic, I would have literally tried to ram her with my car."

The burst of near-homicidal rage left Blackledge shaken. He'd been in therapy for years, took several medications, and thought he was making progress. Now it seemed like he was right back where he had started. Iwona could tell something was seriously wrong the moment he walked through the door, seething after seeing the litterer. "I can't live with myself and what I've become," he told her. "I feel like I just want to kill myself." She blanched and picked up the phone. Within minutes, two of Blackledge's aides—men who had been with him in both Iraq and Jordan—were at the door. They told him that they'd made an emergency appointment with his therapist for the following morning and would drive him there themselves. Blackledge's aide-de-camp, one of his closest friends and most trusted advisors, gestured to the closet where Blackledge stored the handgun he'd been issued after being promoted to general. "Sir, I need to confiscate your pistol," the officer said. "I don't feel comfortable leaving you alone with it." Blackledge nodded his head and handed over the gun.

The following morning Blackledge's two aides took him to see the psychologist who had been treating him since his return from the war zone. She told him that getting better didn't mean he would no longer have flashbacks, nightmares, or sudden flashes of anger. It would instead mean that they were happening less frequently and not hitting him quite as hard. She said that Blackledge could safely return to his job, but she recommended that he leave his gun with his staffers. Six months passed before he felt comfortable asking for it back, and before they felt comfortable returning it to him.

He considered suicide multiple times over the next few years, but with the help of medication and therapy, he always managed to get those dark impulses under control. Many of the soldiers under Blackledge's command weren't as successful. During his two years at Fort Bragg, seventy of his civil affairs and psychological operations troops tried to take their own lives, and twenty-one succeeded. The numbers stunned him, and Blackledge began to wonder how many other troops were experiencing the same kinds of sleeplessness, anger, and depression that had haunted him since Iraq and Jordan.

One afternoon he was about to start a PowerPoint presentation when he set aside his prepared notes and instead began telling the roomful of officers about his own emotional and behavioral struggles. The soldiers nodded their heads and said they had been wrestling with similar issues since returning from Iraq and Afghanistan. A few days later the Blackledges hosted a family day for the soldiers of his unit and their spouses. Walking around the room, David Blackledge heard the surprise and relief in the women's voices when they discovered that they weren't the only ones struggling to adjust to the changes in their husbands' behavior. "It was clearly a relief for them to be able to compare notes and say 'Oh, I didn't realize that your husband was also getting angry and having trouble falling asleep,'" Blackledge said. "The wives were all living with the same kinds of things. The more they talked, the more they realized that it wasn't just their relationship that was under strain and that it wasn't just their husband who had come home differently than when he'd left."

With that, Major General David Blackledge, West Point class of 1975, threw himself fully into the fight against stigma. He made TV and radio appearances, sat for newspaper interviews, and addressed large crowds at events put on by civilian groups such as the National Alliance on Mental Illness. Speaking at the Pentagon and at army bases across the country, Blackledge preached a simple message: Seeking help is a sign of strength, not weakness, and it is absolutely nothing to be ashamed of.

Iwona Blackledge was deeply uneasy about her husband's decision to speak out. She felt that the move would hurt—or potentially end—his career. Blackledge knew she was right, but he felt morally obligated to use his position to try to persuade troubled young soldiers that they could seek help and still be promoted.

"I'm a two-star general, and I've had a great run," he told her. "If it ends tomorrow because I'm talking about PTSD, that's a fair price to pay."

Blackledge soon came to the attention of Brigadier General Loree Sutton, an army psychiatrist leading the Pentagon's main effort to develop new methods of understanding and treating PTSD and TBI. Sutton had been trying to find senior officers willing to publicly discuss their own experiences with the emotional disorder, and Blackledge fit the bill perfectly.

"I look at it as just like a physical injury," Blackledge said in a video segment recorded for the Real Warriors Campaign, a Pentagon mental health awareness effort that Sutton helped to create. "If you break your leg, you're going to go to the doctor, you're going to get help, you're going to be on crutches for a while, you're going to have a cast, but then you're going to get through it. You're going to be tougher afterward. We need people—the whole chain of command, as well as the soldiers themselves—thinking that way."

The messenger was just as important as the message. The video notes that Blackledge had been promoted from brigadier general to major general while getting help for his PTSD. If he could advance through the ranks while going through therapy, the video clearly implies, other soldiers could too. Iwona Blackledge later recorded a Real Warriors Campaign video describing her own struggles to come to terms with the carnage she saw as a trauma nurse at a large military hospital in Iraq. She gave speeches about the nightmares she suffered after returning home from Iraq and an earlier deployment to Somalia. Like her husband, she reassured young soldiers that they shouldn't feel ashamed about needing help or reluctant to seek it.

Blackledge, like Mark Graham, broke the military's code of silence about mental health and spoke about depression and suicide openly and without shame. He was empathetic toward troubled soldiers at a time when that was the exception, not the norm, and he didn't get that kind of empathy in return. When he was in command at Fort Bragg, Blackledge's PTSD would flare up at unpredictable times, sometimes forcing him to arrive at work late or abruptly leave his office to go see his psychiatrist. That rubbed several of his subordinates the wrong way, and one filed an anonymous complaint with the Department of Defense's inspector general accusing Blackledge of paying too little attention to his job. Blackledge submitted an affidavit from his civilian psychiatrist attributing the behavior to the severity of his war-related PTSD and noting that he caught up with work at home, but it wasn't enough. He was formally reprimanded for a having "a poor work ethic," a ruling that blocked his chances for another promotion and effectively ended his career.

"It came as a total surprise, and frankly, I was devastated by the accusation," he said. "It made me question just how serious the army is about reducing stigma and wanting soldiers to get help. Actions speak louder than words."

Blackledge retired in 2012 after thirty-seven years in the army, five Bronze Stars, and two Purple Hearts. He has no regrets about telling his own story publicly and wishes more of his fellow generals would be willing to do the same. The United States has been at war for nearly thirteen years, and dozens of generals have cycled in and out of the war zones. Many of those senior officers privately acknowledge that they have some form of PTSD. But the stigma surrounding mental health issues in the armed forces remains so strong that only a handful of generals have been willing to acknowledge their suffering publicly. Mark Graham had been equally reluctant to talk about his own personal pain, but that was about to change.

CHAPTER 15

Arlington, Virginia, May 2007

Mark Graham looked out at the packed hotel ballroom, took a deep breath, and prepared to deliver a speech he had never expected to give. It was the first time he was going to speak publicly about his two sons, and Mark wasn't sure how his remarks about Kevin would go over with the hundreds of parents, spouses, and children of service members who had lost their lives in combat or training accidents rather than by their own hand. He also wasn't sure how it would feel to tell total strangers about the waves of guilt that washed over him and Carol whenever they thought about their failure to have understood the depths of Kevin's depression or to have done more to prevent their son from taking his own life. Still, Mark felt compelled to speak out. In the four years since Kevin's suicide, he and Carol had become increasingly uneasy with how differently the deaths of their two sons were treated by friends, relatives, and even other army officers. Mark's colleagues regularly told him that Jeff died a hero, and that he and Carol should be proud of their son's bravery and sacrifice. They didn't say much of anything about Kevin, and acted as if his suicide was a tragedy better ignored than discussed. The silence wounded Mark to his core. His younger son had been sick, not weak, and

Mark felt that Kevin's death was no less worthy of acknowledgment and respect than Jeff's. In the early days of the military's suicide epidemic, Mark Graham was one of the only ones who thought that way. Bonnie Carroll was another.

Carroll, an air force reservist with a seemingly boundless supply of energy, was the president and founder of the Tragedy Assistance Program for Survivors, a nonprofit devoted to helping bereaved military families learn to deal with their grief. Carroll had founded TAPS in 1992 after her husband, Brigadier General Tom Carroll, the commander of Alaska's Army National Guard, was killed when his military plane crashed near Anchorage. The number of families reaching out to her organization began to increase sharply in 2005 and 2006 as the death toll from the battlefields of Iraq and Afghanistan climbed steadily higher. But Carroll and her staff soon began to notice something disturbing: A small but growing percentage of those contacting her organization said they'd lost their loved ones to suicide, not to combat. Many widows of soldiers who had taken their own lives complained of being shunned and ostracized by those they'd once considered friends, including the troops who had worked most closely with their husbands. They didn't know what to tell their children about how their fathers had died, and they didn't know how to deal with the volatile mix of shock, anger, and guilt that hammered them every day. Mostly, they felt isolated and alone. Suicide was still a taboo topic in military circles, and few of the bereaved families knew that there were hundreds of others quietly going through the same struggles. Carroll wanted to change that, but she needed someone to help persuade the wives, parents, and children that they weren't to blame for their loved ones' decisions to take their own lives and that they would eventually be able to move past their grief. The ideal messenger would be someone who spoke their language, a soldier who had personal experience with suicide and could talk about it openly and without shame. When a friend told her the story of Brigadier General Mark Graham, Carroll knew she'd found the right person.

Mark initially felt differently. When Carroll contacted him that spring to see if he would be the keynote speaker at the TAPS national conference, his first reaction was to say no. He assumed that Carroll wanted him to speak solely about Jeff's death in Iraq and was stunned when she told him that she was actually just as interested in Kevin.

"We need you to share Kevin's story even more than Jeffrey's," Carroll told him. "We have so many families that are trying to pick up the pieces of their lives after losing someone they loved to suicide, and they need to hear that it can be done."

Her words struck a chord with both Grahams, who had long drawn comfort and solace from others whose loved ones had taken their own lives. During their time at Fort Sill, Carol was part of an informal group of suicide survivors who met at local restaurants or in one another's homes and spent hours talking about those they'd lost. It was one of the only places where Carol felt free to share graphic details about Kevin's death without worrying about being judged. "No one recoiled when I talked about seeing Kevin's body or made me feel ashamed that we hadn't seen the warning signs in time," she said. "I could just say anything and know that everyone would know what I was talking about. I felt safe, and that was such a kindness."

Years had passed, and Mark and Carol felt that it was time to try to provide others with the kind of support they'd received during the darkest moments of their own lives. On a sweltering evening in late May, one night before Memorial Day, Mark Graham stepped to the microphone of the DoubleTree hotel in Arlington, Virginia, glanced down at his notes, and began telling the story of his two sons.

"Eight months before Jeffrey was killed in Iraq, we lost our son Kevin to a different kind of battle," he told the crowd. "The devastating realization that we had lost one son was the heaviest burden imaginable at that time, but the thought that both of them were gone was beyond comprehension."

The Grahams, like all of those in the audience, had become members of an intimate fraternity none had ever wanted to join. Each person there was mourning a fallen soldier, sometimes one who had taken his or her own life, and each person there had to face the daunting struggle of getting out of bed each morning and trying to navigate a world that seemed darker and emptier. Mark told the audience that the loss of his two sons took the moments that should have been among the happiest parts of his professional and personal lives and instead made them almost unbearably painful. "I made speeches as soldiers deployed and redeployed," he said. "We celebrated their homecomings and watched as families were reunited after long separations. Our friends' children had birthdays, graduated, got married and had babies, which left us always wondering how the world could even keep spinning without Jeffrey and Kevin in it. At church we tried desperately to hold back the tears as other people's prayers seemingly were answered."

Mark closed by reciting a line from an Archibald MacLeish poem engraved on Fort Riley's memorial wall for America's fallen in Iraq and Afghanistan. "'They say: We leave you our deaths. Give them their meaning,'" Mark read. It was easy to apply those words to Jeff, who was a war hero so celebrated that a sergeant at Fort Sill had named his son Jeffrey Graham Beemer not long after the fatal explosion in Khaldiyah. It had always been harder to talk about Kevin, but Mark and Carol had spent years waging a quiet war of their own against suicide. Kevin had died at the University of Kentucky. The Grahams' lonely fight had begun there as well.

The envelopes arrived by the dozen, some containing store-bought cards, some containing handwritten notes. Many of the people who'd heard about Kevin's death assumed the Grahams needed money for funeral expenses. They sent checks and cash to help convey a pair of simple messages: We're sorry for your loss, and we want to help.

It was the fall of 2003, and Mark and Carol were still reeling from Kevin's suicide. Their pain was so overwhelming that they were desperately trying to find meaning and purpose in his death. The unexpected flood of money gave them an idea. The University of Kentucky, like many cash-strapped public universities, didn't have enough mental health counselors to ensure that every troubled student who reached out for help would be seen quickly. Its undergraduate enrollment at the time of Kevin's death was around twenty-four thousand, but it had just eight full-time counselors on staff. The International Association of Counseling Services said that schools should have one counselor for every fifteen hundred students, which meant that the University of Kentucky had about half the mental health professionals it needed. A shortfall that significant meant that the university's therapists often had less time to spend with students than they would have liked. Kentucky had been lucky—only a handful of students had taken their own lives during the Grahams' time at the school—but administrators worried they didn't have the resources to prevent those numbers from rising.

The Grahams were stunned when they learned how small Kentucky's counseling staff was, and they wanted to figure out how to expand the school's suicide prevention efforts. As thousands of dollars in donated money began rolling in during the initial months after Kevin's death, Mark and Carol realized they had a way of doing so. They set up a meeting with Dr. Lee Todd, the University of Kentucky's then president, and offered to fund a new campus-wide suicide prevention effort. Mary Bolin, the head of the school's counseling department, suggested implementing an initiative known as QPR, for "question, persuade, and refer." The program was designed to teach students, faculty, and residential advisors to be on the lookout for indications that someone might be preparing to commit suicide, including signs of depression or hopelessness and unusual behavior such as giving away prized possessions or significantly ramping up alcohol or drug consumption. They were then taught to try to persuade troubled students to seek help or, in a pinch, to refer them for emergency treatment themselves. "The idea isn't to have students walking around campus and having the first question to their friends be 'Hey, are you suicidal?'" Bolin said. "The goal is for students and faculty to be trained listeners and trained observers so they feel comfortable going up to a student and saying, 'I noticed that something seems different. How are you doing? Do you have a few minutes to sit down and talk?'"

The beauty of the QPR system, in Bolin's view, was that those who completed the training were encouraged to teach it to others. That meant the number of people at the University of Kentucky with rudimentary suicide prevention training could expand exponentially in a relatively short time. Mark and Carol loved the idea. They had wanted to get a sizable suicide prevention program under way as quickly as possible, and this was clearly the way to do it. They received roughly $10,000 in the first months after Kevin's death, and they donated all of it to the University of Kentucky in his name. They received $30,000 more after Jeff was killed in Iraq the following spring and funneled it to the university as well. Bolin said that money from the Kevin and Jeffrey Graham Memorial Fund has helped the university give QPR training to roughly six thousand students, campus police officers, dorm counselors, and faculty members, with the number rising every semester.

Checks continued arriving in 2006 and 2007, though in smaller amounts, and Mark and Carol donated the money to the QPR suicide prevention efforts they'd launched at Kentucky and at Cameron University, the Oklahoma school where Melanie finished her undergraduate degree. They saw the programs as a living memorial to their two sons and a concrete way of preventing other troubled young people from deciding that death was the only way of escaping the sadness and loneliness that seemed destined to haunt them for the rest of their lives. Most of the people Mark and Carol met reacted with sympathy and kindness when they learned about Kevin's suicide, but some spoke of him derisively, even cruelly. Kevin, they implied to the Grahams, had been a weakling, a coward, and even a sinner. The callousness of those comments taught Mark, Carol, and other suicide survivors a painful lesson. Families shattered by suicide desperately needed their friends and colleagues to provide them with comfort and solace. All too often, they were instead left to feel isolated, alone, and ashamed.

It was an evening church event in Oklahoma, one of the dozens Carol had attended near the Grahams' home at Fort Sill since the deaths of their two boys. The congregation had recently lost a member to suicide, and Carol had been asked to offer advice about how to best comfort the bereaved family. She brought along her Bible and began by telling the small group of women that she'd gotten through many of her own sleepless night and pain-filled days by holding on to her faith and learning as much as she could about the science of depression and suicide. "The most important thing about caring for a family who loses someone to suicide is to treat them the same way as you would if their loved one had died of a car wreck, drowning, cancer, or a heart attack," she told the women sipping coffee in the living room of one of the church members.

When Carol finished speaking, many of the women began sharing their own stories about relatives who had been quietly treated for mental illnesses or who had died by their own hand. It was a deeply religious Baptist congregation, and Carol was surprised that the women spoke about suicide with empathy rather than condemnation. There was one very vocal exception, however. A woman sitting near the back of the room kept interrupting the stories about depression and suicide to say that nothing in life was insurmountable and that all people had to choose between good and evil and whether to follow the path to heaven or the path to hell. "Satan is real and he is powerful and his evil spirit prowls around like a hungry lion looking for souls," she said.

Carol sat back in her chair, trembling and trying to keep herself from crying. The clear implication of the woman's remarks was that Kevin's decision to kill himself meant that he had turned away from God and willfully chosen to go with Satan. "I just remember feeling so much shame and guilt and left there in worse shape than I had been in when I arrived," Carol said. "I received phone calls, e-mails, and letters from quite a few of the ladies who had attended that evening thanking me, but the one voice that haunted me was of that one lady who clearly sent a strong message that Kevin and anyone who killed themselves was in hell."

Some months later the shopkeeper at a local store told Carol that she'd heard about the deaths of Kevin and Jeff and wanted Carol to know that her entire church was praying that God would lift the family curse that could be the only rational explanation for the two tragedies. Carol grew up a Methodist, but she was feeling so rattled that she took the comments seriously and began calling all the local Catholic churches to see if they had priests who would be willing to perform an exorcism on her and Mark. None of them did, and Carol quickly dropped the idea.

Melanie Graham had been facing her own struggles to come to terms with her brother's decision to take his own life. In the immediate aftermath of his suicide, she had a difficult time walking around a campus full of classroom buildings, lawns, and bars that all reminded her of Kevin. She also began to feel alienated from her fellow students. "I'd be at these parties where everyone was smiling and joking around, and I'd just start feeling really angry, like no one there had any idea what it was like to lose people you loved," she said. "It was like everyone was in a nice little bubble except for me."

Her grades were the next thing to go. Melanie began earning Ds in anatomy and the other classes that she'd need to get into nursing school. Melanie's academic advisor bluntly told her to pick a different major. "Nursing's too hard for you with all you've been through," she said at the time. "You probably need something easier." Melanie dropped out of the University of Kentucky in October 2004 and moved in with some friends. The local Olive Garden where she worked as a hostess became a second home of sorts, with her coworkers serving as a surrogate family while she slowly healed from the trauma of losing her brothers.

In January 2005, Melanie flew to Oklahoma to celebrate Mark's promotion. As a newly minted general, Mark was entitled to have an aide-de-camp, which was a fancy way of describing a young officer who accompanied him wherever he went and handled such tasks as managing his schedule and coordinating his travel. Mark's aide was an army lieutenant named Joe Quinn, an Iraq veteran with a thick Brooklyn accent and a self-deprecating sense of humor who had been serving near Ramadi when Jeff was killed. Joe was a regular visitor to the Grahams' official residence, and Carol thought he and Melanie would be good for each other. Joe's older brother Jimmy had been killed in the World Trade Center on September 11, so both had lost someone they'd cherished, and each had spent years struggling to move on. "I wasn't trying to meddle in Melanie's life, but part of me was definitely playing matchmaker," she said.

One morning Joe stopped by the Grahams' house to pick up Mark's dress uniform. Carol slipped him a piece of paper with Melanie's e-mail address and cell phone number written on it. "You should reach out to her," she told him. Joe wasn't sure how to respond. He'd seen photos of Melanie and thought she was beautiful. At the same time, she was his boss's daughter. Contacting her would be risky. He didn't know how she'd respond, and he didn't know how Mark would react when he found out. Joe decided to roll the dice anyway. He e-mailed Melanie, and she e-mailed back. They began texting throughout the day and speaking by phone at night. They clicked, just like Carol had hoped they would.

In early March, Mark and Carol asked Melanie to fly in from Kentucky to look after their beloved Yorkie, Wicket, while they were away on a two-week trip. Melanie said she'd be happy to do it. She and Joe talked almost every day but had barely spent any time together. A few weeks at Fort Sill would change that, and her parents, in an added benefit, would be hundreds of miles away. The trip, Melanie thought, would give her a real sense of whether she and Joe had a future.

Initially it wasn't even clear that they'd have a present. Joe asked Melanie out for dinner at a local Chili's on her second night in town. She assumed this would be their first real date, but when she walked into the restaurant, Joe was sitting at a table with his two roommates and one of the roommates' girlfriend. He tried to explain that evenings back home always involved hanging out with large groups of friends, but Melanie did little to hide her annoyance. "She'd been looking for a date, not dinner with three complete strangers," he said. "I was lucky my Irish charm convinced her to just laugh it off."

Melanie and Joe spent the next two weeks at each other's side, going to movies and eating dinner at the Outback Steakhouse and other restaurants just outside Fort Sill. By the time Mark and Carol returned home in mid-March, the e-mail flirtation had developed into a full-fledged romance. The night before her flight back to Kentucky, Melanie came home after a date with Joe, lay down on her bed, and smiled at her mother. "He's the guy I'm going to marry," she told Carol. "He's the one."

Melanie's burgeoning relationship with Joe left her wrestling with feelings of guilt and uncertainty. She knew that she'd mourn Jeff and Kevin for the rest of her life, and a large part of her thought that was the way it was supposed to be. Was she betraying her brothers, Melanie wondered, by allowing herself to feel as happy as she did with Joe? She was also struggling with how to tell people she met in Oklahoma and Kentucky about Kevin's suicide. Melanie, like her parents, found it relatively easy to talk to strangers about Jeff's death in Iraq. It was a tragic and simple story: Her brother was a soldier, and he'd been killed in combat. Talking about Kevin was much harder. She loved her brother and had come to understand that he died of a depression that was as deadly as any physical illness, but she sometimes felt embarrassed telling people that he'd killed himself. She worried that friends or strangers would subconsciously decide that she and her parents had failed Kevin, or that he had been a weakling and a coward, and she simply didn't feel up to the challenge of changing their minds. "People would say, 'Are you an only child?'" she said. "Sometimes I would say I did have two brothers, but sometimes I would find myself saying I had an older brother who was killed in Iraq and then not mention Kevin at all. I just worried that people were going to judge me."

For many suicide survivors, that's exactly what happens. Kim and John Ruocco had what Kim described as a storybook marriage, but John, a marine pilot, was almost unrecognizable when he returned from Iraq in 2004. He had flown seventy-five combat missions over some of the most violent parts of the country and been given a medal for exemplary service. Back home in Massachusetts, however, he had trouble sleeping and ate so little food that he dropped an alarming amount of weight. He distanced himself from his two boys and would criticize them relentlessly for not playing well enough in their hockey games. Once a devout Catholic, he stopped going to church. He walked around the house with a blank look in his eyes and regularly told Kim that he could no longer see any beauty in the world. She told her husband that he needed help, but he insisted that he could handle things himself. Reaching out to a counselor, John told her, would end his career as a pilot.

In the fall of 2004, John's unit was sent to California, hundreds of miles from where Kim lived with their boys, and given word that it should prepare for another deployment to Iraq. He moved into a hotel and told his wife that he didn't think he'd be able to make it through another six months in Iraq. In December, John flew to Boston to spend Christmas with his family. He was gaunt and disheveled and showed flashes of a temper that Kim didn't know he had. She could see how hard her husband was fighting to keep his emotions in check, and she could see how badly he was failing. On John's last night in Boston, Kim bundled her sons into the car and drove him to the airport. The boys were asleep in the backseat as John took his luggage out of the trunk. Kim suggested waking them so he could say good-bye, but John quickly shook his head. "Don't wake them," he told her. "I don't want them to see me like this." John Ruocco disappeared into the airport without saying another word.

Six weeks later Kim watched John's beloved New England Patriots beat the Philadelphia Eagles in the Super Bowl for their second straight title. One of Kim's sons called John to celebrate but abruptly passed her the phone. "Daddy's not okay," he told Kim. "He didn't watch the game, and he's crying."

Alarmed, Kim told John that she was going to tell his superior officers about his problems unless he immediately sought help on his own. He said that he was going to drive to an outpatient behavioral health clinic on the base and promised to call her as soon as he arrived. When the phone never rang, Kim raced to Logan Airport and bought a red-eye ticket to California. She called the clinic as soon as she landed, but they told her that no one with her husband's name had shown up for help. The main base hospital told Kim the same thing, and the marines in John's office said he hadn't come to work that day. When she drove to her husband's hotel and asked about John Ruocco, the hotel clerk stared at her for a moment before scrambling into a back room, slamming the door shut, and then quickly locking it. John was already dead, but the clerk couldn't summon the courage to tell her so.

"He treated me like I was contagious," Kim said today. "His entire sense of humanity disappeared. He wouldn't tell me what room John was in, take me there, or even bring himself to say 'I'm sorry.' He just closed that door and pushed me away."

The Catholic priest who'd been summoned to the hotel after John's body was found was no more sympathetic. Kim had just watched, shell-shocked, as her husband's corpse was wheeled out of his hotel room under a white sheet. She asked the priest what she should tell her boys.

"You know what the church thinks about suicide, right?" he asked.

Kim, who'd grown up a Methodist, shook her head.

"It's a sin," the priest said. "It's a mortal sin."

"Are you telling me that I not only have to tell my kids that their dad is dead, but that he's in hell?" she replied, incredulous.

Kim spent days wrestling with what to say to her boys, but Joey, the older of the two brothers, effectively made the decision for her. She had initially told them that John died in an accident, a lie that she hoped would spare them from even more pain. A few days later Kim was driving Joey to a birthday party at a pizza restaurant when he tapped her on the shoulder and said that he thought he had killed his father. Kim stopped the car, put her arm around her son, and quietly asked what he meant.

"When Dad was home at Christmas we had nachos. I asked if I could put salt on the nachos, but he said, 'No, because too much salt isn't good for your heart, and you can have a heart attack and it can kill you,'" Joey told her. "Well, when Dad wasn't looking, I salted the nachos, and I think that something must have happened to his heart."

Kim decided, then and there, to tell her son the truth about John's suicide. She told her younger son a short time later. Nine years later Kim still wonders if she made the right decision. "I sometimes think I should have told them something else, at least until they got older," Kim said. Today Kim runs TAPS's suicide prevention efforts. "Suicide is a hard enough thing for adults to understand," she said. "I don't know if it was the right time to try to explain that to such young boys."

In the first months of 2005, Melanie Graham and Kim Ruocco weren't the only ones wrestling with whether, or how, to speak about those who'd chosen to take their own lives. Thousands of miles away, one of the army's most highly regarded generals was facing the same painful question.

When General Peter Chiarelli arrived in Iraq in March 2004, a year after U.S. forces first streamed into the country, it was the culmination of a lifelong dream. Chiarelli had spent decades aching to lead troops into combat, but he'd come to accept that he'd probably never get the chance to do so. That changed when he got orders to take his 1st Cavalry Division to Baghdad, the center of Iraq's growing insurgency. Chiarelli had once pictured himself leading columns of tanks into battle against Soviet forces. Instead, he and the twenty thousand soldiers of his division were essentially told to man checkpoints throughout Baghdad, mount patrols on foot and in their Humvees, and do their best to prevent the tenuous security situation in the city from deteriorating even further. It was occupation duty, not full-blown war against a global superpower, but Chiarelli was excited all the same.

A stocky man with thick forearms and a firm handshake, Chiarelli looked like a wartime general straight out of central casting. His imposing physical appearance, however, obscured the fact that he was an unusually compassionate and emotional officer. Chiarelli had deployed to Iraq in February knowing that his youngest son, Patrick, would have left home and begun college by the time he returned to the States. In his journal Chiarelli wrote candidly about the sadness and guilt he felt over leaving his wife, Beth, to wait for him by herself in a large, empty house. "Knowing I will never live in the house again with Pat makes me tear up," he wrote in an entry quoted by Greg Jaffe and David Cloud in their book *The Fourth Star.* "I will never forget Beth whispering in my ear through tears that she was afraid to be alone."

Chiarelli had arrived in Baghdad with ambitious plans to fix the city's shattered electrical grid, improve its decrepit sewage system, and create enough jobs to jump-start the local economy and give angry young men reason to lay down their guns. Those dreams collided with the reality of Iraq's escalating guerilla war. On April 4, Shiite insurgents ambushed a convoy of Chiarelli's trucks and Humvees as they escorted sewage tankers through the militant stronghold of Sadr City. Other 1st Cav troops raced in to rescue their comrades, only to be ambushed themselves. Nineteen soldiers had been in the initial convoy; by the time the shooting stopped, one was dead and seven were wounded. Seven of the rescuers had been killed and more than sixty wounded. Chiarelli went to visit the survivors and was shaken by the sight of so many bloody, maimed soldiers. The deaths hit him even harder. He wrote the names and hometowns of each fallen soldier on note cards that he kept in the breast pocket of his uniform, ensuring they were with him wherever he went.

When he returned to the United States the following spring, Chiarelli oversaw a somber ceremony in which the names of 168 dead soldiers from his division were inscribed onto a memorial wall at Fort Hood. There was only one problem: 169 of his men had left for Iraq and not returned, not 168. The missing man was Private First Class David Potter, a shy twenty-two-year-old from Tennessee who'd killed himself in Baghdad shortly after the unit deployed to Iraq. Potter had tried to take his life once before, but press reports from the time said that the military had ignored a psychiatrist's recommendation that Potter's anxiety and depression were so severe that he should be sent home from Iraq immediately and taken off active duty. On August 11, 2004, Potter pulled a gun from under a fellow soldier's bed and shot himself through the mouth.

As word of Potter's suicide spread throughout the division, Chiarelli's subordinate commanders were adamant that he didn't deserve to have his name listed alongside those who had fallen in battle against the enemy. Chiarelli agreed, a decision he describes as one of the worst of his nearly four decades in the army. "The saddest thing, the thing that I regret the most, was leaving the kid off of that wall," Chiarelli said.

Potter's name wasn't added to the wall until years later, long after Chiarelli had given up command of the 1st Cavalry Division and began steadily ascending the ranks of the military. He served as the senior military advisor to then defense secretary Bob Gates and then as the vice chief of staff of the army. He would also become a leading, if controversial, figure in the fight against military suicide, using the powers of his office to help steer hundreds of millions of dollars to researchers developing new methods for identifying and treating at-risk troops. And he would try to eliminate the army's institutional reluctance to talk about soldiers who'd taken their own lives by requiring individual generals to conduct detailed investigations into any suicides in their units and then personally brief him on the findings. In 2005, however, Chiarelli was still a typical army general with a typical army view of suicide. "We were Neanderthals, just like the rest of society was, and we thought that people who killed themselves were just weak," Chiarelli said.

In the early years of the army's suicide epidemic, the families of troops who'd taken their own lives were treated callously, even cruelly, by the nation's military and political leaders. The relatives of those killed in combat received full military funerals, complete with twenty-one-gun salutes and folded American flags. They were given gold stars to commemorate their loss and condolence letters from the president.

There were no hard-and-fast rules for how soldiers who had committed suicide should be buried, by contrast, so many didn't receive full military funerals. Their names weren't added to the memorial walls at many bases. They didn't receive letters from the White House, and their families often had to fight to receive the pensions, health insurance, and other benefits accorded to relatives of other fallen members of the armed forces. By the time those policies began to change, hundreds of soldiers had already committed suicide. The year 2005 had set an all-time record for army suicides, with 87, but the record was shattered in 2006, when 102 soldiers took their own lives, and then again in 2007, when the number spiked to 115. The suicide epidemic had erupted, but few people inside or outside the army knew how to think about those who'd taken their own lives, or how to try to prevent others from following suit. Mark Graham had some ideas, and he was about to get the opportunity to put them into practice.

On an unseasonably cold evening in the spring of 2007, Mark heard a knock at the back door of his house at Fort Sam Houston in San Antonio. He opened the door and froze, his heart sinking. Lieutenant General Robert Clark and his wife, Karen, were standing on the landing, and Mark's immediate thought was that his boss had come to personally tell him that something horrible had happened to Melanie, just as Dave Valcourt had done when Jeff was killed in Iraq. He exhaled when he saw the bottle of champagne in Clark's hands. The general hadn't come with bad news; he'd come to share a much happier development. Clark had just learned that Mark had been selected for a second star and was about to move even higher up the military hierarchy, and he wanted to be the first to tell his friend the good news.

A few months later Major General Mark Graham received his next assignment. He was put in command of 1st Army Division West, which oversaw more than forty thousand soldiers stationed on bases west of the Mississippi River, and Fort Carson, an enormous base in Colorado that had a reputation for being one of the most physically beautiful installations in the entire army. He and Carol packed up their house in Texas and set out for the long trip to Colorado. The biggest and most important fight of Mark's professional life was just about to begin.

CHAPTER 16

Fort Carson, Colorado, September 2007

Carol Graham looked out the passenger window and gasped as her car approached the main gates of Fort Carson. Fields of emerald-green grass stretched out for miles, broken only by clusters of bright yellow wild-flowers and towering pine trees. The Colorado Rockies stood in a jagged line behind the base, patches still covered by pristine white snow. Fort Carson was called "the Mountain Post," and Carol thought it was a perfect name. She hadn't seen anything so beautiful since her time in Germany more than a decade earlier.

Carol and Mark had driven the nine hundred miles from San Antonio in an aging green Honda Accord that Kevin owned before his death, and it had been a bittersweet trip. The Grahams were leaving Fort Sam Houston, a small base that they'd come to know and love, and moving out to a huge facility that was home to nearly one hundred thousand soldiers and members of military families. Mark had passed through Fort Carson a few times on day trips, but Carol had never been to the base before. She was used to uprooting herself whenever Mark got a new assignment, but the moves had gotten more difficult after the deaths of her sons. She knew that Mark's position as the commander of the base meant that they'd receive an enormous official residence, and she knew the house would feel empty and lonely without Kevin and Jeff. The peaks in the distance hit her particularly hard. "It looks like those mountains can touch heaven," she told Mark. "Do you think the boys are standing up there?" Driving onto the most beautiful army base in the United States, her newly promoted husband at her side, Carol began to cry.

Mark's formal change-of-command ceremony at Fort Carson took place in mid-September, and it didn't go as smoothly as he'd hoped. He had been told that he'd be doing a military ritual known as a mounted review of his troops. Usually this means a new general standing in an open-backed Humvee while being driven past rows of troops standing at formation on the base's parade ground. Fort Carson took the idea much more literally. The day before the ceremony, a young soldier called Mark to ask if he wanted to come down to the base's stables and practice riding the horse he'd be using during the change of command. Mark was speechless; he hadn't ridden a horse since attending a local carnival with his mom when he was nine years old. It was too late to back out, so Mark dutifully spent several hours at the stables learning how to get on and off a horse and use the reins to turn it left and right. It turned out to be time well spent. During the ceremony Mark's brown horse abruptly whinnied, reared up onto its hind legs, and began trotting backward. Mark managed to get it moving forward again, but not before hearing nervous laughter from the large crowd of soldiers and civilians who'd gathered to see Fort Carson's new commander for the first time.

Mark's former boss, Lieutenant General Russel Honoré, flew to Colorado to present him with the flag signifying his new command over Fort Carson and the army's Division West. Honoré couldn't resist a lighthearted joke at his onetime subordinate's expense. "Next time, Mark, we'll let you pick your own horse," he said, drawing laughter from the crowd.

The Grahams settled into their official residence, a light-filled man-

sion that Mark named Ouray House after the Indian chief who had nego-
tiated a peace treaty with the famed frontier explorer Kit Carson. Mark
and Carol could see bears stumbling down their street, knocking over
trash cans while looking for food, and hear coyotes howling when taps
echoed from loudspeakers throughout the base at dusk. The Rockies
sparkled in the late-afternoon sunlight, and the rows of pine trees that
dotted the base swayed gently in the wind. "It felt like Mark and I were
living in a postcard," Carol said.

They soon learned that Fort Carson's physical beauty masked a cancer that was steadily spreading throughout the base. On December 1, just
months after Mark took command, a newspaper deliveryman found the
bullet-riddled body of a young Fort Carson soldier named Kevin Shields
lying on the sidewalk of a quiet residential neighborhood of Colorado
Springs, the town closest to Fort Carson. Three other soldiers from the
base were arrested for Shields's murder, rattling the entire community
and shaking Mark Graham to his core. He had heard of soldiers beating
one another up badly enough that they needed to go to the hospital, but
one soldier shooting another in the head? That was something Mark had
never encountered. He hoped Shields's death was a one-off crime carried out by a few unbalanced troops, but every day seemed to bring news
of more fatal shootings by troops from the base. Fourteen Fort Carson
troops would eventually be linked to eleven killings or attempted killings between 2005 and 2008, far and away the most violent crimes ever
committed by soldiers from a single base over such a short period. The
victims ranged from a Fort Carson soldier named Robert James to a pair
of young Colorado Springs residents, Amairany Cervantes and Cesar
Ramirez Ibanez, who were gunned down in front of their two-and-a-
half-year-old nephew as they pasted up posters advertising a yard sale.
What, powerful lawmakers and senior Pentagon officials began to ask,
was going so terribly wrong at Fort Carson? Mark wondered the same
thing, and he wondered if he'd be around to find out. Late at night, alone

in Ouray House, Mark sometimes confided to Carol that he thought he might be fired.

The murders weren't all Mark had to worry about. Thousands of Fort Carson troops had returned home from the battlefields of Iraq and Afghanistan with PTSD and severe depression. An alarming number fell through the cracks of the base's mental health system and wound up killing themselves before receiving the help they desperately needed. In 2008, Mark's first full year at the base, 8 Fort Carson soldiers killed themselves, giving the base a suicide rate of 66 per 100,000, triple the rate of the army itself and more than four times the national average. Some of the base's failures to spot troubled soldiers came down to simple mathematics. The Pentagon had moved so many troops to Fort Carson after the start of the two wars that it tripled the size of its population. The behavioral health department at Fort Carson's Evans Army Community Hospital simply wasn't able to hire new staff fast enough to keep up. Between 2006 and 2008, the bloodiest years of the Iraq War, more than a third of the overall behavioral health positions at the hospital were unfilled. That meant soldiers seeking help at the hospital's fourth-floor mental health clinic usually waited several hours for appointments that lasted less than thirty minutes and generally ended with little more than prescriptions for powerful medications, many of which were addictive or had severe side effects. Those kinds of problems were far from unique to Fort Carson, but the base's previous commanders had failed to take action against the ingrained callousness, and even cruelty, that many of its veterans were confronting when they returned. The army's later investigations concluded that Fort Carson's deeply flawed mental health system was failing to give troubled soldiers the help they needed.

In June 2007, just weeks before Mark took command of Fort Carson, National Public Radio reporter Daniel Zwerdling spotted an unusual memo tacked to a bulletin board in the office of Dr. Steven Knorr, an army colonel who was the chief of mental health at Fort Carson's Evans military hospital. The subject line was "Common Mistakes Made When Dealing with Troubled/Problem Soldiers," and its language was jarring:

1. **Trying to Save Every Soldier.** We can't fix every Soldier, and neither can you. Everyone in life beyond babies, the insane, and the demented/mentally retarded have to be held accountable for what they do in life.

2. **Procrastinating on Discipline and Separation.** Delaying administrative separation and NJP [Nonjudicial Punishment] is counterproductive.

   We see Soldiers monthly that had their Chapter evaluation [performance evaluation] six months ago, and now are worse off and more of a management problem than before. Get rid of dead wood . . .

3. **Assuming Psychiatric Hospitalization Works Like a Reform School or MP Holding Cell.** Psychiatric hospitalization has its limits. We can't put them there just because they break barracks restriction and go get drunk, or get in fights, or engage in similar misconduct . . .

4. **Assuming Psychiatric Diagnosis Is Just a Common Sense Process.** Prematurely concluding a Soldier's complaints and symptoms are invalid or malingered. We're not naïve, and shouldn't automatically believe everything Soldiers tell us. The truth is usually somewhere in the middle.

Bonnie Carroll had warned Mark before he even left Fort Sam Houston that Fort Carson had a serious suicide problem. "Be careful," she told him. "The handwriting's on the wall there, and it's ugly." Knorr's memo was a literal illustration of precisely what Carroll had been talking about.

Mark was horrified when he listened to the NPR report and heard about Knorr's apparent belief that many of the troops who sought help at Fort Carson were "dead wood" who faked their symptoms to mask their own inadequacies. The memo, Mark thought, sent a clear message that Fort Carson's military mental health system looked down on soldiers who said they were suffering from PTSD, making it far less likely that those troops would be willing to come forward for treatment. "I couldn't believe that our top psychiatrist was part of the stigma," Mark said. Knorr had been in the process of deploying to Iraq but planned to return to Fort Carson and assume his old job as soon as his tour was finished. Mark made sure he didn't come back. "I said I wanted someone else," he said, "and they sent me someone else." Mark later contacted Major General Doug Carver, the two-star officer overseeing the army's chaplains, after one of Fort Carson's senior chaplains made an even more shocking comment: The base's suicide problem, the chaplain said shortly before Carver transferred him to a new post, was because witches living in the surrounding mountains had cursed Fort Carson and the soldiers who lived there.

The real causes of Fort Carson's suicide spike were far more prosaic: pervasive stigma that left soldiers afraid to seek help for fear of harming their careers or appearing weak in the eyes of their colleagues, and an understaffed mental health clinic that failed to identify at-risk soldiers or give them the personalized care they needed. Sergeant First Class Kenneth Lehman was a medic in the army's Special Forces, one of the best of the best, but he never fully recovered from the memory loss, headaches, and double vision that had set in after a training accident at Fort Carson in the fall of 2006. In February 2007, about six months before Mark Graham arrived at the base, Lehman swallowed so much Valium that his roommate came home and found him unconscious on the couch, barely breathing. Lehman was rushed to a clinic at Fort Carson, but doctors there released him after he denied trying to kill himself. In November,

Lehman again took so much Valium that he needed to be hospitalized, and doctors again released him after he said it wasn't a suicide attempt. Lehman was a tough guy, one who told friends that he prided himself on never admitting weakness or asking for help. He did his best to mask his problems, but Fort Carson's doctors should have realized that something was dangerously wrong with a soldier who twice overdosed on Valium.

On February 1, 2008, Lehman ran into Andrew Pogany, a retired member of the Special Forces who had become an unofficial advocate for Fort Carson troops who felt they were being mistreated by the army because of PTSD or other behavioral health issues. Pogany's willingness to go to bat for individual soldiers—fighting to ensure that those suffering from PTSD received full medical benefits, for instance—made him a deeply unpopular figure at Fort Carson, and senior commanders routinely tried to bar him from setting foot on the base. Rank-and-file troops such as Lehman, by contrast, saw Pogany as a trusted ally, one who understood what they were going through because he had gone through it himself. Pogany had deployed to Iraq in September 2003, just months after U.S. forces first swept into the country. Less than a week into his tour, Pogany watched an Iraqi get cut in half by machine-gun fire. Horrified, Pogany vomited and trembled for hours. He told his bosses that he was having a panic attack and needed help, but Special Forces commanders instead sent him back to Fort Carson and charged him with "cowardly conduct as a result of fear," a crime that can bring the death penalty. Pogany and his lawyers argued that his erratic behavior in Iraq stemmed from exposure to an antimalarial drug called Lariam whose known side effects include paranoia, nightmares, and hallucinations. It took nearly two years, but he won the case. The army gave Pogany an honorable discharge and acknowledged that he had "a medical problem that requires care and treatment." Pogany settled in Colorado Springs and made himself available to any troubled soldier who wanted to talk. Lehman, who was rapidly spiraling downward, was one of them.

"Andrew, I'm not doing well," Lehman told him. "I have PTSD. I need help, and I'm not getting it."

Pogany suggested they get together a few days later to talk about Lehman's issues and plot out a way of getting him better treatment. Lehman told Pogany that he had to rush off to a mental health appointment but said he'd call to set up a specific time and place. Pogany never heard from him again. On February 2, Pogany was standing in a hallway at Fort Carson's hospital when he heard a doctor casually tell a colleague that he'd been assigned to do the autopsy of a Special Forces soldier named Ken Lehman. Lehman, the doctor confided to the other physician, had killed himself. Pogany quickly found out the details. Lehman, who'd been taught to save lives, had instead used his medical knowledge to take his own. He walked into his barracks bathroom, injected himself with a syringe full of anesthetic, and then slashed open his left wrist with a surgical blade. Lehman, thirty-one, bled to death on the cool tile floor. "I had to go outside and get some fresh air when I heard," Pogany said. "I was just in complete shock that it had happened the day after we'd talked. The tragedy was that you had this guy who wanted help but couldn't quite bring himself to ask for it from the doctors on the base."

Soldiers who were willing to acknowledge that they needed counseling faced another problem: mistreatment at the hands of fellow troops who mocked them as weak or cowardly. Some soldiers from the 3rd Brigade Combat Team of the 4th Infantry Division, another Fort Carson unit, designed a fake "Hurt Feelings Report" and left copies near a sign-out sheet troops used when they were going to see one of Fort Carson's doctors. The document began, "Reasons for filing this report: Please circle Yes or No." The choices included, "I am thin skinned; I am a pussy; I have woman-like hormones; I am a queer; I am a little bitch; I am a cry baby; I want my mommy; all of the above." There was a blank space for soldiers to fill in the "Name of 'Real Man' who hurt your sensitive feelings."

The suicides and near suicides kept coming, one troubled Fort Carson soldier after another deciding that life was no longer worth living. A few weeks after Lehman's suicide, a young army private named Adam Lieberman, twenty-one, gobbled down a pile of prescription painkillers, sleeping pills, and antianxiety medication, dipped a brush into a can of black paint, and scrawled a suicide note onto one of the walls of his tiny barracks room. "I FACED THE ENEMY AND LIVED," he wrote, in all caps. "IT WAS THE DEATH DEALERS THAT TOOK MY LIFE!" Lieberman had tried to take his own life. Unlike Lehman, he didn't succeed.

Lieberman had taken the GED so he could enlist at seventeen without finishing high school. He was eighteen when he deployed to Iraq, and he celebrated his nineteenth birthday near the end of what had been a long, bloody, and emotionally grueling tour. He had fought in Iraq as part of the 1st Battalion, 67th Armor Regiment, a unit known as the Death Dealers, and he returned home in December 2006 haunted by the carnage he'd seen in the war zone. During one mission an insurgent bomb decapitated the gunner standing in the turret of Lieberman's Humvee, sending the headless body collapsing into his lap. Later in his deployment, Lieberman saw an IED shear the legs off a close friend and watched, horrified, as the soldier tried to move his arms and speak before he died. Lieberman, who was promoted to corporal during the deployment, had several close calls of his own. During one foot patrol, he kicked down the front door of a house and came face-to-face with an insurgent bomb that had been booby-trapped to go off as soon as the first soldier stepped inside. The bomb didn't explode, but Lieberman told his mom that he was trembling for days. On a different mission, a sniper shot Lieberman right in the chest, destroying a digital camera and gouging a deep hole in his body armor but leaving him otherwise unscathed. "He counted nine incidents where he should have died and didn't, and that just made him feel terrible guilt whenever someone else from his unit was killed," his mother, Heidi, said.

Lieberman had always been a bit rowdy, but his behavior deteriorated rapidly once he got back from Iraq. He had panic attacks in public places like the local Walmart and 7-Eleven. He drank heavily and got into shouting matches and fistfights with other troops. In December 2007, Lieberman slugged one of his unit's top enlisted personnel after the sergeant insulted his roommate, a serious offense in the rank-sensitive world of the U.S. military. A few weeks later he told doctors at Fort Carson that he was suffering from nightmares, bursts of uncontrollable anger, insomnia, and emotional numbness. Death Dealer commanders didn't give Lieberman a bit of slack because of his admitted emotional problems. They instead demoted him to private and threatened to court-martial him for drinking, fighting, and other comparatively minor offenses such as breaking into a candy machine or leaving Fort Carson without permission, which he did in order to say good-bye to a friend who was preparing to leave for Iraq. "They chose not to see the problem," Heidi said. "They were going to punish the symptoms, not the cause."

Heidi Lieberman believes that the court-martial threat was what made her son suicidal. By the spring of 2008, Adam Lieberman was trying to decide between shooting himself in the head or driving his car off a cliff. Lieberman's anger, insomnia, and suicidal thoughts were among the classic symptoms of PTSD, but Fort Carson's behavioral health staff said that he was suffering from depression and anxiety that predated his time in the military and weren't tied to his combat experiences in Iraq. It's impossible to know whether Fort Carson doctors simply failed to spot Lieberman's PTSD or whether they were making a diagnosis of preexisting psychological problems so the army could dishonorably discharge him and avoid having to provide lifetime medical and financial benefits.

Either way, the doctors soon made a far more dangerous miscalculation. On October 30, according to medical records obtained by *Salon,* Lieberman's army psychologist said he was harboring thoughts of killing other people and was suffering from "alcohol dependence," depression, and anxiety. Still, the psychologist concluded that Lieberman had "no suicidal ideation" and wasn't actively thinking about taking his own life. She was wrong. Lieberman scrawled his note about the Death Dealers on the wall of his barracks room a few hours later when he tried to kill himself, though he didn't succeed. Groggy from the pills, he crawled out of his room and dialed 911. An ambulance rushed him to Evans, and doctors managed to purge the drugs out of Lieberman's system. His problems, though, were just beginning.

Heidi traveled to Fort Carson a few days after her son's suicide attempt to ask his commanders why Adam wasn't being moved into a unit devoted solely to treating soldiers with physical or psychological wounds. Lieutenant Colonel Lance Kohler, the commander of Lieberman's battalion, told Heidi that the military was thinking of court-martialing Adam for his candy machine break-in and other misdemeanors. Kohler paused and said that the army was considering charging Adam with one other offense: defacing government property. Heidi was stunned. "By painting his suicide note on the wall?" she asked.

Desperate to protect her son from being punished for his PTSD, Heidi called the captain in charge of Adam's company and offered to repaint the wall herself. To her surprise, the officer said yes. Heidi and her sister spent the next day painting the wall and covering up her son's scrawl about the Death Dealers, but it wasn't quite enough. Fort Carson's military police had Adam brought to a holding room, kept him there for hours, and chastised him for scrawling his note on the wall before they finally let him go.

Carol Graham was watching the local news a few days later when she saw a report about the Lieberman case and immediately called Mark. Mark listened, incredulous, to her description of what had taken place. He asked one of his aides to get Kohler on the phone.

"Please tell me this has not actually happened on our post," Mark said.

"Yes, sir, it did happen," Kohler replied, explaining that he was simply trying to give Heidi honest answers to her questions about Adam's treatment.

That answer made Mark even angrier. "Soldiers' moms don't paint barracks walls," he barked.

Mark believed that both Kohler and the young captain who had been in charge of Lieberman's unit had abjectly failed a young soldier who was desperately in need of help. "It was just unfathomable to me that this had occurred," he said. Mark called Kohler into his office to verbally reprimand him and ordered Lieberman's brigade commander to investigate the incident and consider whether to punish Kohler and the captain. Mark didn't follow up on the case to see if anything was actually done to either officer. At the time, he thought that making the two men's direct boss aware of the incident was enough. Today Mark believes he was far too light on Kohler and the captain. "In hindsight, I wish I had done more," he said. "I should have intervened personally to make sure they were given some type of disciplinary measure."

Heidi Lieberman said that she has long since forgotten the names of the men involved in her son's case and doesn't mind that they were never formally punished. She has much bigger things to worry about. Adam's army psychologist changed her diagnosis shortly after he tried to kill himself, attributing the suicide attempt to "chronic post-traumatic stress disorder." The PTSD has never gone away, and Adam was medically retired in June 2009. The army pays his medical bills and gives him a monthly stipend, but Adam lives at home and hasn't held a full-time job since leaving the army. Heidi isn't sure that he ever will. "He has good days, and he has bad days," she said. "On the good days he's fun to be with. On the bad days he knows not to be around people because of his mood changes and flashes of anger."

Adam Lieberman's time at Fort Carson ended with a failed attempt to take his own life. Far too many of the base's most troubled troops succeeded. Fort Carson's suicide rate in 2009 was 49 per 100,000, down slightly from 2008's rate of 66 per 100,000, but still far higher than the overall rates in both the military and civilian worlds. Carol and Mark went to the memorial services for all Fort Carson soldiers, regardless of how they died. They arrived early to spend some private time with the bereaved families and to share their own stories of loss. They spoke about Jeff if a soldier had been killed in combat, and about Kevin if it had been a suicide. "Rarely would we tell the families about both because it was just too much," Carol said. "We wanted them to know we understood and connected with their pain and sorrow, but we didn't want to add to it or try to make it about us." Some of the others who joined the Grahams in trying to comfort family members of the soldiers who took their own lives eventually chose to follow suit. Jeffrey Cartee, one of the base's chaplains, presided over hundreds of funerals of dead troops, including dozens who'd committed suicide. Cartee killed himself shortly after transferring from the base.

Mike Mullen, then the chairman of the Joint Chiefs of Staff, paid a visit to Fort Carson in the summer of 2008 and asked Mark to accompany him, alone, on the drive back to his waiting airplane. The invitation seemed ominous, and Mark thought he was about to be relieved of his command. *This*, Mark thought, *is not going to be a good ride.* Mullen didn't fire Mark, but he emphasized that the large numbers of murders and suicides at the base were unacceptable. Mark's charge was clear: Figure out what was causing the violence, and then figure out how to stop it.

In the months to come, Mark would turn Fort Carson into a laboratory for testing new methods of eliminating the stigma around mental health issues and getting troubled soldiers the help they needed before it was too late. Some of the experiments would work, and some would not. But even Mark's detractors would come to understand the magnitude of the challenge he had taken on. Mark wasn't looking for a set of easy fixes. He was trying to change the culture of an entire base, and of the military itself.

CHAPTER 17

Fort Carson, Colorado, February 2009

Sally Darrow picked up her cell phone and dialed the 800 number, praying that someone would pick up on the other end. Darrow's son, a young Fort Carson soldier named Michael Crawford, had just told her that he was about to kill himself, and she was frantically looking for a way to save his life. Darrow lived in rural Michigan, which meant that it would be impossible for her to travel to Fort Carson in time to prevent her son from harming himself. She'd never served in the military and didn't know whom to contact for assistance. She went to Fort Carson's website, hoping to find a name or number of someone who might be able to help. To her surprise, she found it. The page had Mark's photo and office phone number. "Got problems? Need help?" the site read. "Call this number." Darrow dialed, expecting to go to voice mail. But someone answered. "This is the commanding general's hotline," a soft female voice said. "How may I help you?"

Since returning from Iraq in December 2008, Darrow's son had been a wreck, shaken by what he'd seen and done as a sniper. Many of the men he killed looked like teenagers, not terrorists, and Crawford couldn't stop imagining their parents' grief. He was haunted by memories of the day he watched, powerless to help, as several friends burned to death when their Humvee was hit by an IED. His body was just as battered as his psyche: Crawford suffered three concussions from IED blasts, including one that sent him flying into a concrete wall and tore the leg off another soldier. He had come home to Colorado Springs moody, paranoid, and hypersensitive to slights, real or perceived. In February, he accused a group of Fort Carson soldiers of exaggerating their war stories; they responded by chasing him into the parking lot of a local Hooters, knocking him to the ground, and taking turns kicking him in the head. The assault left Crawford with a broken nose, a latticework of gashes on his face, and a severe brain hemorrhage that made it difficult for him to remember to show up for formation or keep his uniform in order. Crawford's sergeant treated him like a pariah, took away his gun, and prevented him from taking part in combat drills. Crawford had wanted to be a soldier since he was a child and had a hard time accepting that his military career was essentially over. He had also just found out that a baby he'd thought was his actually had a different father. He'd barely been holding on before, and the twin blows sent him careening over the edge. "Good-bye, Mom," he said shortly before Darrow called the hotline. "They tell me that I'm damaged in the head and that there's nothing they can do to help. I'm sorry, Mom. I'm sorry."

Darrow told Sergeant First Class Robin Foe, the woman who answered the phone at Fort Carson, that her son was serious about killing himself and that there was only a small window of time to prevent him from doing so. She didn't try to mask the fear in her voice. Darrow's son Justin had killed himself a few years earlier, and she told Foe that she couldn't imagine how she'd survive losing a second son to suicide.

"I'm just the mother of a soldier," Darrow said, crying. "I don't know how this stuff works. But my son is going to die soon if he doesn't get help."

"Give me ten minutes," Foe said.

Foe called Mark at home as soon as she hung up the phone, and they cobbled together a makeshift rescue plan. A soldier from Crawford's unit was sent to his barracks room to keep an eye on him and make sure that he didn't try to hurt himself. Mark arranged to get Crawford immediately transferred into a unit at Fort Carson that offered specialized psychiatric care. He was in treatment less than a day later.

Mark had built the hotline two years earlier, shortly after taking command. Fort Carson's former system sent callers straight to voice mail, a potentially fatal flaw that meant some troubled soldiers who reached out for help at a moment of crisis were unable to reach a live operator. Mark junked the existing hotline and had all of the calls routed to Foe's BlackBerry, trusting that the sergeant's calm demeanor and innate kindness would make her the ideal person to speak to a scared, jumpy soldier or concerned family member. Foe kept the phone with her around the clock and took calls late into the night, straining her marriage to the breaking point. "At a certain point my husband said it's either him or the BlackBerry, and of course the BlackBerry won," she said. "I kept thinking about the people who might have been falling through the cracks, the ones we lost because they didn't have anyone to talk to, anyone who would listen." Foe, the only soldier assigned to the hotline, tried to be that person. A soldier dialed in one night to say that he'd been AWOL for more than a month and was so afraid of being court-martialed that he was sitting at home with a gun, getting ready to shoot himself in the head. Foe kept him on the phone while she raced to his house with one of Fort Carson's chaplains. They managed to talk the soldier into putting down his weapon and accompanying them to Evans so he could be kept in a locked psychiatric ward for observation before being rushed into therapy. He survived, as did Michael Crawford.

The hotline system was an illustration of how Mark Graham tried to change Fort Carson during his years there. He would learn about a problem with one of the programs for helping war-damaged soldiers, look for what seemed like a good fix, and then try to put it into place as quickly as he could. When Mark took command, an individual unit had to be notified within seventy-two hours if one of its soldiers missed a mental health appointment. Mark, who worried that the three-day window gave troubled soldiers more than enough time to harm themselves, put in a new rule requiring that the unit be alerted the same day a soldier failed to show up for a counseling session. Mark would go so far as to directly intervene on behalf of individual soldiers he thought were being mistreated by their own commanders. It was virtually unheard-of for a general to get personally involved in standard disciplinary cases, and some of Fort Carson's officers and sergeants were furious that Mark was willing to reach all the way down into their units and overrule their decisions. Others, particularly within the base's medical community, resented that Mark intruded on their turf and sometimes tried to force them to change how they were doing their jobs. The complaints were often justified: Mark alienated some talented officers and enlisted personnel by imposing his own views and not giving enough deference to theirs. For better or worse, it was a fight Mark was willing to wage. He took behavioral health issues such as suicide far more seriously than his predecessors had, and for far more personal reasons. He and Carol felt invisible wounds were just as deadly as physical ones, and they were willing to do anything in their power to try to help heal them.

In the fall of 2007, just weeks after taking command, Mark summoned dozens of Fort Carson's highest-ranking officers to the Elkhorn Conference Center, a one-story redbrick building that overlooks nearby Cheyenne Mountain. Mark told them that the base was failing to provide adequate care to troops who were returning from Iraq or Afghanistan with PTSD or depression. Troops who sought help, he said, were often made to feel like they didn't deserve to serve alongside their fellow soldiers. In one case, Mark said, a soldier who told his chain of command that he needed to see a psychiatrist was ordered to drink from a sink in the bathroom instead of the water fountain used by the rest of his unit. "You are all going to stop things like this from happening and you're going to stop it now," he said to the assembled officers. "You're going to pay attention and look after your soldiers."

Then Mark did something none of the officers had ever seen before. He told them about Kevin's suicide, stressing that he and Carol were haunted by the thought that they could have done more to prevent their younger son from taking his own life. His voice cracked as he spoke. By the time he finished, Major General Mark Graham, meeting with many of his officers for the first time, was crying.

Lieutenant Colonel Gaylene Weber was sitting in the audience during Mark's remarks, and she was stunned by the scene unfolding in front of her. Weber had gone to dozens of military memorial services over the years, and the generals she'd seen in the front rows of the churches seemed to go out of their way to avoid crying or displaying any sign of emotion. When Mark started talking about Kevin's suicide, Weber noticed some of the officers sitting nearby shifting in their seats and looking away from the podium; they were clearly uncomfortable watching a general show his emotions so openly. That changed once the officers realized that Mark cared about suicide prevention so much that he was willing to risk being ridiculed behind his back. "When Mark started crying, there wasn't a peep in the room," Weber said. "It was clear that he was really different from other general officers."

Mark also surprised many at the base by making a point, early in his tenure, of sitting down with Andrew Pogany, the former Special Forces noncommissioned officer who'd emerged as an unofficial advocate for soldiers diagnosed with PTSD or other psychological wounds. Pogany was persona non grata at Fort Carson, and Graham's predecessor, Major General Robert Mixon, had refused to talk with him. Other officers tried to get Pogany banned from the post, and some called the military police whenever they spotted him talking to one of their soldiers. Angela Gilpin, who worked as Mixon's executive assistant, said Pogany was seen as a self-promoter who was out to harm Fort Carson's public image because of his own past battles with the army.

Mark was willing to give Pogany the benefit of the doubt. Bonnie Carroll, one of Mark's closest friends, told him that Pogany was genuinely committed to helping war-damaged troops and that he often had detailed and accurate information about individual soldiers who were being mistreated by others on the base. "She said that if I wanted the ground truth, I should listen to Andrew Pogany," Mark said.

Mark invited Pogany into his tidy, sunny office on the top floor of the base's central command building shortly after the Elkhorn speech and listened to the story of Ryan LeCompte, a young soldier who had served a pair of lengthy tours in Iraq before returning to Fort Carson in January 2006. LeCompte sought medical help in early June 2007, telling doctors at Fort Carson that he couldn't sleep or get through the day without having flashbacks to his time in Iraq. He also developed a host of physical problems. He had a hard time getting out of bed, walking, or finding the energy to brush his teeth. His wife, Tammie, effectively became a full-time nurse, bringing her husband food to ensure that he didn't starve, walking him to the shower when he couldn't get there himself, and pushing him to his unit's 5:30 A.M. formations in a wheelchair when he had trouble even standing. She seriously considered leaving him.

LeCompte's superior officers thought he was simply a substandard soldier. They saw a young man in the prime of his life who showed up late to drills, skipped his daily physical fitness training, appeared dazed and disheveled, and regularly claimed to have forgotten his orders. A few months after his return, LeCompte was arrested after allegedly assaulting a pair of other soldiers at their barracks. LeCompte's brigade commander, Colonel Butch Kievenaar, had had enough. He felt LeCompte was faking his problems and was simply a bad soldier who wasn't worthy of continued service in the United States Army. Kievenaar slapped LeCompte with an Article 15, the strictest punishment a soldier can receive short of a full court-martial. It reduced his rank from specialist to private, sharply cut his pay, and paved the way for him to be kicked out of the military with a dishonorable discharge.

Mark heard about LeCompte through the base's legislative liaison officer in the fall of 2007 and asked his aides to bring him all of the details of the case that they could find. Something immediately seemed off. LeCompte had never been accused of misconduct before his time in Iraq, and he'd won plaudits from his commanders during the years he spent in the war zone. The young soldier's behavior was out of character, and Mark couldn't help but conclude that his combat experiences in Iraq had caused the changes. He got LeCompte transferred from Fort Carson to Walter Reed, and it didn't take doctors there long to decide that LeCompte's problems were real and that he had lost the capacity to care for his own physical needs. In a memo dated December 13, 2007, Dr. Geoffrey Grammer, the chief of inpatient psychiatry at Walter Reed, diagnosed LeCompte with "severe catatonic depression" and PTSD. "There is no doubt about the validity of his symptoms and no evidence on the ward of embellishment or malingering," Grammer wrote in LeCompte's medical records.

In the spring of 2008, Mark signed a memorandum that entirely reversed the punishments Kievenaar had imposed. Mark wrote that LeCompte had been diagnosed with "mental health problems due to a traumatic brain injury and post-traumatic stress disorder from two tours in Iraq" and noted that he had sought medical help almost immediately after returning to the United States. Mark restored the young soldier to specialist, gave him back pay for the salary he'd lost while at the lower rank, and removed the Article 15 from his military record. His ruling cleared the way for LeCompte to be medically discharged from the army, allowing him to receive free medical treatment and other financial benefits for the rest of his life.

The decision infuriated Kievenaar, who felt that Mark had basically given a free pass to a soldier who'd falsely claimed that he was suffering from PTSD to escape punishment for his own personal failings. "There was a belief that the chain of command was seen as guilty unless proven innocent, and that if there was a problem, it was because we didn't do something," Kievenaar said. "We weren't allowed to hold the soldier accountable to the standards and values of our institution."

Mark believes that officers such as Kievenaar were simply reluctant to acknowledge the severity of PTSD. "I had a different set of beliefs from some of the other officers at Fort Carson, and some of the commanders disagreed with me because it was a new way of doing things," Mark said. "I erred on the side of the soldier and didn't want to punish someone if there were reasons to think his problems came from PTSD."

LeCompte was just one soldier, and Mark knew that other troops risked being treated exactly the same way unless Fort Carson's systems for identifying and treating those with physical and mental wounds were fundamentally restructured. The longer he was at the base, the more Mark came to understand just how many parts of the military would need to change.

Master Sergeant Denny Nelson read and reread the deployment orders, but he couldn't make sense of them. Nelson, a nineteen-year veteran with a Bronze Star, had suffered severe leg and foot injuries in the fall of 2007 while playing on his daughter's trampoline. That November doctors at Fort Carson said that he shouldn't run, jump, or carry anything weighing more than twenty pounds for at least three months. The doctors were emphatic: Nelson shouldn't be sent anywhere near the war zone.

His bosses disagreed, and they shipped him to Kuwait less than a month after the diagnosis. In a January 3, 2008, e-mail obtained by the *Denver Post*, Captain Scot Tebo, the surgeon for Nelson's brigade, explained that the unit had "been having issues reaching deployable strength, and thus have been taking along some borderline soldiers who we would otherwise have left behind for continued treatment." Two days later Major Thomas Schymanski, a doctor in Kuwait, e-mailed Tebo to ask that Nelson be shipped back to Fort Carson. "This soldier should NOT have even left [the United States]," Schymanski wrote. "In his current state, he is not full mission capable and in his current condition is a risk to further injury to himself, others and his unit."

Nelson was sent home in mid-January, but the case alerted Mark to a serious problem: Some Fort Carson soldiers were being sent to the war zones despite injuries so severe that the base's doctors wanted them kept back in the United States for treatment. He ordered Fort Carson's inspector general to investigate. The resulting report found that there was "no initial indication that the units deliberately deployed medically unfit soldiers against explicit medical advice" but said that Nelson and at least thirty-five other soldiers from the 3rd Brigade Combat Team of the 4th Infantry Division had been sent to the Middle East despite having been diagnosed as "nondeployable" because of their wounds.

As Mark dug into the issue, he came to believe that the practice was a direct result of the military's desperate need to recruit new soldiers and retain the ones it already had as the long wars in Iraq and Afghanistan dragged on. The army had tried to find more troops by lowering its eligibility standards, allowing in growing numbers of troops who lacked high school diplomas, were obese, or had criminal records. It had tried to buy its way out of the personnel shortage by offering officers retention bonuses of more than $30,000 and giving $20,000 bonuses to enlisted soldiers who agreed to go straight to Iraq after basic training. It had tried to persuade wavering soldiers to make a career in the army by promoting record numbers of officers and enlisted personnel to higher ranks. When the moves didn't bring in enough troops, the army shifted to a pair of far more controversial initiatives. One was a "stop-loss" policy that forced tens of thousands of soldiers to remain in the military after their enlistments ended. The other was the widespread, if informal, practice of sending troops such as Denny Nelson to the war zones even if doctors wanted them to stay back in the United States. Pentagon records show that at least forty-three thousand such soldiers from across the army were sent overseas between 2003 and 2008.

Mark thought the deployment policy was profoundly misguided. Iraq had no fixed front lines, so wounded troops given noncombat jobs could easily find themselves thrown into sudden firefights that they were physically unprepared to handle. He also feared for the troops' emotional well-being. Soldiers who were unable to serve alongside others from their unit risked feeling like they were letting their friends down, particularly if colleagues were hurt or killed. Mark had no ability to affect what the rest of the army was doing, but he had the power to change Fort Carson's own procedures for deciding which troops could safely be sent overseas. On July 9, 2008, he issued an order requiring commanders to get his personal approval for any individual soldier they wanted to bring overseas despite a doctor's recommendation that the soldier be held back for medical treatment. Policy 25 marked a change in how the army went about its business. Colonels commanding combat brigades normally had full autonomy to decide which troops to deploy to the war zones, and in what capacities. Mark was now taking that power for himself, a move that many officers saw as an unwarranted intrusion into their ability to run their own units. "It's hard for me to overstate how unpopular that policy was," said Heidi Terrio, a retired army colonel who ran Fort Carson's Soldier Readiness Processing Center. "The commanders really didn't appreciate that policy because it took the decision making out of their hands. General Graham began weighing in on specific soldiers, and a lot of commanders saw it as micromanaging."

Colonel Kelly Wolgast was particularly uneasy about Mark's involvement in her work. Mark was in charge of the base's overall operations, with one major exception: its hospital and sprawling medical system. That was the purview of Wolgast, who had a view of mental health profoundly different from Mark's. Mark was willing to trust that soldiers who came forward to seek help were actually suffering from PTSD. Wolgast believed that many of the troops were faking their symptoms to avoid being sent back to Iraq or Afghanistan, and she urged her staff to be careful about devoting too much of their time and resources to troops who might not be as badly off psychologically as they claimed. Pogany recalls sitting down with Wolgast once to discuss whether to hospitalize a certain soldier with severe depression. "She basically told me that he wasn't suicidal enough to warrant hospitalization," Pogany said. "I was flabbergasted. How do you know when a guy is going to snap? How can you just wait for someone to deteriorate to the point where they may or may not do something and may or may not ask for help? It was a profoundly unsettling conversation."

Wolgast was turf-conscious, and she made no effort to hide her belief that Mark should leave her to run Evans and the base's medical operations as she saw fit. Gaylene Weber had been tapped to oversee Fort Carson's Warrior Transition Unit, a new and controversial organization that the army had created to give troops with physical, mental, or psychological wounds a safe place, far from the front lines, to recover. Mark made a point of visiting the unit once a week and sitting down privately with the soldiers to hear about whether they felt satisfied with their treatment. The answer, all too often, was no. Some soldiers complained about waiting far too long to see a counselor, others about being given so many prescription drugs that they felt like they were going through life in a haze.

Mark would bring those concerns directly to Weber, who commanded the unit, or to Wolgast, Weber's boss. His comments weren't always welcome. Wolgast told other officers that she was a registered nurse with decades of medical experience. A layman like Mark, she said, should stay in his lane and not try to change how the hospital staff did its jobs. "No one likes having a general officer coming down into their units and telling them what to do," Weber said. "I eventually got used to it, but it really grated on Kelly."

On a purely bureaucratic level, Wolgast had a point: She was part of the army's medical command, which meant that Mark wasn't technically her boss. Still, she was a colonel, and Mark was a two-star general. He hated to pull rank on her, but Mark wasn't afraid to do so when he felt she'd left him no other choice. The biggest dispute erupted over a soft-spoken psychiatric nurse and retired army captain named Alison Lighthall.

Lighthall had been brought to Fort Carson in 2008 to try to help answer the two most important questions facing the base: What was causing so many of its soldiers to take their own lives, and what could be done to prevent it? Six soldiers had killed themselves in 2007, Mark's first year in command, setting a new record. Lighthall quickly came to two conclusions. First, the most logical explanation for the suicide spike—that the troops were simply breaking down under the stress of repeated deployments—didn't hold up to scrutiny. The majority of troops had gone through multiple tours to the war zones, but more than a third had either never deployed or had done just a single tour. Her second takeaway was that Fort Carson needed to ensure that the different programs that dealt with troubled soldiers shared information about which troops might be most at risk. The behavioral health staff on the fourth floor of Evans, for instance, didn't talk to personnel from the base's substance abuse program even though increased alcohol or drug use was often a sign that a soldier was depressed and thinking of suicide.

One of Lighthall's initial attempts to improve Fort Carson's behavioral health system almost ended her career. She had read a book called *Why People Die by Suicide* by Thomas Joiner and been struck by its argument that troubled men and women typically took their own lives only after they'd had firsthand exposure to death, started to feel that they didn't fit in with their friends or family anymore, and decided that they had become a burden to their loved ones. Lighthall felt that the work offered a clear, cohesive theory for why soldiers committed suicide—troops serving in Iraq or Afghanistan surrounded by violence often had serious problems readjusting to life at home—and a potential way to identify those most at risk before they could actually do so. She turned the book's central thesis into a PowerPoint presentation and e-mailed it to Carol. Carol forwarded the file to Mark, who invited Lighthall to his office to walk him through the presentation and teach him how to deliver it to others. Wolgast went ballistic when she heard about the meeting. Lighthall was her employee, and Wolgast felt that she'd deliberately gone outside the chain of command by going to see a two-star general on her own. Lighthall was certain that she was about to be fired, but Mark fought to protect her. "Kelly, we need Alison here," he told Wolgast at a reception. The military's strict hierarchy made it highly unusual for a general to weigh in on personnel decisions, particularly those involving low-ranking staffers such as Lighthall, but Mark's intervention worked and she kept her job.

Mark's relationship with Wolgast deteriorated so much after the Lighthall incident that he took the unusual step of reaching out to her boss, Major General James Gilman, to complain. He worried that the bureaucratic tussling with Wolgast could actually put soldiers' lives at risk. "I told him I was frustrated that she wasn't on the team as much as she should be," Mark said. "She wasn't in sync with me or what I was trying to do on the base, and I thought he needed to know that."

Gilman flew to Fort Carson and spent time with Mark and other officers from the base with similar concerns about Wolgast's behavior and worldview. He concluded that Mark's disputes with Wolgast stemmed from a philosophical disagreement about whether soldiers with PTSD should be held to the same standards as other troops when it came to drug use or other misconduct.

"Colonel Wolgast sincerely believed that the best approach was to hold a pretty hard line when it came to matters of indiscipline and operating within the chain of command," Gilman said. "Major General Graham was, in my opinion, at the other end of the spectrum—multiple failures before any discipline or punishment."

That same debate had been raging across the army since the start of the long wars in Iraq and Afghanistan. Still, Gilman said, Mark and Wolgast "were less flexible in their stances than the rest of us."

Wolgast, who now teaches at Vanderbilt University, declined to comment for this book, but she disagreed just as sharply with Mark's approach to mental health as he did with hers. She was also far from the only Fort Carson soldier who felt that Mark was too soft on troubled soldiers and too quick to overrule officers and sergeants who wanted to punish substandard troops or boot them out of the army altogether. "People in the hallways would talk about how Mark wanted to babysit all of these troops who should really be thrown out of the army," said Sergeant First Class Kalena Hodges, who'd served as Mark's enlisted aide, a job that put her in charge of organizing official social functions at Ouray House. "They called him a 'limp dick' who wasn't tough enough to run the base during a war."

In 2009, more than two years into Mark's tenure at Fort Carson, Hodges overheard a senior officer tell a colleague that Mark had gotten the job solely because of the military's version of affirmative action. "The only reason he even made general was because of what happened to his sons," she remembered the officer saying.

Mark Graham had more than his share of critics, but he also had more than his share of allies. Gilman used his influence within the army's medical command to increase the size of Evans's beleaguered behavioral health department from 48 counselors in 2007 to 109 counselors in 2009. Henry Yates, Fort Carson's ombudsman, alerted Mark to cases where individual soldiers with PTSD were being mistreated and worked to help him make sure they got the help they needed. Weber tried to persuade skeptical colleagues from inside the Warrior Transition Unit to give Mark a fair hearing and not simply dismiss him as a meddler. Foe made sure that hotline calls were always answered, regardless of the time of day. None of Mark's allies, however, were more important than a battle-hardened army colonel named Randy George.

George had had an unusual army career, starting off as an enlisted soldier before switching to West Point and earning his commission as an officer. He'd done a pair of combat tours through Iraq and Afghanistan, earning a chestful of commendations and medals, and arrived at Fort Carson in June 2008 to take command of the Lethal Warriors, the troubled combat brigade at the center of the base's murder spree. He was still settling into his new offices when he got word that soldiers from the unit had just been arrested for the killings of Amairany Cervantes and Cesar Ramirez Ibanez, the young Colorado Springs residents who had been gunned down in front of their nephew. "I had literally just gotten there," George said. "It was, to put it mildly, a wake-up call."

The brigade was scheduled to deploy to a particularly violent patch of Afghanistan the following summer, and George worried that some of the men might break down under the strain of combat. Many of the Lethal Warriors had been with the unit during its last tour through Iraq, and they'd had barely a year to recover from the pain of losing dozens of friends to insurgent roadside bombs and ambushes there.

George decided to do whatever he could to get his troops psychologically prepared for the difficulties of being far from home, the trauma of surviving attacks that took the lives of their colleagues, and their own fears about being hurt or killed during the tough times ahead. With Mark's permission, George hired a company called the Magus Group to put the four thousand soldiers in his brigade through a four-hour course on deep breathing, meditation, and other techniques for dealing with the stress of combat. George and his top officers and sergeants made a point of going through the class first to show their troops that it was nothing to be embarrassed about. Some of the soldiers privately mocked the program, but most took to it. The military is a strict hierarchy, and troops were accustomed to emulating their commanders and following their lead without exception. Mark snuck into the back of a darkened office one afternoon and saw rows of George's soldiers lying on the floor, practicing how to control their breathing. "It sounded like a Lamaze class," Mark said. "I expected to go in and hear snarky remarks from some of the soldiers, but there was none of that. People took it seriously."

The deep-breathing course was one of the first pilot programs Mark rolled out during his time at the base, part of a series of initiatives that would slowly begin to turn Fort Carson into a laboratory for testing new ideas about suicide prevention and mental health. He encouraged Evans to hire a full-time acupuncturist and pushed units throughout the base to offer voluntary yoga classes to their soldiers. Some of the doctors at Evans opposed both moves, arguing that the medical benefits of acupuncture and yoga had never been scientifically proven. Mark was no fan of yoga—he had tried it once in Korea to help with a sore back, and the stretching only made it worse—but he felt there was no harm in making it available to soldiers who wanted to try it. "Some of the doctors said there was no data and that these things have never been proven to work," Mark said. "My feeling was, 'Okay, but how long should we wait to put something out there that might help?' If yoga wasn't going to hurt the soldiers, I didn't see any reason why we shouldn't try it."

In January 2009, Mark signed off on the creation of an entirely new way of looking after soldiers' emotional and psychological needs, a system that would eventually be replicated across the entire army. When Mark took command, any soldier who wanted counseling had to visit Evans's fourth floor, the sole place to see the base's psychologists, psychiatrists, and social workers. The stigma surrounding mental health issues was so strong that many troops opted not to seek help because they were afraid other soldiers would see them going there. Mark quickly recognized the severity of the problem and he asked the hospital's behavioral health staff to figure out a way of bringing care out to the soldiers rather than simply expecting soldiers to come see them. The idea developed into a concept known as the "embedded behavioral health" program, or EBH, which proposed assigning a team of about a dozen behavioral health specialists to a single combat brigade of roughly 3,500 soldiers. The team would operate out of the brigade's existing medical clinic so soldiers would get used to the idea that seeing a psychologist for depression was no different from seeing a nurse for a sprained ankle. The behavioral health staffers would work exclusively with one brigade, giving them a chance to get to know the unit's soldiers before the troops deployed so they'd be better equipped to spot at-risk personnel when the unit came home. The brigade's soldiers, meanwhile, would see the same therapists repeatedly, giving them a level of comfort and trust that would be impossible to develop with counselors the troops saw only once or twice.

Mark had an icy relationship with Kelly Wolgast, but he signed off on the idea as soon as she formally presented it to him. Randy George, in turn, asked that his brigade get the first of the new teams. There wasn't enough time to build offices for the team before George's unit deployed, so the behavioral health personnel set up shop in the brigade's medical clinic and made themselves available to any troops who wanted to talk. They worked with soldiers from George's unit right up until it deployed to Afghanistan that summer. "We wanted that team down with us so it could become part of the unit culture," George said. "It meant that my guys weren't talking to strangers." A later army report found that the number of soldiers from the brigade who exhibited "risk behaviors" such as suicide attempts, financial problems, or positive drug tests in the six months before their deployments was nearly 60 percent lower than in a comparable frontline unit that hadn't worked with an embedded behavioral health team. Other brigades throughout the army soon started building teams of their own.

Mark Graham had given himself three main goals when he took command at Fort Carson. The Iraq War was intensifying, and Mark believed that his top priority was to make sure soldiers from the base were trained and equipped properly before they deployed. His second mission was to improve the base's systems for identifying troubled soldiers and working to get them help. His third one was to change how the base commemorated troops who took their own lives. Transforming the base's entire mental health system was the more important move because it clearly had the potential to save lives. Making sure that soldiers who committed suicide received the respect they deserved was a much harder, and more personal, fight.

Staff Sergeant Chad Barrett shouldn't have been sent back to Iraq. He had returned to the United States after two previous deployments depressed, lethargic, and prone to suddenly screaming at his wife and picking fights with strangers, according to a detailed account in *Salon*. In 2007, a few months before he was set to leave for his third combat tour, Barrett tried to kill himself by downing a powerful cocktail of prescription drugs. The army diagnosed him with severe PTSD and began the process of formally discharging him.

Barrett wasn't ready to leave. He had grown up listening to his grandfather's stories about World War II and helped pull charred human remains out of the rubble of the Pentagon after the September 11 terror attacks. He was devoted to the army and to his fellow soldiers. When he got word that his unit was preparing for a new deployment to Iraq, Barrett began pressing the army to let him go with them. His brigade was desperately short of men, and Barrett managed to persuade his doctors and commanders to halt the discharge proceedings. In the fall of 2007, Dr. Jonathan Olin, a psychiatrist at Evans, gave Barrett a final examination that concluded he had "no suicidal intent," according to medical records obtained by *Salon*. Barrett was given prescriptions for a range of antidepressants and sleeping pills and cleared for a return to active duty. He had spent his entire career as a frontline combat soldier, but Barrett would be going back this time as an overnight radio operator, a job that wouldn't allow him to carry around a loaded weapon. On Christmas Day he shipped off for Iraq.

It didn't take long for Barrett's depression to return. On January 28, 2008, a massive roadside bomb killed five soldiers from his unit. Barrett told his parents that he felt like he should have died with them. They pleaded with him to get help, but Barrett told them in a February 1 e-mail that the army only cared about having "the correct number of people on the ground . . . no matter what the cost."

"Everyone," he added darkly, "will find out the cost soon enough."

The e-mail terrified Barrett's parents, and they desperately tried to contact their son's commanders in Iraq to ask that he be put into some form of protective custody. They didn't get through in time. Early in the morning of February 2, just hours after sending the e-mail, Chad Barrett killed himself by swallowing a mound of prescription sleeping pills and antidepressants. In a suicide note left in his barracks and obtained by *Salon,* he wrote that he was feeling "hopeless," that he had "no reason or purpose in life," and that he was "wanting to die."

Barrett's suicide came just days after hundreds of soldiers filled an auditorium at Forward Operating Base Marez in northern Iraq to pay tribute to the five soldiers who'd died in the roadside bombing. The top U.S. generals in Iraq flew in from Baghdad for the ceremony, which ended with individual soldiers walking toward the front of the room and saluting the pictures of each of the fallen troops as taps echoed through the large, drafty building. Barrett's service was very different. So few soldiers showed up that only the first few rows of the auditorium were filled, according to a later report in the *Colorado Springs Gazette*. Taps wasn't played, and the soldiers who attended didn't salute Barrett's photo as they marched out of the building. Barrett was a soldier who'd spent years battling the same shadowy militants who'd killed their five friends, but the men of the 3rd Brigade Combat Team of the 4th Infantry Division simply didn't know what to make of a man who'd chosen to take his own life rather than losing it in combat.

A similar debate was raging half a world away in the hallways of Fort Carson. Mark and Carol attended every memorial service for a Fort Carson soldier, regardless of whether the soldier had died in combat or by suicide. They also made sure to spend time with the relatives of soldiers who'd killed themselves, knowing all too well that they were often shunned by other military families. When it came to Chad Barrett, Graham believed that the combat veteran died from the PTSD he'd carried home from Iraq and deserved to have his name engraved on the base's memorial wall for soldiers lost in Iraq and Afghanistan. Barrett's commanders felt just as strongly that the wall should be used to honor only those killed in combat. Mark's opponents weren't coldhearted or cruel men. They simply believed that soldiers who chose to take their own lives, regardless of their personal demons, were fundamentally different from those who had fallen in combat. Even some of Mark's strongest allies felt that giving soldiers who died in combat and troops who killed themselves the same type of burial service risked validating suicide or making it seem like an acceptable way to die. "The difficulty is that we don't want to encourage anyone else to commit suicide," said Lieutenant Colonel Chris Ivany, who ran Fort Carson's behavioral health sciences unit during much of Mark's tenure at the base.

Mark ultimately settled the debate by overruling the other officers and ordering them to add Barrett's name to the memorial. The soldiers complied, but many did little to hide their anger. A handful of troops from Barrett's unit made a point of boycotting the somber ceremony where Barrett's name was chiseled into the granite wall. Mark, other critics on the base began to whisper, was simply not tough enough to be a wartime commander. No one said that about Colonel Randy George, Mark's primary ally at Fort Carson and a man whose previous tours through Iraq and Afghanistan had earned him a well-deserved reputation as one of the base's bravest and most battle-hardened officers. George would soon be confronted with a case much like that of Chad Barrett. To the surprise of many at Fort Carson, he would handle it in much the same way.

The attackers massed outside Combat Outpost Keating in the dark, taking up positions just hundreds of yards away from the remote U.S. base in eastern Afghanistan. They struck just before sunrise on October 3, 2009, lashing Keating with mortars, rocket-propelled grenades, and machine-gun fire. An assault force of more than two hundred Taliban fighters rushed in from multiple directions, breaching the makeshift walls surrounding the outpost and forcing their way into the base itself. "Enemy in the wire at keating," a terrified young soldier messaged to a nearby base. "ENEMUY IN THE WIRE ENEMY IN THE WIRE!!!" The Taliban fighters overran the base, destroying Keating's power generators, ransacking its armory, and setting fire to every building they could. It took U.S. warplanes and helicopters more than nine hours to fully repulse the insurgents. Eight of Randy George's soldiers were killed in the attack, one of the military's worst single-day losses of the Afghan war. Two dozen other troops were badly wounded. George had recommended closing the base months earlier, but his warnings about its vulnerabilities were dismissed by top U.S. commanders in Kabul. The attack vindicated his assessment, though at a horrifically high price.

George and his men suffered a very different type of casualty less than two months later at a small base overlooking the snowcapped Hindu Kush mountains. Staff Sergeant Thaddeus Montgomery was a dreadlocked reggae fanatic who spent three years working at Yellowstone National Park before enlisting in the army in March of 2003, just as U.S. forces were sweeping into Iraq. He did one tour there and was on his second deployment to Afghanistan when his life suddenly went off the rails. Montgomery was stationed at a remote base in the Korengal Valley, a Taliban stronghold where dozens of American troops had died since the start of the war. The base was rocketed virtually every day, and U.S. patrols leaving its fortified perimeter were routinely ambushed by unseen enemies. On January 16, 2010, a young army specialist named Robert Donevski was killed in a Taliban strike, and Montgomery never quite recovered. Back at Keating, Montgomery told commanders that he felt like he could no longer fight, according to a later account in the *Washington Post*. He insisted that he wasn't suicidal, but the captain running the base grew so concerned about Montgomery's mental state that he arranged for him to be flown out on January 20. Montgomery killed himself a few hours before the helicopter landed to bring him home.

Montgomery's death forced George to confront the difficult question of how to properly mark the death of a soldier who took his own life rather than having it taken on the battlefield, the exact challenge Mark faced in the Chad Barrett case. At the start of the two wars the answer would have been simple. Montgomery's death, while tragic, would have been handled far differently from that of a soldier who fell in combat. It would have been commemorated but without the formal battlefield services accorded those killed in battle. By 2010, though, George had come to believe that depression was a physical wound and that suicide wasn't simply a sign of weakness. Montgomery, he decided, had done two difficult combat tours and was in the midst of a deployment to arguably the most dangerous single base in Afghanistan. He was a combat casualty of a different sort, but a combat casualty all the same.

George, the brigade commander, ordered his men to give Montgomery the same service that he'd have received if he'd died in battle. On a sunlit afternoon the men who'd served with Montgomery in Baker Company stood in formation in front of a makeshift memorial constructed from Montgomery's rifle, dog tags, helmet, and boots. Baker Company's chaplain read an invocation, and the unit's top enlisted officer called the company's roll, pausing when he got to Montgomery's name. A bugler played taps, the notes echoing through the barren outpost. "He was a warrior," George, who has since been promoted to brigadier general, said. "He deserved to be remembered as one."

Mark relinquished command in the summer of 2009, leaving Colorado for a new posting at the Army Forces Command (FORSCOM) in Georgia. It had taken a heavy personal and professional toll, but he had won his most important battles at Fort Carson. The changes Mark put in place turned the base into a model for the rest of the army. Other bases launched hotlines of their own, and the Pentagon eventually rolled out an army-wide phone system modeled on the one Mark created at Fort Carson. Nearly three dozen mobile behavioral health teams have since been set up at fourteen army bases, including the military's five largest facilities. Tens of thousands of soldiers have been given classes on meditation and deep breathing, and army-approved yoga courses— informally known as "Joga," a play on the traditional way of calling a soldier "Joe"—can be found on virtually every military base in the country. The army's top leadership mandated that soldiers who killed themselves be given the same type of memorial service as those who fell in combat, formally adopting a policy that Mark had put in place at Fort

Carson over the objections of many of the base's top officers and enlisted personnel.

The changes were motivated by what army leaders could no longer deny was a full-blown suicide epidemic. The number of soldiers who succumbed to their own demons was steadily increasing, setting a grim record each year only to break it the next. In 2008, 143 soldiers from across the army took their own lives; in 2009, that number spiked to 162. Fort Carson was a rare bright spot. In 2008 the base's suicide rate was 66 per 100,000, triple the army average. It fell to 49 per 100,000 in 2009 and to 31 per 100,000 in 2010. Mark had made large numbers of enemies at Fort Carson, but he and Carol had no doubt the fights had been worth it.

CHAPTER 18

West Point, New York, July 9, 2011

The crowd rose to its feet as Mark Graham led his daughter down the aisle of West Point's Cadet Chapel, a century-old church whose towering center spire dominates the skyline of the military academy's low-slung campus. Melanie wore a sleeveless white wedding dress with a long train, a diaphanous veil, and a hidden pocket that allowed her to carry her brothers' dog tags with her. Mark wore a blue army dress uniform with gold striping on the sides of his pants and rows of multicolored military service medals on the left lapel of his waist-length jacket. Joe Quinn was waiting in the front of the sanctuary, smiling at the woman who was about to become his wife.

Joe and Melanie had gotten engaged the previous summer during a walk through the lush greenery of the Boston Common, the young couple's favorite park. Joe dropped to one knee and asked Melanie to marry him, but the engagement ring had somehow gotten lodged deep in the pocket of his suit pants. Melanie was giggling by the time he pulled it out. "You've got to be kidding me," she told him. Joe had broken his knee in elementary school and shook his head, partly from the pain of kneeling down for so long. "I'm dying over here," he told her. "You've got to say yes." She did.

One year later Chaplain Mike Durham, West Point's top religious official, opened a leather-encased Bible and turned to Mark.

"Who giveth this woman to be married to this man?" he asked.

"Her father," Mark replied, lifting the veil from his daughter's face.

Joe and Melanie, flanked by bridesmaids in emerald-green strapless dresses and groomsmen in black tuxedoes, climbed the carpeted stairs leading to the altar at the front of the sanctuary. A wall-sized marble triptych showing Saint Michael the Archangel and a pair of other celestial warriors loomed just above the platform, bathed in the sunlight that streamed through a large stained glass window showing figures from the Old and New Testaments. The flags of West Point and the United States stood at the edges of the altar, tangible reminders that the chapel, despite its beauty, was part of a military base, not a church.

Durham led Joe and Melanie through their vows, asking each of them to treasure the other as a precious gift from God. Joe slid a platinum wedding ring onto Melanie's finger, and Melanie slid one onto Joe's.

"What therefore God hath joined together let no man put asunder," Durham said. "Joe, you may kiss your bride." He did.

Joe and Melanie's friends and relatives cheered a short time later as the newlyweds made their way into the glassed-in banquet hall where the reception was being held. Mark Graham waited for Joe and Melanie to finish their first dance as a married couple before walking to the front of the room and picking up a microphone.

"The roads have been bumpy, and all of you in this room know that because you've ridden the road with us," he told the crowd. "We thank each and every one of you for being with the Grahams and the Quinns during some of our bumpiest times."

Mark raised his glass and asked everyone to stand. "Ladies and gentlemen, I propose a toast to Mr. and Mrs. Joe Quinn," he said, taking a long sip of his champagne. "Let the good times roll."

A few hours later, Mark held Carol in his arms for a slow dance and then leaned in to kiss his wife softly on the lips. The wedding, he and Carol say, was the happiest day of their lives.

Two days later Mark was on his way back to his office at the Army Forces Command in Georgia when his secretary said that General James Thurman, Mark's former boss, was calling from his new post in Korea. Mark took a deep breath. He knew that the four-star general wouldn't have carved time out of his busy schedule to share good news.

"Mark, I'm calling to let you know that you haven't been selected to move forward to being a three-star," Thurman said. "I'm sorry."

Mark immediately understood the significance of Thurman's call. The military has a system known informally as "up or out." In practice it means that generals who aren't promoted are effectively forced to retire at the end of their current assignments. Thurman wasn't simply telling Mark that he wasn't going to get a third star; he was telling Major General Mark Graham that his thirty-four-year army career was over.

The call wasn't a total surprise. FORSCOM has an important role—overseeing the training and mobilization of soldiers worldwide—but it's one of the least-known and least-prestigious commands in the entire military, and many of the officers who are assigned there see it as a clear sign that they won't be promoted. Mark had started his FORSCOM job just days after relinquishing command of Fort Carson in August 2009, and many of his friends inside and outside the army thought it would be his final assignment. Mark loved his work, which involved helping to design and implement FORSCOM's training efforts, but he secretly shared the belief that it would be his last posting. The competition for a third star was fierce, and Mark knew that his lack of combat experience in Iraq or Afghanistan would significantly reduce his chances for promotion. "The chances had always been slim," he said. "Somewhere along the line you're going to be told no."

He was shaken by the call all the same. The army had been his second family, and friends from throughout the military had been the first to reach out to him and Carol after the deaths of their two sons. It was the world he knew, and the one he'd fought so hard to change. The thought of leaving it was jarring and more than a little scary. "All I'd done my whole adult life was be a soldier," he said. "Now the reality began to set in that I wasn't going to be a soldier anymore."

Still, Mark was able to calm himself down enough to thank Thurman for telling him by phone, rather than by e-mail. He also thanked his boss for waiting to break the news until after Melanie's wedding. The delay allowed Mark to celebrate his daughter's marriage to Joe without being distracted by the pain of knowing that his military career was about to come to an abrupt end and the uncertainty about what he was going to do next.

Carol took the news much harder. As a two-star general, Mark had the power to force a major base such as Fort Carson to implement new ways of preventing troubled soldiers from taking their own lives and the prominence to garner significant media attention and to attract large audiences to his speeches about depression and suicide. Carol worried that Mark would be far less effective in the suicide prevention fight as a civilian, and she took the army's decision not to give him a third star far more personally than he did. Carol had heard whispers for years that other senior officers resented how often she and Mark spoke out publicly about the need to reduce stigma within the military and about the importance of treating depression and PTSD as illnesses, not as signs of weakness or cowardice. She had always dismissed the rumors as idle gossip, but now she wondered if there wasn't some truth to them after all.

Mark left the army on May 18, 2012, roughly ten months after Thurman's phone call. He had stayed in his FORSCOM post at the request of the army, which wanted him to help oversee the command's move from Fort McPherson to North Carolina's Fort Bragg. FORSCOM finished settling into its new home in the spring of 2012. A few weeks later, hundreds of Mark's friends, relatives, and fellow soldiers huddled under tents at Fort Bragg on an unusually rainy and chilly day to watch him say goodbye to the army he'd served for so long.

General David Rodriguez, FORSCOM'S new commander, pinned a Distinguished Service Medal to Mark's camouflage uniform and draped another one around Carol's neck. The Grahams, he told the crowd, had managed to find purpose in unimaginable tragedy.

"In the short expanse of nine months, Mark and Carol lost both their sons, and Melanie lost her brothers," Rodriguez said. "You and Carol took this loss and transformed it into hope for so many others."

Mark knew he'd be nervous when it was his turn to speak, so he'd typed makeshift stage directions into the text of his written remarks. "Pause," he wrote. "Breathe . . . Smile."

"Our sons, who died fighting different battles, but are here in spirit today, both decided to serve our nation," he told the crowd. "As we go about our daily lives, I ask that we always remember our fallen who have given the ultimate sacrifice ensuring that our treasured freedoms live on for generations to come. Think also of our wounded, many with wounds we can see and yet so many with wounds we cannot see. Please keep them and their families in your thoughts and prayers as they travel their challenging journey toward recovery."

The ceremony ended with the playing of a song Gene Autry made famous in the years after World War II. "Old soldiers never die, never die, never die," the crowd sang. "They just fade away."

Mark Graham entered a military still struggling to deal with the emotional and psychological toll of the Vietnam War. Three decades later he retired from one struggling to deal with the emotional and psychological toll of the wars in Iraq and Afghanistan. In 2011, his final full year in uniform, 278 soldiers took their own lives. In 2012, the year Mark said good-bye to the army he'd served for so long, a record 349 troops killed themselves, and the number of soldiers who died by suicide exceeded those killed in combat for the first time.

Each of those suicides hit Mark and Carol hard. They thought of the young lives cut short, of the families that would spend the rest of their lives blaming themselves for not seeing how much their loved ones were suffering or doing more to get them the help they needed. Most retiring generals head straight from the army to a defense contractor willing to pay them hundreds of thousands of dollars per year to lobby their former colleagues. Mark has chosen a very different path, choosing to work for organizations dedicated to military suicide prevention rather than to seek a lucrative private-sector job. He and Carol have endowed suicide prevention programs at the University of Kentucky and at Cameron University in Lawton, Oklahoma, the town where Kevin and Melanie were born, and where Melanie, years after her brothers' deaths, eventually finished nursing school. The Grahams crisscross the country each week to tell their story of loss and love at military bases, universities, suicide prevention conferences, and churches, hoping that they might be able to persuade a troubled man or woman in each audience to seek help before making that most final of decisions. In 2011 they made more than twenty-six speeches to military and civilian audiences. In 2012 they made roughly thirty-seven. In 2013 they made more than sixty. Everywhere they go, every speech they give, Mark and Carol think of their sons.

Some reminders are more tangible than others. In October of 2012, Mark and Carol flew to Washington, DC, to watch Melanie run a ten-mile race in a T-shirt that had a picture of Jeff and Kevin printed on the back. There were three words underneath the picture: RUN AND REMEMBER. Mark and Carol cheered their daughter, still glowing like a newlywed, as she crossed the finish line. They couldn't stay long, though. They had a flight early the next day to Camp Pendleton, California, to tell their story to more than two thousand marines.

Jeff and Kevin Graham are buried side by side in a local cemetery in Frankfort that is best known for housing the remains of Daniel Boone. Their graves sit at the center of a small, grassy plateau overlooking the green-tinted, languid Kentucky River and, across the water, the ornate dome of the Kentucky State Capitol. If you squint, you can just about make out the spire of the church where Mark and Carol Graham were married nearly four decades ago and where Jeff Graham and Stacey Martinez planned to have their wedding after he returned from Iraq. Jackie Shroat, Carol's mom, still attends the church every Sunday, though she sometimes finds it hard to stay in the sanctuary during wedding ceremonies. Each of the smiling young couples reminds her of Jeff and Stacey, and each reminds her of the life her grandson and the woman he loved never had the chance to share.

Mark and Carol Graham visit their boys whenever they're in Kentucky. Carol wears a heart-shaped locket with their names engraved on the outside and her sons' pictures inside. She also wears a gold bracelet with Jeff's name engraved next to the symbol of the Big Red One, his division in Iraq, and Kevin's engraved next to airborne wings from the elite unit he was slated to enter after being commissioned as an officer. Mark wears the same bracelet in stainless steel.

Each trip home reopens old wounds. Mark and Carol look out at the headstones and remember Kevin patiently teaching his older brother to speak without mispronouncing any words or letters. They remember

Jeff's joy when he found out that his younger brother would be joining him at the University of Kentucky. They remember the crisp afternoon when their three children gathered into a happy cluster on the Great Wall of China and posed for Mark's camera, eyes wide open and bright. They remember that their children were smiling.

Brian Wade, the former commander of the boys' ROTC unit, drives up from Lexington every few weeks to polish their marble headstones and brush away any dust or stray grass. Wade has been making the trip for more than a decade, and he sees it as both an honor and a sacred duty. He's far from the only regular visitor.

On a hot summer afternoon Jackie Shroat drove to the cemetery from her house, a tidy split-level crammed with framed pictures of the two brothers. She stepped slowly out of her car and gingerly bent down to pick up a piece of trash that had landed near Kevin's and Jeff's headstones. "I have to remind myself that they're not really here," she said quietly. "It's just their bones. But it comforts me to know that they're together again."

She reached out and patted the two headstones, letting her hand linger first on Jeff's, then on Kevin's. The marble was warm to the touch in the bright midday sun.

THE LOST

May 2013

General Ray Odierno is a hulking man who played football at West Point before joining the army in 1976, two years before Mark Graham. Some of Odierno's soldiers dubbed him "Shrek," and the nickname has stuck. He commanded the army division that helped capture Saddam Hussein in 2003 and later helped implement the counterinsurgency strategy that brought Iraq back from the brink of civil war. His professional success in Iraq was marred by a personal tragedy. Odierno's oldest son, Anthony, lost his left arm when a rocket-propelled grenade smashed through his Humvee in the summer of 2004. The younger Odierno, an army captain who dreamed of a long career in the military, almost died from blood loss and had to leave the service. His father, meanwhile, kept ascending through the ranks of the military. In the fall of 2011, Odierno was tapped to be the chief of staff of the army, elevating him to the Joint Chiefs of Staff and making him one of the most powerful people in the entire military.

In an interview for this book, Odierno said that he'd had soldiers take their own lives in every unit he commanded, from the one-hundred-soldier company he led as a young captain to the twenty-thousand-soldier division he oversaw as a two-star general. He also has a personal connection to suicide: His wife's uncle, a retired noncommissioned officer in the air force, took his own life a few years ago after being diagnosed with an incurable physical illness. Odierno said that he's haunted by the large number of soldiers who have killed themselves on his watch. "Every soldier is important, and when we lose a soldier, it's a big deal, regardless of whether it's through suicide, a motorcycle accident, or combat," he said. "Suicides are particularly concerning because that means something is happening in this soldier's life that is so bad, he believes that the only way out is to take his own life. It's incumbent on us to prevent things from getting to that point."

Odierno said, rightly, that the military has significantly changed how it tries to identify troubled troops and get them into care before they can harm themselves or others. The Pentagon has boosted the total number of military mental health professionals by 35 percent, to nearly ten thousand. The entire army undergoes an annual mental health "stand-down" that requires all units to halt their normal work for a day and instead practice how to identify fellow troops who need help and may be at heightened risk of suicide; the Marine Corps, a service hit hard by suicide, requires all of its troops to undergo similar training over the course of each year. The navy and air force don't require stand-downs, but they have poured tens of millions of dollars into their own suicide prevention efforts. The Department of Veterans Affairs runs a twenty-four-hour telephone crisis line that connects troubled troops and veterans with trained mental health professionals. Jan Kemp, the VA's top suicide prevention official, said that the hotline has received more than 850,000 calls since its creation in the summer of 2007 and referred more than 65,000 people to government counselors for further treatment. Fourteen of the army's largest posts have adopted one of Mark's signature policy changes from his time at Fort Carson and created behavioral health teams that are assigned to individual combat brigades. A group of retired admirals and generals led by Pete Chiarelli were instrumental in eliminating a National Rifle Association–backed piece of legislation that barred commanders from seeking information about a soldier's personal weapons.

The military, backed by the Obama White House, has worked to reduce the stigma surrounding mental health issues. Army Specialist Chance Keesling, twenty-five, shot himself in the head in Iraq in the summer of 2009. The military gave the Keeslings a full military burial, complete with a twenty-one-gun salute and the presentation of a folded American flag to his grieving mother. The one thing the Keeslings didn't get was a condolence letter from the White House; Chance, an army official told them, wasn't eligible because he had taken his own life. The Keeslings felt that the White House was effectively telling them that their son's death didn't matter, and they spent two years lobbying to change the rule. In July 2011 the efforts paid off. President Obama announced that he would begin sending condolence letters to the families of troops, like Chance Keesling, who killed themselves in Iraq or Afghanistan. In a written statement Obama said he was "committed to removing the stigma associated with the unseen wounds of war" suffered by the hundreds of troops who had committed suicide in recent years. "This issue is emotional, painful, and complicated, but these Americans served our nation bravely," Obama said at the time. "They didn't die because they were weak. And the fact that they didn't get the help they needed must change."

The Pentagon has also been throwing huge amounts of money at the suicide problem. It has spent more than $700 million on research into traumatic brain injuries since 2007 and funded an additional $700 million of research into PTSD. The army and the National Institute of Mental Health have also launched a $65 million project called the Army Study to Assess Risk and Resilience in Servicemembers, or Army STARRS, which is tracking the mental health of tens of thousands of military personnel over the course of their military careers, from basic training to combat deployments to their return home. The STARRS project resembles the famed Framingham Heart Study, which has been following thousands of patients over their entire lives to help identify the specific behaviors—such as smoking, obesity, and lack of exercise—that help cause heart disease. Framingham data led to the creation of a sophisticated diagnostic test that allows physicians to calculate an individual patient's likelihood of developing a cardiovascular disorder. The doctors running the STARRS initiative hope to do the same for PTSD and suicide. "When it comes to mental health, we can think of the army as a haystack with an enormous number of needles," said one of the lead researchers, Dr. Michael Schoenbaum. "Our goal is to help the army build smaller haystacks with a smaller concentration of needles."

The new research into PTSD and suicide, much of it funded by the Pentagon, has the potential to revolutionize how the military identifies and treats troubled soldiers. Several studies have found that the portions of the brain that regulate the ways troops with PTSD respond to fear and stress function differently from those in troops who don't have the disorder, a finding that could help neurologists assess whether troops who return home and begin drinking heavily or jumping at loud noises have PTSD or are simply blowing off steam after difficult and bloody overseas deployments. Other research has shown that traumatic brain injury can cause PTSD, establishing a definitive link between the signature physical wound of Iraq and Afghanistan and the signature psychological one. More recent studies suggest that injecting troops with morphine immediately after they suffer a serious brain injury can significantly reduce their chances of developing PTSD, a potential indication that proper medication and treatment can prevent wounded troops from developing the disorder most closely linked to military suicide.

For the moment, though, the ongoing research has mainly served to illustrate how hard it will be for the military to bring its suicide rate down. Multiple deployments to the war zones of Iraq and Afghanistan have long been seen as a primary reason so many troops take their own lives, which led to a widespread hope that the suicide rate would gradually decline once those conflicts came to a close. A wide array of new research suggests that that optimism is misplaced. The Pentagon's most recent examination of military suicide data found that 52 percent of the active-duty troops who killed themselves between 2008 and 2011 had never served in either Iraq or Afghanistan. In the summer of 2013, the *Journal of the American Medical Association* published the results of the most comprehensive examination of military suicide ever undertaken. Its central finding was striking: 57.8 percent of the troops who took their own lives had never deployed. Instead, the survey said that troops who committed suicide were often heavy drinkers who suffered from preexisting mental health problems such as depression or bipolar disorder, the same factors that have long been linked to suicides in the civilian world. "It's more complicated than 'war is hell,'" Schoenbaum said. "That wouldn't explain what's happening to those who have never gone to war."

The more likely scenario, many researchers believe, is that deployments are just one part of a complex web of factors that determine which troops take their own lives and which don't. Some of those, such as the genuine sadness that can be caused by divorce or the death of a child or loved one, are common to both civilians and soldiers. Some, particularly the ease with which soldiers can get handguns and other firearms, are far more pronounced in the military. In 2011, several years into the military's suicide epidemic, the commanders of an army brigade that had just returned from Afghanistan commissioned .45-caliber handguns stamped with the unit logo and urged soldiers to buy them. No one seemed to have given much thought to the wisdom of making it even easier for combat veterans to buy weapons to keep in their homes. In early 2012 an army specialist named Kip Lynch shot his wife in the back as she held their infant daughter, killing them both, and then turned the gun on himself in a failed attempt to take his own life. Just over a year later, on Valentine's Day 2013, Lynch's commanding officer, army captain Alpheaus Lamar, a married father of five, killed himself. Both men used the commemorative handguns they'd received for their service in Afghanistan. Odierno, who was the chief of staff at the time of both deaths, believes the number of soldiers who take their own lives will continue to rise in the years to come. "I don't think we've hit the top yet on suicides," he said. "For the next five to ten years, I think we're going to continue to see some issues here. They're not going away anytime soon."

He's right. Our all-volunteer army reflects the society in which its soldiers were raised, and any problem that affects the country also affects those sent overseas to fight in its name. Suicide is one of those problems, and it's getting worse. More people take their own lives than die in car crashes, a vivid illustration of the skyrocketing civilian suicide rate. In 2010, the most recent year for which official data is available, 38,364 people took their own lives, while 33,687 died in road accidents. D. J. Mathis, one of Jeff Graham's best friends, was one of them. In August 2013 he shot his estranged wife five times, leaving her a quadriplegic, before killing himself. Veterans accounted for 9,000 of those suicides, an eye-opening number given that our nation of more than 360 million people has just 22 million people who have worn a military uniform over the past fifty years.

The increase has been particularly pronounced among baby boomers and other middle-aged Americans. From 1999 to 2010, the suicide rate for adults aged thirty-five to sixty-four jumped nearly 30 percent, to a record 17.6 deaths per 100,000. Male baby boomers were hit particularly hard, with the suicide rate for men in their fifties jumping by nearly 50 percent, to a record 30 per 100,000. The nation's long recession certainly pushed many of them to take their own lives; middle-aged men who are laid off face the very real prospect that they may never again find steady employment. Ease of access to powerful prescription drugs is also a factor. Many antianxiety and antidepressant medications can cause an initial spike in suicidal thinking, while powerful painkillers such as Oxycontin can be both addictive and deadly when taken in large doses. Most Americans who choose to end their own lives do it with firearms, but a growing number are intentionally overdosing on prescription medications, as detailed in this book.

All of the factors driving up the civilian suicide rate exist in the military world, but they're even more pervasive among troops and their families, and even more potent. The military medical system, for example, is so short-staffed that its physicians don't have time to devote much attention to individual patients, particularly those with PTSD. All too often, that means doctors give troops prescriptions for powerful medications and simply send them on their way. A wide-ranging army study from 2011 found that psychiatric medications and opioid painkillers were being prescribed throughout the military at record levels because soldiers were surviving grievous injuries that would have been fatal just a few years earlier, while others who emerged from combat relatively unhurt were still dealing with aches and pains from their repeated overseas deployments. The flip side was that 25 to 35 percent of the wounded troops waiting to be discharged from the army because of their injuries were hooked on prescription medications. Others were medicating themselves by abusing alcohol and drugs such as marijuana, crystal meth, and heroin. The military's rates of drug addiction and alcoholism dwarf those of the civilian world. Once out of the military, veterans have to battle those addictions while simultaneously trying to adjust to a civilian world they often can barely recognize or understand. It can be a lethal combination.

Tens of thousands of troops will also soon face the same types of financial pressures that lead desperate civilians to take their own lives. Looming budget cuts mean that the army will have to fire eighty thousand soldiers by 2017, forcing soldiers who'd expected to spend their entire careers in the military to find private-sector jobs at a time of sky-high unemployment. Bob Gates, the former defense secretary, believes that veterans who can't find work will be at high risk of taking their own lives, particularly if they are also suffering from PTSD or TBI.

"A lot of these guys are going to feel betrayed," Gates said. "The question will be whether there are enough dollars to help prepare those young men and women to reenter a civilian economy in terms of teaching them how to write a résumé, teaching them how to convert a military skill into a salable civilian skill. If you don't have programs for that, you're going to have a lot of problems with this large number of young people coming out of the military before they'd expected." Gates, like Odierno, expects the military's suicide rate to increase in the years ahead.

The growing number of sex crimes within the military poses an additional threat. A Pentagon report in 2013 said 3,374 troops were sexually assaulted in 2012, while roughly 26,000 troops were victims of "unwanted sexual contact," a catchall term that covers crimes ranging from groping to rape. Both figures were up sharply from 2011, and military commanders privately believe the true numbers are far higher because many victims are afraid to come forward for fear of harming their careers. The male troops who were the victims in 53 percent of the sex-crime cases were particularly reluctant to report the attacks, partially because of pure shame and partially because they were worried about being kicked out of the military if they admitted to having homosexual contact with other men, even if it was forced and unwanted. The 2011 repeal of the military's "don't ask, don't tell" restrictions on gay service members has made some male troops more willing to step forward, but most are still thought to suffer in silence.

The pervasive stigma surrounding sexual violence in the military means that troops who need help the most often choose not to seek it, leaving them at elevated risk of developing lasting emotional and psychological problems. Rachel Kimerling, a researcher for Veterans Affairs, has found that troops who are sexually assaulted can develop PTSD at rates that are just as high, and sometimes higher, than troops who have taken part in intense combat. Rape does lasting harm to all of its victims, but Kimerling believes that service members are hit especially hard. The men and women who volunteer for the armed forces see themselves as physically and mentally stronger than their civilian counterparts. Being sexually assaulted shatters those beliefs and leaves the troops with an overwhelming sense of powerlessness and betrayal. "Sexual assaults in the military are more toxic than in the civilian world," she said. "You are living and working with the perpetrator in these cases. There is no going home or going away. And these are the people who are supposed to have your back."

Kimerling's research has shown that sexual assaults at the hands of other troops lead many soldiers to attempt to commit suicide. Her current work is looking at whether it also causes them to carry through with it. Other researchers privately say they are virtually certain that there's a direct link between military sexual assault and military suicide. Tia Christopher enlisted in the navy straight out of high school. She was raped a few months into her first deployment by a sailor she'd been casually dating and developed the symptoms of what she later realized was PTSD. Loud noises startled her, and she couldn't stand being in public places. She had trouble eating and lost nearly thirty pounds. She pleaded with the navy to shift her to a different room, but they refused, forcing her to sleep in the bed where she'd been raped. A few months later she used a pocketknife to make three deep gashes in her left wrist. Christopher survived, but many female troops aren't so lucky. In 2010, women accounted for just 5 percent of the military's total number of active-duty suicides. The figure jumped to 6.7 percent in 2011 and 7.1 percent in 2012.

It is projected to increase again in 2013, potentially pushing the military's suicide numbers even higher.

Completely eliminating the military's suicide problem will be impossible; there will always be some soldiers who feel darkness enveloping their lives and grasp at the only thing that they think will end the pain. Still, there are steps that could help. The science is far from conclusive, but the military should expand its financial support for research into next-generation scanners and diagnostic machines that could show whether troops with severe head wounds have also suffered a traumatic brain injury, putting them at high risk of developing PTSD or one day taking their own lives. It should change the policies that make it easy for soldiers to automatically renew their prescriptions for powerful prescription drugs, enabling them to build stockpiles that they can use to kill themselves through intentional overdoses or to swap for other medications whose side effects include heightened suicidal thoughts. The military should also finance new research into why rapidly increasing numbers of National Guard and Reserve troops are killing themselves and what can be done to prevent them from doing so. Guard and Reserve personnel account for nearly a third of the military's total number of suicides, a vastly disproportionate percentage given the relatively small number of those troops currently serving at home or abroad.

Restricting troubled soldiers' access to guns, as quixotic as it may seem, is another step that could save a significant number of lives. Suicide is an impulsive act, which means that it's critically important to make it as hard as possible for troubled troops to act on their sudden urges to kill themselves. It's a concept known as "means restriction," and it's been shown to work in a variety of military and civilian contexts. In 2006, after a spate of military suicides, the Israel Defense Forces prohibited its troops from taking army-issued weapons home with them; the number of suicides promptly fell by 40 percent. American commanders can disable or take away the military-issued weapons of troops who are seen as potentially suicidal or violent, but they can't take similar steps with the personal weapons soldiers keep at home, including the handguns used in 68 percent of military suicides. The Pentagon can help U.S. troops do the next best thing: ask colleagues who are behaving erratically, drinking heavily, or showing other signs of major depression to temporarily turn over their firearms, install trigger locks that prevent the weapons from being fired, or lock them away in safes that require keys or combinations to open. "The idea is to eliminate access to potential sources of harm before something sparks a suicidal impulse," said Craig Bryan, the head of the University of Utah's National Center for Veterans Studies. "That impulse normally passes fairly quickly, so you just need to buy a bit of time." The Pentagon has begun to tentatively embrace means restriction. Jackie Garrick, the head of the Defense Department's Suicide Prevention Resource Center, said the military gave out roughly 75,000 trigger guards in 2013 and launched a public awareness campaign designed to persuade troops to store their personal weapons in armories on their bases rather than in their homes. It's a good start, but the military should give trigger guards and gun safes to all of its active-duty troops, putting the onus about whether to use them on the soldiers themselves.

The most important changes, though, are the ones that will be the hardest to put in place because they require fundamental changes to the military's culture and value system. The army is the literal definition of a hierarchy, and younger soldiers won't truly believe that they can seek help without destroying their careers until top generals and senior sergeants begin to publicly share stories of their own struggles with combat stress, PTSD, and depression. So far, only a distressingly small number of them have been willing to do so. Dozens of generals and high-ranking sergeants served in Iraq and Afghanistan, many at bases that came under regular insurgent attack. A significant number lost close friends, and all of them had to wrestle with the emotional impact of attending battlefield memorial services, writing condolence letters to grieving families, and visiting field hospitals where young troops who had lost limbs or suffered horrific burns writhed in pain. It is extremely difficult for anyone, including generals specifically selected for their resiliency and inner strength or sergeants selected for the image of toughness they project, to live through those types of experiences and return home exactly the same as when they left. In more than a year of research for this book, however, I was able to identify only three generals who have gone public about their nightmares, jumpiness, flashes of anger, or other PTSD-related symptoms. Dave Blackledge was the only one of those generals who was willing to speak to me on the record and acknowledge that he sometimes thought of taking his own life. Even now, at the very pinnacle of their professional lives, most of the generals afflicted with PTSD suffer in silence because they are afraid other soldiers will see them as weak.

It's possible that younger soldiers, raised in a time when psychiatric drugs such as Xanax are advertised on television and sold at every pharmacy in the country, will be more willing to publicly discuss their own struggles with PTSD than their elders have been. One prominent veteran, Medal of Honor winner Ty Carter, already does. Carter was stationed at Combat Outpost Keating, the remote base in eastern Afghanistan that Colonel Randy George had wanted to shut down, when it was overrun by Taliban fighters. He repeatedly braved enemy fire to carry ammunition to a trio of troops who were cut off from the rest of the unit, and later he dragged a badly wounded soldier, Specialist Stephan Mace, to safety. Mace died anyway, and Carter returned to the United States haunted by feelings of guilt over surviving a battle that had claimed the lives of eight of his friends. He had trouble falling asleep and suffered from nightmares so vivid that he would wake up in the middle of the night trembling. It took him months to accept that he had PTSD—something he'd long believed to be a myth—and needed help. Carter started seeing a counselor shortly before finding out that he was going to be awarded the Medal of Honor, the military's highest commendation. Like the Grahams, Carter believes that soldiers will continue killing themselves until they feel safe seeking help. Like the Grahams, he travels the country sharing intimate details of his own struggles with PTSD and depression in the hopes of persuading troubled troops to reach out for assistance before it's too late. And like the Grahams, he remains very much the exception: No other living Medal of Honor winners have talked about their own difficulties reacclimating to the civilian world.

The military has other ways of persuading its top officers and non-commissioned personnel to commit themselves to the suicide prevention fight. It should begin by making the ways commanders and enlisted personnel handle mental health issues within their units a formal part of the written evaluations that help determine whether they're promoted. Commanders who develop innovative ways of improving the mental health of their units should be recognized and rewarded, just like those who did the best job of training their soldiers for frontline combat in Iraq and Afghanistan. Senior leaders who fail to take care of soldiers suffering from PTSD or traumatic brain injuries or who allow other soldiers to ostracize, harass, or bully them should be relieved of command and drummed out of the force. More than thirteen years after U.S. troops first swept into Afghanistan, the military hasn't taken either step, and there are no signs that it will do so anytime soon. Many of the suicides and murders I write about in this book could potentially have been prevented if commanders and senior noncommissioned personnel had better monitored the emotional state of their troops or done more to ensure that those who needed assistance got it before they harmed themselves or others. I couldn't find any examples of those officers and enlisted personnel being held responsible for failing to act. Nothing was done to the officer who made the mother of a troubled soldier spend a day painting over the suicide note her son had scrawled onto the walls of his barracks room before trying to take his own life. Nothing was done to the commanders and enlisted personnel who allowed nine troubled veterans of an army unit called the Lethal Warriors to fall through the cracks and eventually kill more than a dozen people. Dr. Steven Knorr, the Fort Carson psychiatrist who wrote that many of the troops who sought help were "dead wood" and fakers, returned to the base as a civilian after he retired from the army and currently works as a senior member of its behavioral health department.

The military's handling of its sexual-assault crisis, which mirrors and fuels the suicide epidemic, offers further reason for pessimism. In June 2013 the Joint Chiefs of Staff, Odierno included, were summoned to a packed Capitol Hill hearing room to face angry questions from lawmakers outraged by the new statistics about rape and sexual violence within the ranks of the armed forces. Senator Jack Reed, a Democrat from Rhode Island and former Army Ranger, asked the generals if any of their commanders had been relieved for failing to take stronger steps to curb sexual assault in their units or on their bases. Odierno said the army had removed roughly a dozen commanders over the previous four years for their handling of sexual assault and unspecified other issues. The commandant of the Coast Guard, Robert Papp, said he'd fired one officer involved in a sex case. But Odierno and Papp were the exceptions. Far more typical was Reed's exchange with Admiral Jonathan Greenert, the chief of naval operations. "Have you relieved a commander specifically, not generally because of bad climate, but specifically because of a failure to respond to sexual abuse in his or her command?" Reed asked. Greenert shifted uncomfortably in his seat before answering. "Not explicitly due to sexual abuse within a command," he said. The heads of the Marine Corps and air force also admitted that none of their officers had ever been sacked because of their handling of sexual violence within their units.

There is no single cause for the spike in military suicide, and there is no single solution to the problem. But that doesn't mean we should give up. The nation sent more than 2.5 million of its sons and daughters to fight in Iraq, Afghanistan, and other distant lands, and many have returned with invisible wounds that will haunt them for the rest of their lives. PTSD symptoms often don't manifest until years or even decades after a soldier has come home from war, and they don't fade over time. In 2003, researchers found that four out of every five Vietnam veterans who developed PTSD because of the war were still suffering from the disorder decades after the conflict ended. That means hundreds of thousands of Iraq and Afghanistan veterans with PTSD may still be battling their personal demons long after the guns of war have fallen silent, leaving many at risk of one day choosing to take their own life. The Iraq War is over and Afghanistan is winding down. The military's fight to save its troops from taking their own lives will rage well into the future.

Carol and Mark Graham are out on the front lines of that fight, telling their story again and again. Reliving the loss of their two sons has not gotten easier over time. Carol routinely breaks down midspeech, and Mark often has to pause, catch his breath, and dab his eyes before he can finish telling strangers about his lost sons. They savor small victories— parents approaching them after a speech to say that they finally understand that their sons and daughters have returned home from war with psychological wounds that are as deadly as physical ones, marines hugging them and whispering that the remarks have persuaded them to seek help. Mark and Carol have devoted their lives to trying to save as many war-damaged troops as they can, regardless of the cost. We, as a country, should do no less.

On a rainy day in the summer of 2013, Mark Graham sat down behind a table in a windowless auditorium at Columbia University for a panel discussion on the military's suicide rate, which was beginning to attract widespread media and congressional attention. More than 120 soldiers had killed themselves in the first five months of the year, and military officials were already worrying that 2013 would set another record.

Mark's appearance was part of a daylong conference organized by Give an Hour, a nonprofit that matches troubled troops with civilian mental health professionals willing to see them for free for at least one hour a week. Barbara Van Dahlen, the clinical psychologist who founded the organization in 2005, sees it as a way of trying to help fill the void created by the military's chronic inability to hire enough psychologists and psychiatrists of its own. "There are hundreds of thousands of troops returning home with invisible wounds that have no place to go for help," she said. "We're trying to be one of those places." Van Dahlen was named one of *Time*'s 100 Most Influential People in 2012, and her group has forged formal relationships with all five branches of the military. By 2013, Give an Hour had a network of roughly seven thousand mental health providers in all fifty states. Mark served on its board, and he had flown to New York to spend the day with a roomful of mental health professionals who might one day confront the kinds of demons that had claimed his son.

"We learned about the impact of mental health in the worst way possible," he said, choking up. "We truly wish we knew then what we know now. We truly wish we had known that we were part of the stigma. But we didn't hear what our son was trying to tell us, and nothing we do will ever bring him back."

Mark continued with a story from one of Jeff's last nights in the United States. Shortly before deploying to Iraq, a young soldier knocked on Jeff's door and quietly asked if he was the officer who had lost a brother to suicide. The soldier told Jeff that his father killed himself and that he was having the same dark thoughts but didn't want to tell anyone in his unit for fear of being kicked out of the military. Jeff told him to get help immediately. Nothing, he said, was more important than the soldier's life, and there would be other ways of serving the country if he had to leave the army. In the fall of 2003, with U.S. troops already fighting and dying in Iraq, Jeff called Mark and said that he wouldn't have known what to say that night if his brother hadn't committed suicide. Kevin's death, he told his father, had given him the knowledge to help save the young soldier's life.

"That's one reason my wife and I do what we do," Mark concluded. "Before he died, Jeff had told us to promise that we wouldn't stop doing what we're doing. He told us there were too many Kevins out there. So here we are. We won't stop."

AUTHOR'S NOTE

This book draws from hundreds of hours of interviews with Mark, Carol, and Melanie Graham over the past eighteen months, both on the phone and in person, as well as family journals, e-mails, letters, pictures, and cards. I also had access to Mark's and Jeff's written military evaluations and Kevin's otherwise confidential health records and autopsy reports. I spent a week in Kentucky with Carol's sisters, brothers-in-law, and cousins, who sat for lengthy interviews about the family's life in Frankfort and their memories of Jeff and Kevin. Carol's indomitable mother, Jackie, hosted me in her home and chauffeured me around the city so I could see the house where Carol grew up, the church where she and Mark got married, and the grave sites of Carol and Mark's two sons. I'd also like to thank Carol's sister, Sandra Shroat Bush, for sharing intimate details about her own struggle to overcome mental illness in the hope of helping others do the same. At the University of Kentucky, Jeff and Kevin's former ROTC instructor, Brian Wade, gave me a tour of the facilities where they did their military training. The Iraq section draws from my own time embedded with military units operating in and around Anbar Province, the bloody region where Jeff was killed. I also spent significant amounts of time in both Fallujah and Ramadi while I was living in Iraq and running the *Wall Street Journal*'s Baghdad bureau.

When I started working on this book, I chose to write it as a purely chronological narrative that would take readers inside the Grahams' world and allow them to experience the high and low points of Mark's and Carol's lives as they did, in real time and without the benefit of hindsight. To take one example, Kevin's final months were full of small clues that in retrospect make clear that he was a deeply troubled and potentially suicidal young man. Those signs, though, were only clear after the fact. In the moment, Mark and Carol simply didn't see them.

This style of writing avoids the normal journalistic practice of attributing every discrete fact and quote. Instead, each section of the narrative incorporates material from an array of interviews and primary source materials. The conversations depicted in the book were re-created, whenever possible, by interviewing everyone involved. Some scenes, particularly those involving Kevin and Jeff, were drawn from a single source. I didn't describe anyone as having "thought" or "felt" something unless I'd interviewed the person myself, read through primary documents that described a state of mind at a given moment, or interviewed sources who had discussed those thoughts and feelings with the person contemporaneously. Jeff's journal from Iraq was an invaluable window into his mind-set during the last months of his life.

I spent a year reporting and writing this book, primarily from a cozy office at the Center for a New American Security, an institution that punches far above its weight and has built a well-deserved reputation for intellectual rigor and top-notch research.

Over the course of my research, I interviewed more than one hundred people, civilians and military alike, and am deeply appreciative of their willingness to help me better understand both the Grahams and the army itself. I am particularly indebted to Ray Navarrette and the other members of Jeff's platoon in Iraq, who have been wrestling with their own pain and guilt over his death for more than a decade.

In addition to those listed below, I want to pay special tribute to four fine journalists whose coverage of the army's suicide problem, particularly at Fort Carson, deeply influenced my reporting and writing: David Philipps of the *Colorado Springs Gazette,* whose book, *Lethal Warriors,* is a searing indictment of the military's failure to spot the unit's problems before several of its soldiers went on a killing spree at Fort Carson; Daniel Zwerdling, of National Public Radio, a legendary investigative reporter who broke an array of stories about the base's deeply dysfunctional mental health system; and Mark Benjamin and Michael de Yoanna, formerly of *Salon,* who were the first to call attention to the disturbing cases of Chad Barrett, Adam Lieberman, and other Fort Carson soldiers whose deaths or psychological problems could have been averted by better, more caring commanders. All of them were kind enough to share contacts, advice, military investigative reports, and other raw materials with me over beer or coffee or by e-mail. I also want to cite the work of *Vanity Fair's* Maureen Orth, who was the first to detail the Fort Bragg murders, and *Rolling Stone's* L. Christopher Smith, who did a lengthy reconstruction of the Fort Carson killings.

Several books provided essential background material for several sections of *The Invisible Front.* In particular, I recommend Bill Murphy Jr.'s *In a Time of War,* which details the casualties that hammered the unit Jeff Graham would eventually join in Iraq, as well as the life stories of many of those wounded and killed; E. B. Sledge's classic World War II memoir, *With the Old Breed,* which vividly describes the psychological traumas of war; Drew Gilpin Faust's *This Republic of Suffering,* which details PTSD's impact on the soldiers and veterans of the Civil War; Karl Marlantes's *What It Is Like to Go to War,* a haunting memoir about his own struggles to overcome the psychological toll of service in a combat zone; Nancy Sherman's *The Untold War,* which looks at PTSD and other invisible wounds; Jonathan Shay's landmark *Achilles in Vietnam,* which charts how humans have struggled to overcome the psychological damage of going to war for as long as wars have existed; Marvin Gettleman et al.'s *Vietnam and*

America: The Most Comprehensive Documented History of the Vietnam War, which looks at the practice of fragging; and Richard Boyle's *Flower of the Dragon: The Breakdown of the U.S. Army in Vietnam,* a detailed look at the drug-addicted, ill-disciplined force Mark entered as a young officer. I also learned a lot from Eric T. Dean's *Shook Over Hell* and Dave Grossman's classic *On Killing.*

Interviews, though, form the backbone of this book, and I wanted to thank all of the following below for their willingness to talk to me, often more than once: retired major general Mark Graham, Carol Graham, Melanie Graham Quinn, retired captain Joseph Quinn, former defense secretary Robert Gates, former Joint Chiefs of Staff chairman Admiral Mike Mullen, army chief of staff General Ray Odierno, Lieutenant General Ray Mason, Betty Cerrone, Debbie Hull, Jamison Hull, Alison Lighthall, Dr. Barbara Van Dahlen, Ben Baxter, Benjamin Chavez, Bonnie Carroll, retired lieutenant colonel Brian Wade, Colonel Butch Kievenaar, Dr. Elspetch Cameron "Cam" Ritchie, Dr. Charles Hoge, retired colonel Charlie Baer, retired colonel Michael Thompson, Brigadier General Randy George, Dr. Craig Bryan, David Miller, Dr. Philip S. Wang, Emily Ullmer, retired lieutenant general Russel Honoré, retired lieutenant general Dave Valcourt, Grant Breithaupt, Heather Willis, Heidi Lieberman, retired colonel Heidi Terrio, retired colonel J. Chesney, Jackie Shroat, Dr. Jan Kemp, retired colonel Jefferson Ewing, Jeff Hohman, John Bradley, Jon Burns, D. J. Mathis, retired staff sergeant Jon Pennington, Karen Halverson, Katie Clark, Brenda Shusko, Dr. Kerry Ressler, Kim Henry, Kim Ruocco, retired brigadier general Loree Sutton, Lori Molenaar, retired lieutenant colonel Nate Huggins, retired lieutenant colonel Toby Martinez, Lieutenant General Robert Clark, retired major Dwayne Edwards, Lieutenant Colonel Mike Taylor, Dr. Mary Chandler Bolin, Pat Conrad, retired major general David Blackledge, Major Michael Thompson, Michele Cassida, retired general Peter Chiarelli, Georg-Andreas Pogany, Terri Tanielian, Sergeant First Class Robin Foe, Ryan Lai, Sally

Darrow, Major Sam Preston, Sandra Shroat Bush, Sergeant First Class Mike Crane, Stacey Martinez, Ted Thoerig, Colonel Wayne Boyd, retired colonel Whiz Broome, Lieutenant Colonel Chris Ivany, Sergeant First Class Ray Navarrette, retired lieutenant colonel Preet Singh, Henry Yates, retired colonel Jeff Swisher, Adrienne Bory, Major Amy Pestona Buck, Colonel Emmett Schaill, retired specialist Richard Wagner, Matt Vangjel, retired sergeant first class Kalena Hodges, Lieutenant Colonel Gaylene Weber, retired lieutenant colonel Nicholas Palarino, Reverend Jack Brewer, retired colonel David Haught, Angela Gilpin, retired major general Douglas Carver, retired major general James Gilman, Dr. James Churchill, Dr. Michael Schoenbaum, Tia Christopher, Dr. Rachel Kimerling, Gregg Keesling, John Madigan, Dr. Matt Miller, Jackie Garrick, Carrie Saunders, Allison Broughton (née Saunders), and Carol Triesch.

ACKNOWLEDGMENTS

This book couldn't have been written without Mark, Carol, and Melanie Graham, whose deep love for Jeff and Kevin gave them the strength to share the most intensely intimate and painful parts of their lives. Although all of the editorial decisions were my own, one of my goals in writing this book was to try to bring Jeff and Kevin back to life in its pages; to the degree I succeeded, the Grahams deserve most of the credit.

I was deeply fortunate to work with my editor, Vanessa Mobley, who came to be both a close friend and my most trusted collaborator. Her passion for the subject and her keen gifts for shaping the narrative and tightening the writing made this book much better than it would otherwise have been. A colleague of mine from the *Wall Street Journal* once told me that good editors don't substitute their writing voice for yours. Instead, he told me, they make your voice louder and clearer. By that measure, Vanessa isn't just a good editor, she's a great one.

I was also lucky to work with a talented team at Crown whose professionalism and dedication to this project were evident from day one. I want to especially thank the publisher of Crown, Molly Stern, and her deputy, Jacob Lewis, for their personal involvement in every step of this process. I also want to thank Sarah Breivogel, my tireless publicist; Sarah

Pekdemir, a skilled marketer who helped build my personal website; and Claire Potter, whose skill and good cheer augur a long and successful career in publishing.

My agent, Gary Morris, believed in the project from the beginning, was a trusted adviser and friend, and helped nurture this work from an idea to a finished book.

At the Center for a New American Security, my home for the year in which I wrote the book, I want to single out my friend Nate Fick, an accomplished writer in his own right and CNAS's former chief executive officer; Richard Fontaine, its president; Ellen McHugh, who made all the trains run on time; Joel Smith, who helped with some of the research; and Bob Work, Nate's successor as CEO. Phil Carter, a senior scholar at CNAS who has devoted his professional life to veterans' issues, has been both a trusted adviser and an extremely close friend.

My career has been enriched by the counsel and mentoring of a large circle of talented journalists, several of whom were kind enough to read the manuscript and offer comments, advice, and moral support. I want to thank Greg Jaffe and Jonathan Eig, two former colleagues from the *Wall Street Journal*, and Jim Tankersley and Adam Kushner, from my time at *National Journal*. David Rothkopf, the editor and publisher of *Foreign Policy*, has been supportive of the project since I began working at the magazine and generously gave me the space and time to properly finish it.

I also feel blessed to have a large circle of friends, many of whom have effectively become members of my family over the years. In Chicago, they include Danny, Alida, Tye, Marnina, and Dodi Harris; Rick and Judy Katz; and Rabbi Michael Myers, who has been a beloved teacher and role model. In Washington, they include Matt Early, Margaret Allen, Seth Edlavitch, and Goli and Adam Tiffen, to whom I owe a debt that can never truly be repaid.

ACKNOWLEDGMENTS

I come from a small family, and I hold my relatives close. Growing up, Dan Kaplan was the older brother I never had; as an adult, that relationship has expanded to include his wife, Reva, and their beautiful sons, Levi and Izzie. Dan's father, Kal, used to take me to father-son baseball games so I wouldn't be the only one there without a dad. I will forever be grateful.

When I married my wife, I joined an utterly extraordinarily family. Annie's brilliant and accomplished father, Jamie, effectively adopted me as a son; her equally brilliant and accomplished mother, Loren, welcomed both me and my mother into her home and heart. Jamie read my manuscript, and his kind words about it touched me more than he could possibly know. Annie's sister Rachel has made me feel like a protective older brother; it took me awhile to realize that she was so strong and mature beyond her years that she didn't really need one. Annie's brother David has an innate kindness and goodness that is truly remarkable and humbling to see.

My mom raised me by herself, sacrificing and scrambling to get me into private schools and ensure that I had the same toys and, later, clothes as my friends. She is an accomplished pianist, and some of my happiest memories involve climbing on top of her piano as a small child, laying out a pillow, and napping to the sounds of her playing. She has spent her life taking care of others, first her own parents and then me, without asking for anything for herself. She has taught me what it means to truly love another person, and I am proud to be her son.

Several years ago, a close friend asked me to think through the things I would want in a wife. I had a long list: beauty, intelligence, a sense of humor, a love of adventure, a willingness to go to crazy places, and a passionate attachment to dogs. Just as importantly, I said that I wanted to find someone who I could love fully and unconditionally and would love me that way in return. We laughed, because finding that sort of woman seemed impossible. Then I met Annie. She brings out the best in me and has given me a sense of peace I have never felt before. She is my best friend and I cannot imagine a life without her. These last words of dedication are the easiest to write. Without my beloved Annie, there would be none preceding them.

INDEX